Arts in the Margins of World Encounters

Edited by

Willemijn de Jong
University of Zurich, Switzerland

Eriko Aoki
Ryukoku University, Japan

John Clammer
O.P. Jindal Global University, India

Curating and Interpreting Culture
VERNON PRESS

Copyright © 2022 Vernon Press, an imprint of Vernon Art and Science Inc, on behalf of the authors.

All rights reserved. No part of this publication may be reproduced, stored in a retrieval system, or transmitted in any form or by any means, electronic, mechanical, photocopying, recording, or otherwise, without the prior permission of Vernon Art and Science Inc.
www.vernonpress.com

In the Americas:
Vernon Press
1000 N West Street, Suite 1200,
Wilmington, Delaware 19801
United States

In the rest of the world:
Vernon Press
C/Sancti Espiritu 17,
Malaga, 29006
Spain

Curating and Interpreting Culture

Library of Congress Control Number: 2021933073

ISBN: 978-1-64889-356-8

Also available: 978-1-62273-602-7 [Hardback]; 978-1-64889-275-2 [PDF, E-Book]

Product and company names mentioned in this work are the trademarks of their respective owners. While every care has been taken in preparing this work, neither the authors nor Vernon Art and Science Inc. may be held responsible for any loss or damage caused or alleged to be caused directly or indirectly by the information contained in it.

Every effort has been made to trace all copyright holders, but if any have been inadvertently overlooked the publisher will be pleased to include any necessary credits in any subsequent reprint or edition.

Cover design by Vernon Press. Cover photo by Eriko Aoki, 2015: "Clayworks by Masami Yamagiwa in the Atelier Yamanami."

Table of Contents

List of figures — v

Prologue
Arts, world encounters, markets and marginality: a decolonising perspective — vii
Willemijn de Jong
University of Zurich, Switzerland
Eriko Aoki
Ryukoku University, Japan
John Clammer
O.P. Jindal Global University, India

Part I. Re-Creating Art Conventions in the Margins of World Encounters — 1

Chapter 1
Dress as art: portrait of an ikat weaver in Eastern Indonesia — 3
Willemijn de Jong
University of Zurich, Switzerland

Chapter 2
The enchantment of *topeng*: thinking art through Balinese masks — 27
Maria Bonome Pederneiras
Museu Nacional/Universidade Federal do Rio de Janeiro, Brazil

Chapter 3
Aboriginal art, transits and transitions: exhibitions in Japan and the US — 43
Sachiko Kubota
Ashiya University, Japan

Part II. Appropriating and Resisting the Global Art World — 57

Chapter 4
Life, art and commoditisation: how disabled people's works in Japan encountered gazes of the international art world — 59
Eriko Aoki
Ryukoku University, Japan

Chapter 5
Heritage and identity: contemporary art practices of Pacific peoples in New Zealand 81

Matori Yamamoto
Hosei University, Japan

Chapter 6
Indigenous arts in Brazil: aesthetics, cosmology and politics 103

Ilana Seltzer Goldstein
Federal University of Sao Paulo, Brazil

Chapter 7
Artwork and performances in the creation of Martinican history and culture 125

Magdalena Sophia Toledo
Universidad Alberto Hurtado, Chile

Part III. New Forms of Art and Ethnography in Museums and Development 145

Chapter 8
Material culture and art practice in Ladakh: notes from a collaborative art project 147

Abeer Gupta
Achi Association India

Chapter 9
Poets from the refugee camps in Rwanda talk to the world 169

Andrea Grieder
University of Technologies and Arts of Byumba, Rwanda

Epilogue
Art in/from the margins: some comparative and theoretical reflections 191

John Clammer
O.P. Jindal Global University, India

Contributors 209

Index 213

List of figures

Figure 1.1 Mama Ango is tying a *lawo gamba* at her ikat frame. 12

Figure 1.2 Mama Ango shows several types of sarongs: *lawo pundi, lawo luka semba, lawo gamba*. 12

Figure 1.3 *Lawo gamba* made by Mama Ango in 2016 with motifs of the ritual sacrifice, the sacred snake, gold jewellery, the national eagle emblem and the photographer. 15

Figure 2.1 *Topeng Sidhakarya*, performed by I Made Djimat in an anniversary ceremony. 33

Figure 2.2 *Topeng Dalen* (mask of the king) performed by I Made Djimat in a funeral ceremony. 36

Figure 2.3 I Dewa Gede Mandra, in his house, finishing a *Jauk Manis* mask by nailing the eyebrow with a bamboo nail. 38

Figure 4.1 The shop corner of Good Job Centre. 71

Figure 4.2 Artworks in process by Hideaki Yoshikawa at Atelier Yamanami. 72

Figure 5.1 Installation view, the exhibition *Bottled Ocean* curated by Jim Vivieaere, City Gallery Wellington, 17 May–7 August 1994. 88

Figure 5.2 Vaimaila Urale, "Lepo," 2017, acrylic on canvas, 3000 x 1800 mm (centre) and "Typeface: Enjoy," 2018, vinyl mural, dimensions variable (wall). 94

Figure 5.3 John Vea, "import/export," 2008–2016 (foreground) and "Finish this week off and that's it!," 2014 (background). 96

Figure 6.1 Map of important artmaking ethnic groups in Brazil in 2019. 107

Figure 6.2 Stool shaped like a jaguar, by a Kuikuro artist. BEI private collection, exhibited at the Ibirapuera Park, 2018. 109

Figure 6.3 Ceramic vase made by Libência Rufino, from the Kadiweu people. 111

Figure 6.4 Draft of a tile made by Sofia de Souza, from the Kadiweu people. 112

Figure 6.5 Headdress made of plastic straws, unidentified artist. 114

Figure 6.6 Mural painting by the indigenous collective Mahku. 116

Figure 6.7 "Forest standing, fascism on the ground." Serially-produced political sign by Denilson Baniwa, print on paper, 2019. 120

Figure 8.1 Mother Spindle, Installation by Chemat Dorjey at IGRMS. 163

Figure 8.2 Welcome to Ladakh, Installation by Chemat Dorjey at IGRMS. 164

Prologue
Arts, world encounters, markets and marginality: a decolonising perspective

Willemijn de Jong

University of Zurich, Switzerland

Eriko Aoki

Ryukoku University, Japan

John Clammer

O.P. Jindal Global University, India

Forms of art created in so-called marginal regions and contexts get too little recognition in the national and global art worlds. Whereas the anthropological case studies of this edited volume impressively problematise this fact with respect to different world encounters and their colonial histories, in the prologue we try to explore the reasons behind it. We do so with a decolonising stance, in particular by challenging the hegemony of the West with its specific canonical views on art. As a first step, we look at the fascinating dialogue between anthropology and art that has intensified during the last decades, in particular at the concept of the agency of art and making art as social and cultural practice. Then we consider the history of the relation between art and marginalised people in the context of the development of capitalism and Western centric ideas about art, and search from an anthropological perspective for alternatives. Finally, we delve into the issue of local or regional arts, margins and decolonisation in the contexts of museums and development. We advocate a stronger dialogue between the field of art and the field of development and promote the idea of "aesthetic democracy". Thereby, we also introduce the three parts of the book: re-creating art conventions in the margins of world encounters; appropriating and resisting the global art world; and new forms of art and ethnography in museums and development.

Keywords: regional art, margin, social agency, decolonialisation, aesthetic democracy

> "This is an intervention. A message from that space in the margins that is a site of creativity and power, that inclusive space where we recover ourselves, where we move in solidarity to erase the category colonized/colonizer. Marginality as site of resistance."
>
> bell hooks
> "Marginality as a Space of Resistance", in *Out There: Marginalization in Contemporary Culture* (1990, 343)

In this edited volume we present innovative contributions on intricate forms of art that are given insufficient recognition in national and global contemporary art contexts. Most of the contributions were initially submitted and discussed in the panel "Arts on the Margins of World Encounters" at the 18th IUAES Conference with the title *World (of) Encounters: The Past, Present and Future of Anthropological Knowledge* that took place from 16 to 20 July 2018 in Florianopolis, Brazil. The book consists of ten chapters written by scholars in the field of anthropology. The chapters deal with a wide variety of art forms, such as clay figures, textiles, paintings, poems, and theatre performances, based on committed anthropological fieldwork in Brazil, Martinique, Rwanda, India, Indonesia, Japan, Australia and New Zealand. Some of these art forms are often called "traditional", but we think that they are better understood when we relate them to processes of modernity and contemporaneity. The relationship of local or regional arts, marginalisation, tradition and contemporaneity is hardly systematically dealt with in recent publications on art and anthropology. The people and the works, we are focusing on, are marginalised in different ways, due to various processes and structures of social and political inequalities, locally, regionally, nationally and transnationally. The artistic actors are living in allegedly peripheral areas, they are categorised as ethnic minorities, or as people with immigrant background or disabilities. Often, these social inequalities and discriminations result from long histories of uneven encounters of trade and exploitation between colonial powers and local populations. We also take into account that the term "margin" itself is contested, as the last chapter in this volume intriguingly shows.

Over the last decades and earlier, many excellent outlines on the anthropology of art have been published (e. g. Bell 2017; Coote and Shelton 1992; Kisin and Myers 2019; Morphy and Perkins 2006; Price 1989). Well-known illuminating edited volumes by Arnd Schneider and Christopher Wright especially deal with issues of film, video and photography by contemporary artists from an anthropological perspective (Schneider and Wright 2006, 2010, 2014). As indicated, we focus on visual and performative arts. In doing so we pursue a relational approach of persons and things with a stress on agency and social relations (Gell 1998; Sansi 2015, 2018; Strathern 1998). We refrain from an approach of "inbetweenness" (Basu 2017), as this concept departs from binary thinking and unintentionally may reify it. We are less experimental than the fascinating thought-and-practice provoking volume *Between Matter and Method: Encounters in Anthropology and Art* (Bakke and Peterson 2018). Our main interest is also not in the exchanges between local artists and those of European descent, as in a recent important volume by art historians on "modernisms" (Harney and Phillips 2018).

Instead, our intention is to focus on arts that were and are to a large degree marginalised. Thereby, we try to grasp that marginality is a particularly constructed inclusive analytical site of creativity, power and inclusion in the vein of bell hooks' introductory quote above. At the same time, we acknowledge with Anna Tsing that, although being a site of creativity, marginality is often constituted as an excluding site with little or hardly any visibility, appreciation, and recognition on the global stage (Tsing 1993, 1994). In dealing with the paradoxes and tensions of marginality, we also tackle and problematise the movements of marginalised art to global centers. In doing so, we can expand on aspects of important earlier studies on Aboriginal arts that have experienced trajectories from craft to "fine art" or "experimental art" since the 1980s (Biddle 2018, Morphy 2007, Myers 2002).

We basically are confronted with hierarchical or unequal relations of different sites and different domains of art, work and life of artists, art works and participative external actors. These relations are often born out of colonial and postcolonial encounters. At the same time, we assume with other scholars (Blanes et al. 2016; Bourriaud 2002; Sansi 2015) that art practices entail micro-utopias, i. e. the process of making art enables to imagine the social in different terms. Moreover, we build on anthropological studies of contemporary art that reject universalising notions and canons of art but look at them as locally or regionally determined (Fillitz and van der Grijp 2018). Through our specific decolonised view on art, encounter and marginality, we hope to enrich the current debate among scholars and practitioners of art and anthropology.

Encounters between anthropology and art: basic arguments and concepts

Since the 1990s, with the booming of the market of contemporary arts (Smith 2009), the dialogue between anthropology and art has intensified (Sansi 2015). As a reaction to the commercialisation of art and to civil society movements, many artists started to define their work as "social practice". They increasingly worked in public spaces, with social groups in participative ways on issues of political relevance. In a leading article "The Artist as Ethnographer" (1995), Hal Foster discussed the growing interest of artists in anthropology and ethnography and initiated the "ethnographic turn" in art. Vice versa, anthropologist borrowed from arts. For example, by considering fieldwork as a form of social intervention, coined as "ethnographic conceptualism" (Sansi 2015, 146–150).

We present here some important arguments and concepts of the current anthropology of art that frame the following contributions. Theoretically and practically, a crucial point of departure of the book is the agency of persons and things, also problematised by scholars of material culture (Henare et al. 2007; Gell 1998; Strathern 1998; Tilley et al. 2006). Material things evince shifting agencies depending on the social relationships in which they enact, and especially depending on how they interact with commodity chains and processes of commoditisation, and anti-commoditisation or the process of becoming gifts (Appadurai 1986; Sansi 2017; Tsing 2015; Binsbergen and Geschiere 2005).

Certain objects may advance to works of art, due to their technological virtuosity, the complex intentionality of the makers, and the particular transactional quality of their aesthetics. Thus, we can identify art objects according to the influential anthropological theory of art by Alfred Gell (1998, 1999 [1992], 1999 [1996]). There has been a lively debate about Gell's work during the last decades. Several anthropologists have commented on Gell's work and presented alternative ideas or approaches to art. For example, James Leach (2007) maintains that Gell posits an individual mind within a single person as the source of creativity, which he questions. Howard Morphy (2007, 2010) departs from a cross-cultural category of art as action and focuses on the aesthetic experience right from the beginning, which Gell explicitly does not. Tim Ingold (2013) does not adhere to looking at the work of art as an "object" of ethnographic analysis in a context of social relations, which he ascribes to Gell. But he concentrates from a phenomenological perspective on the correspondence of the practices of art and anthropology, on their "movement of growth or becoming" (Ibid, 8). Like Gell, Philippe Descola (2018) is interested in how material objects are invested with agency, and he develops an own theory of figuration. Nevertheless, he conceded Gell's theory to provide "a means to escape the Eurocentric iconological criteria of occidental aesthetics" which he qualifies as "an immense merit" (Ibid, 27).

Even considering these alternatives, we think that Gell's work continues to be an unexhausted and eminently rich source of inspiration from which we can tap and critically proceed further to make innovative studies, as important publications by both anthropologists and art historians have shown until today (e. g. Chua and Elliott 2013; Küchler and Caroll 2020; Osborne and Tanner 2007; Pinney and Thomas 2001; Sansi 2015). Particularly, his approach is highly revealing with regard to ethnographic micro-analyses and continues to enable fresh insights in new contexts with complex and subtle power relations which the chapters drawing on Gell in the volume demonstrate.

We present now some of Gell's basic notions and concepts. Let us begin with his approach to aesthetics and his concept of methodological philistinism. What does methodological philistinism mean? It is a cross-culturally applicable methodology and implies an epistemological break with aesthetics, which is at the centre in most theories of art. As a legacy to British social anthropology, in his book *Art and Agency* Gell created an anthropology of art that focuses on "the network of social relationships in the vicinity of art objects" (Gell 1998, 25). He distances himself from scholars that look at representational aesthetic and semantic properties of art objects in a cultural context (cf. Morphy 1994, 2007, 2010). That does not mean that Gell is disinterested in ideas and values of aesthetics or in meaning, as he could easily be misunderstood. But these aspects make only sense for him within the social relationships of the cases that are studied, as aesthetics and symbolic meaning vary according to these relationships. He compares this approach with the anthropology of law. That is not the study of the ideas of right and wrong of other people but of the process of litigation in which such ideas may be put forward. Gell criticises the "indigenous aesthetics" programme, a legacy of Boasian cultural anthropology, by saying that "it tends to reify the 'aesthetic response' independently of the social context of its manifestations (...)" (Gell 1998, 4). He sees art as a system of action, and art works as performances, that intend to change the world. Thereby he reflected on both contemporary artworks after Duchamp and on indigenous artefacts and artworks, such as Asmat shields, Maori painting and Melanesian lime-containers. Instead of symbolic communication, he stresses agency, intention, causation, result, and transformation (Gell 1998, 6). Even objects with complex patterns should not be judged principally according to their aesthetic qualities. For example, intricately decorated lime-containers of Melanesian big men are locally primarily considered as "vehicles of personhood, to be owned, exchanged, and displayed". Gell argues: "The aesthetic properties of a lime-container are salient only to the extent that they mediate social agency back and forth within the social field" (Gell 1998, 81).

The concept of methodological philistinism was introduced in the groundbreaking article "The Technology of Enchantment and the Enchantment of Technology" (Gell 1999 [1992]). There, he proposed already that similarly as a break with theology in the anthropology of religion, we should make a break with aestheticism, or more precisely with Western art cult, in the anthropology of art. Alternatively, Gell suggested considering the various arts first and foremost as parts of a technical system. He called that system "the technology of enchantment". This again was based on "the enchantment of technology", meaning the power of technical activities of casting a spell over us. It is generally difficult to grasp the making of artworks, he asserted, they are easily perceived as magical, and the artist as an occult technician. But the creative agency of the artist is always connected to a social collectivity. The social complex, assemblage of social relations, or encounters in the vicinity of artworks were later conceptualised as the "art nexus", including material things, called indexes, and their possible prototypes, artists, and recipients (Gell 1998, 12–27).

Moreover, intentionalities play a crucial role in Gell's theory, on which he elaborates in his second important article "Vogel's Net". He analyses a Zande hunting net, showcased in an exhibition by Susan Vogel in 1988, and other hunting traps as artworks. Devices such as these embody ideas and communicate meanings, as transformed representations of the social relationship of the hunter and the prey animal. In this article, Gell goes so far as to characterise artworks in general as traps and to make the complex intentionalities of the actors in the art nexus a defining criterium of artworks (Gell 1999 [1996], 203).

As already indicated, Gell deals with art phenomena from a micro-relational perspective on persons and things, whereby things "do duty" as persons do (Gell 1998, 9). Similar as British anthropologists like Marilyn Strathern (1998), he builds on Marcel Mauss' theory of the gift: "Given that prestations or 'gifts' are treated in Maussian exchange theory as (extensions) of persons, then there is obviously scope for seeing art objects as 'persons' in the same way" (Ibid, 9).

In his book *Art, Anthropology and the Gift* Roger Sansi discusses important aspects that "complement" Gell's theory (Sansi 2015, 18). Although his focus is on Western contemporary art, these aspects are also important with respect to the local or regional arts that we deal with. Sansi departs from Strathern and Gell, in that he looks at what art does in the process of production. But he argues that not only intentionality but also chance and bricolage play a role. This is particularly relevant in the history of art since Dadaism and Surrealism, and in anthropology these aspects have been put forward by Lévi-Strauss. Particularly for Duchamp choice of his ready-mades meant chance, and art is found in the encounter, or the event, less in the object. For Lévi-Strauss the issue of chance and the term bricolage became pivotal in his study *The Savage Mind* (1966). The mind continuously transforms contingent events into structure. In this process, chance plays an important role. Our book thus draws on Mauss' and Gell's transactionism, intentionality and agency, but at the same time we acknowledge the importance of chance and bricolage.

Moreover, Sansi complements Gell's theory, and is important for us, in that he points to the importance of "devices" that are associated with "regimes of power" (Sansi 2015, 59). Interestingly, artistic devices in current forms of participatory art can function as a mechanism of domination but also of empowerment. With a somewhat different approach, but also looking at art works as an extension of the agency of their makers, Fred Myers (2002) has already earlier pointed to the regime of the art market and the governmental regime, particularly educational institutions, as powerful contextual spheres of social life. These regimes enabled the recognition of the value of the acrylic paintings of the Western Desert Australian Aboriginal people, and their inclusion into the global art scene. Thus, we can infer that, apart from specific contemporary manifestations of participatory art, most art works themselves do not contain including or excluding mechanisms, but their "social-relational matrix" does (Gell 1998, 7). And particularly the (failing) institutional entanglements have a dominating or empowering effect (Myers 2002; Sansi 2015).

We suggest that it is essential to problematise issues of local and global encounter, including hierarchisation and marginalisation, much deeper than has been done to date (cf. Kisin and Myers 2019; Sansi 2015; Schneider 2017). Indigenous art is often discursively and practically positioned in the margins of the art world and of mainstream society—and thus in the margins of past, present and probably future world encounters. In a similar way this is the case with folk art and art brut which are the subject of some of the articles. In recent contemporary art theory, the dynamism of interpersonal social encounters in situations of everyday life, with the participation of the public is considered as highly fruitful, and relations of equality are stressed (Bourriaud 2002). Sansi and others comment that hierarchies are not necessarily weakened but strengthened, also in participative non-commercial or gift-like art encounters (Sansi 2015). Nevertheless, as we have seen, in the production of art promises of a different future, or micro-utopias, may gleam (Sansi 2015, 157). Based on Gell and Sansi, we thus argue that art builds social relations both through gifts and commodities, that art works are produced both through intentionalities and chance, or bricolage, and that art-making enables micro-utopias. This is particularly important when it comes to the issue of development and art on which we elaborate below.

In this volume we look at arts in a global context. Regarding globalisation we distinguish different phases, for example those related to processes of colonialism, post-colonialism and neoliberalism. They shape interpersonal encounters in different ways. As already mentioned, in the anthropology of art today much attention is given to the "global modern" and the "global contemporary" in art (Schneider 2017). But to what extent is the contemporaneity of "traditional" arts, or "folk arts", presently acknowledged in the art world? Our strong impression is that this is hardly the case, despite current efforts of cooperation between "alternative artists" and anthropologists (Schneider 2017). We suggest that "folk arts", including forms such as outsider art, are still marginalised, and thus continue to be positioned, discursively and in social practice, in the margins of the global art world. Moreover, we would like to point out that both artists and anthropologists tend to create subtle, mostly implicit but consequential binaries between "folk arts" and "contemporary arts". This is even the case, when "traditional arts" are part of or point of departure of exhibitions, or when they are included in projects of transcultural art research and art collaboration. Some examples presented in the edited volume by Schneider (2017) bring that clearly to light.

The most revealing example for our discussion here is a collaborative project in art research and art production between Bhutan and Switzerland (Bucher et al. 2017a), starting from Gell's premise that art is social action. A group of Bhutanese and Swiss art teachers and art students met in both countries to present their concepts of local Buddhist "traditional arts" and European exclusive "contemporary art" respectively, theoretically and practically, and subsequently that they made a joint mural in Bhutan. The authors, who are the teachers of the project, explicitly contend that they are not interested in existing and imaginary dichotomies, such as we vs. others and contemporaneity vs. tradition. In a similar vein, the result of the discussions was that "both forms have their traditions *and* are contemporary, suggesting that their usual designations are somewhat misleading and imply value judgments" (Bucher et al. 2017a, 173). These assertions, nevertheless, do not remove the impression of many following statements that the concepts tradition and contemporaneity implicitly are still of questionable relevance, if not in the joint artwork itself, then still in the knowledge and social practices of the participants. In a conversation three years after the project, one of the Swiss teachers admitted that to create a setting on equal terms was difficult due to the "highly judgmental terms (within art discourse) of 'contemporary art' and 'traditional art'" (Bucher et al. 2017b, 186), despite the solution mentioned above. And the other Swiss teacher said that the individual artist's ego of Swiss students hindered a deeper engagement with the Bhutanese context (Ibid, 185).

Through the creation of dichotomies between "traditional" and "contemporary" art forms, the former are more or less devalued, mostly implicitly, with the problematic result that their dynamics and factual potential as contemporary art are excluded. And it has economic consequences as well. It still seems difficult to go beyond a metropolitan conversation between contemporary art and anthropology, as Schneider (2017) and others (Fillitz and van der Grijp 2018) have the merit to advocate.

Let us come back, again, to the issue of arts, social transformation and marginality. Not only in the making of contemporary arts micro-utopias emerge. This is even more the case in "arts in the margins" that we are dealing with in this volume. As already hinted to, we are interested in the "creative living" in the margins. This is a site of paradoxes of constraining and empowering moments, of heterogeneity and dispute, as Tsing reminds us, and it cannot be understood without its wider interconnections. Correspondingly, she asserts: "The 'local' is a form of positioning in the regional, national, and global, and 'local' here is contested" (Tsing 1994, 286). Thereby, she also brings the important issue of gender into play. From a somewhat different angle, but with a similar emancipatory stance, the black American author bell hooks makes us understand that from the "lived experience" in the margins, not only informed by gender but also by race, artists may use their creativity "to imagine alternatives, new worlds" (hooks 1990, 341). Marginality is thus much more than a site of deprivation. It can be a "site of radical possibility, a space of resistance", and most important in our view, it can be a site of remembrance "giving us ways to speak that de-colonize our minds, our very beings" (hooks 1990, 341, 342).

Re-creating art conventions in the margins of world encounters

All the chapters in this volume depict how historically, socially and politically marginalised people live with and within art practices. In order to illustrate how art and anthropology can be harnessed to change a site of vulnerability into that of possibility and resistance, in the following we would like to consider historically the relationship between art, anthropology and marginalised people in a broad perspective.

In his article dealing with the modern visual arts, Gell points out that the formative period of modern visual art (i. e. 1890–1925) coincides exactly with that of anthropology, in which the intellectual currents that created the distinctively "modern" sensibility in visual arts were active (Gell 2013 [1985], 88). In spite of this historical homology, modern visual art and anthropology have followed related but different trajectories concerning people and their artefacts in the areas marginalised by Western mainstream society. In the early formative period, artists like van Gogh and Gauguin went beyond the boundaries of their familiar lives to experience marginalised areas. In the later formative period, avant-gardists such as Picasso and Léger, living in Paris, the world capital city at that time, came to appreciate "enchanting" artefacts from the marginalised "primitive" areas. The main providers of these artefacts were often anthropologists. In contrast, anthropology left armchairs and established the methodology of long-term fieldwork in "primitive" areas as an indispensable part of its discipline. While anthropological practices were carried out in the political milieus of colonisation, as was critically illustrated in *Writing Culture* (Clifford and Marcus 1986), modern Primitivism in Western art was also realised against the backdrops of colonial politics and hegemonic consumerism, as Clifford points out:

> "Picasso, Léger, Apollinaire, and many others came to recognize the elemental, 'magical' power of African sculptures in a period of growing *négrophilie*, a context that would see the irruption onto the European scene of other evocative black figures: the jazzman, the boxer (Al Brown), the *sauvage* Josephine Baker" (Clifford 1988, 197).

As the Western artists and art world have appropriated non-Western artefacts as artworks, non-Western people have likewise appropriated Western art and its system of museums, art schools, collectors, dealers, appreciators and so on in the context of power imbalances which has historically marginalised non-Western people. In the 19th century, Western art was appropriated by the non-Western young elites under the strong influence of colonial governments such as the Dutch East Indies (Suwarno 2010, 14–16), or the governments of the newly formed modern states such as Japan. Due to a combination of the strong governmental influence and crises of identity, those young elites were willing to appropriate Western art. Through global encounters in the formative period of modern art, the mutual appropriations between the non-West and the West began—specifically by the avant-gardists, who belonged to the middle-class, and by the non-Western elites.

After the Second World War, art education and appreciation, which had tended to be monopolised exclusively by the upper classes, became popular among the masses as well, in both the West and the non-West. Since then, the mutual appropriations have spread even further. They might have been positive if the relationship between the non-West and the West were equal and reciprocal. However, since the aesthetic judgements are mostly based on Western art world-centred criteria, there is always a tendency that existing marginalisation and inequalities are intensified.

As mentioned above, despite the historical homology, modern art and anthropology have followed distinctively separate trajectories. The criticism against orientalism and second-wave feminism in the 1970s as well as the shock that the book *Writing Culture* (Clifford and Marcus 1986) brought about in the 1980s led anthropology toward self-reflection. It was seriously disputed whether anthropology was possible in terms of political correctness and epistemological relevance. As a result, anthropologists relativise and scrutinise their own viewpoints strongly in order not to take their ethnocentric view as universal. In contrast, it seems that artists and other art experts in the mainstream art world are not sceptical about the universality of art and their aesthetic judgements (Foster 1995; Nagaya 2104, 35).

Clifford puts forward a critical consideration of an exhibition entitled *'Primitivism' in 20th Century Art: Affinity of the Tribal and the Modern* held at the Museum of Modern Art (MoMA) in New York in December 1984 (Rubin ed. 1984). In the exhibition, the artworks by modern Primitivists and "tribal" artworks were displayed side by side according to their affinity and appeal to modern taste.

> "The affinities shown at MOMA [*sic*] are all on modernist terms. The great modernist 'pioneers' (and their museum) are shown promoting formerly

despised tribal 'fetishes' or mere ethnographic 'specimens' to the status of high art and in the process discovering new dimensions of their ('our') creative potential" (Clifford 1988, 195).

According to Clifford, the MoMA exhibition is based on Western modern aesthetic judgements and allegedly on humanistic generosity. It ignored "Third World modernisms" and the "disturbing questions about race, gender and power" (Clifford 1988, 195, 197).

This method of display, putting ethnographic artefacts and Western artworks side-by-side, has also been adopted by other exhibitions such as *Magiciens de la Terre* held at Pompidou Centre, the National Modern Art Museum, in Paris in 1989 (Shimada 2018, 53–54). In 2006, former French president Jacques Chirac opened the Quai Branly Museum. With high-tech lighting and devices, and without explanation of the ethnographical background or colonial deprivation, the museum displays artefacts from non-Western marginalised, non-occidental or non-oriental areas in such a way as to make the artefacts look not only exotic but also stylish like high-grade commodities. The effect produces an atmosphere reminiscent of an amusement park. Visitors enjoy consuming their experiences in the museum with the museum shops and restaurants. With the exception of Australian Aboriginal paintings, it can be pointed out that since most of the items were collected during colonial times and the "Third World modern arts" are not included, the museum, especially its permanent exhibition, seems to enhance tacitly the superiority of the West over the areas where those items originated from (Yoshida 2007; Kawada 2007; Ogino 2009).

The non-marked category "art" or "Kunst" has worked as an exclusive category in the art world, which has influenced mainstream society—the Western, colonising, developed, metropolitan, urban and upper-middle-class society—in the globalising world. For example, crafts, souvenirs and kitsch are all excluded from art. Although the concept of art is specific to this kind of mainstream society, it is regarded as essential and universal. As long as the art world acknowledges them, any artefacts can be artworks. If Shelly Errington's conception is applied, not only the works created by Western artists but also those created by non-Western artists can be categorised as "art by intention," while non-Western enchanting artefacts appreciated in the circles of the modern Primitivism have become "art by appropriation" (Errington 1998; Svašek 2007, 11). Modern or contemporary artworks produced intentionally by non-Western artists tend to fit poorly in the Western centred art world. When those artefacts produced outside the art world are admitted into the art world, they are given marginal positions indicated by particular, often devaluing, labels such as primitive art, tribal art, folk art, naïve art, art brut, pop art (Becker 1984; Danto 1964, 1988, 1992; Gell 1999 [1992]; Svašek 2007). Even in these cases, the license of being art is issued by the art world based on its own aesthetic judgement.

Against this backdrop, displaying in authoritative art institutions "Third World modern arts" by intention (Chapter 5), artefacts with ritual performances based on non-Western cosmology (Chapters 2 and 6), everyday goods of the marginalised people (Chapter 8), performances by excluded people like refugees (Chapter 9), and shamanistic art practices (Chapter 6) is disturbing and subverting not only to the art world but also to mainstream society. In other words, the performative display of these objects and performances can ignite the world to change (cf. Butler 1999). It is from this perspective that all the contributors to this volume explore marginalised people's "art" practices. Especially, the chapters in the first part of this book argue how those "art" practices can enrich and even re-create art conventions through world encounters.

Appropriating and resisting the global art world

Even within or in the margins of the art world, there have been various "art practices" challenging, contesting, resisting and trying to change the hegemony of the mainstream art world and mainstream societies since the formative period of modern art. In the late 19th century, some artists left their hometowns to search for innovative inspiration by marginalising themselves from mainstream society. This tendency has often been referred to as Bohemianism, which still lingers to provide us with popular images of artists (Firth 1992). In the early 20th century, avant-gardists, such as Dadaists and Surrealists, emerged. The word "avant-garde", which was first used as a military term to mean the frontier between "our land" and the enemy's land, then came to be used to mean socialists, and was finally applied to people who tried to go beyond the frontier of the conventions of art. In this generation artists also placed themselves on society's margins.

Since the formative period of art, while various art movements denying the authority of the art world have emerged with hopes to democratise and improve the world dominated by the mainstream society with "art" as cultural capital, the artworks and discourse that these movements produced have ironically been reincorporated into the art world (Minami 2014). The art market has played an indispensable role in the process of reincorporation.

Following the end of the Cold War, the neoliberal economic system has extended its influence, and economic disparity has spread, leading to a greater number of people living insecure lives (Abramovitz 2014; Ferguson 2009; Standing 2014). Under these historical conditions, the role of the art market has been enhanced, which in turn deprives the art movements of their resisting power. Claire Bishop, an art historian and art critic, points out that in the beginning of the 1990s the "social turn" in art occurred and artists' interest in participation, collaboration and multitude in global arenas resurged as political reaction to the abasement of communist regimes (Bishop 2012).

In his article in *Traffic in Culture: Refiguring Art and Anthropology* (Marcus and Myers 1995), Hal Foster, an art historian, pointed to the artists' growing interests in identity, otherness and its representation in which, artists thought, ethnographers (anthropologists) were experts. As mentioned above, he expressed this change as "ethnographic turn" in art (Foster 1995). This implies that artists carry out their socially engaged projects in much the same way as anthropologists do fieldwork. However, in doing so, they may end up projecting their own vision on "others" inadvertently without awareness. It is because they have not questioned or criticised the "universality" and authority of art in what they are doing as artists. Using this argument, Foster warned artists of the danger of the patronisation of the concerned community in carrying out a socially engaged project in the vein of postcolonial and postmodern art resistance. In the article "The Author as Producer" Walter Benjamin provided a similar warning to authors in the socialist resistance movement (Benjamin 1978 [1934]). While Foster pointed to the limits of art, Marcus and Myers disenchanted and politicised art by showing "in contemporary cultural life, art is becoming one of the main sites of cultural production for transforming difference into discourse" (Foster 1995; Marcus and Myers 1995, 34; Sansi 2015).

In the recent decades, however, art has become more and more enchanting, and art practices have globally flourished in various spheres. The three kinds of entangled currents producing the unprecedented flourishing of art practices may be differentiated: pro-neoliberal, contra-neoliberal, and currents driven by the international organisations such as the United Nations and UNESCO, which we will see later.

The West-centred art world has spread its horizons recently. It has been keeping "art" exclusive, while going hand in hand with art-like consumer (sub)cultures such as fashion, design, animations, comics and so on. In the neoliberal climate, the art market has become one of the most important arenas for investments and has been looking for *terra incognita* in artworks to satisfy the ever-changing tastes of dealers and art consumers. Accordingly, the range of commoditisation of artworks has been expanded. Even in developing countries, extremely rich people have appeared and have become art collectors, not only for investment purposes but also for prestige and moral acknowledgement. New middle classes have also emerged and demonstrated a class distinction by appreciating West-centred art (Miyazu 2014; Hook 2014, 2017).

With the advent of the 21st century, stylish museums for Contemporary Art such as the Quai Branly Museum in Paris, France, the 21st Museum of

Contemporary Art, in Kanazawa, Japan, and the Museum of Modern Art and Contemporary Art Nusantara in Jakarta, Indonesia, have increased worldwide. Well-designed shops, cafes and restaurants are set up in the museums, in one way or another linked to galleries and art fairs, which aim at selling artworks. The acts of appreciating art are in a sense embedded in a series of activities and the lifestyle of consumer culture. Cyberspace and social media play indispensable roles in the flourishing of visual arts. Art agents such as museums, galleries, art fairs, art magazines and so on spread real-time information on visually attractive homepages. Social media platforms make it possible even for small organisations and individuals to spread and respond to written and visual information. Through cyber space and social media, people have developed new ways of experiences (Miyazu 2014; Benjamin 1968 [1936]). Stephane Martin, the president of Quai Branly Museum, says "there are no partitions between corners nor fixed routes in our museum. Visitors can walk around freely. While a conventional ethnological museum is a book and visitors read it page by page, our museum has been evolved into that like a cyber space" (Martin 2007, 82). The great popularity of Quai Branly Museum might be explained in part by its space design which may be more closely aligned with the new ways of experiences.

Against the neoliberal currents, which further marginalise vulnerable people, such as the poor, refugees, ethnic minorities, the disabled, immigrants, the indigenous, and people in postcolonial conditions, various socially engaged art movements have been advocated and initiated. Of these art movements, some try to promote dissent to uncover the difficult reality as Bishop radically proposes (Bishop 2012), while others are more moderate, and aim to foster "friendship cultures" as Nicolas Bourriaud suggests (Bourriaud 2002), or to adapt to the current situations as many art management promoters recommend (Helguera 2011).

The flourishing of art has attracted the attention of many scholars. A special issue entitled *Artification* was published in an online journal *Contemporary Aesthetics* in 2012. The contributors are scholars and practitioners in various fields, such as philosophy, education, aesthetics and mass media. In the introduction, the editors of the special issue, Naukkarinen and Saito, propose to use the neologism "artification" to refer to "situations and processes in which something that is not regarded as art in the traditional sense of the word is changed into (…) something that takes influences from artistic ways of thinking and practicing" (Naukkarinen and Saito 2012, 1). Moreover, they "believe that the concept of artification is useful for understanding a topical and important cultural phenomenon that currently affects our ways of thinking about art and its relation to other spheres of culture" (Ibid.). The articles in the special issue argue how useful artification is in such fields as business, scientific research, natural history museum, health care, welfare, sports, environmental activism and education, which lack creativity or other features typical of art.

In a volume entitled *Aesthetic Capitalism,* the contributors, who are mostly engaged in cultural sociology and social aesthetics, argue that because the 2008–2010 Global Financial Crisis revealed that "the age of the post-industrious economy was over" and various advanced economies turned out to be much less high-tech or info-tech, "aesthetic capitalism" works as "the promise of something on the horizon" (Murphy and de la Fuente 2014, 1, 7). They maintain that the innovative, creative and inspiring faculty of aesthetics and art is important to understand and activate the economies and the world, based on the assumption that capitalism is the necessary condition at present and in the future (Murphy and de la Fuente 2014).

Although investors in the art market, art critics in the media, curators of museums opened recently, artists participating in exhibitions, radical and moderate art activists, and scholars in various fields related to art all have diverse politico-economic stances, they seem to share the Western centric idea of the creative, innovative and inspiring power of art, and focus their concerns mostly on Western urban issues. With this in mind, what can anthropologists do for the marginalised people highlighted in the chapters of this volume?

Since the above-mentioned art-related experts influence the public greatly, it is important for anthropologists to form a dialogue with them in order to resist the hegemony that tends to marginalise the people whom the experts unconsciously tend to leave outside their scope. For the dialogue, first of all, anthropologists should draw the experts' attention to the issues, including those dealt with in this volume, in the right and relevant ways. It seems that Clifford's critical consideration and Gell's persevering analysis concerning "art" are still so inspiring not only to anthropologists but also to the art-related experts. If anthropologists can develop their considerations and analyses, it will help to facilitate such a dialogue. Gell's as well as Clifford's analytical and critical insights can work as "catalyst to further exploration, innovation and, most intriguingly, cross-disciplinary engagement" (Chua and Elliot 2013, 17).

Besides forming a dialogue with art-related experts, anthropologists can also witness, accompany and even collaborate with the marginalised people resisting and appropriating the hegemony amidst the flourishing of art practices, the entangled currents, ambiguous consumer cultures and the discursive cyber spaces of the globalising world today.

Anthropologists' engagements with marginalised people as witnesses, companions and collaborators are not at all static or determined. This is because they are always part of a process in which anthropologists are likely to be displaced not only in their "fields" but also in their places of origin as was the case with Michel Leiris (Clifford 1988, 165–174). As Clifford suggests in his book *Routes*, practices of displacements might emerge as constitutive of cultural meanings, and people's movements and encounters keep marginalising and centring as two sides of the same coin in entangled ways (Clifford 1997, 3). While the West has been geopolitically centred since the time of colonisation, endeavours to decentre the West among many native peoples have been going on simultaneously. Especially the native histories of survival, struggle, and renewal have become widely visible since the late 1990s and the native endeavours to centre themselves in their life are much activated in the 20th century (Clifford 2013). The art-culture system, in which the West has divided the artefacts of virtuosity into artworks by Western individuals and cultural artefacts by non-Western collectives, has been challenged and subverted. The museums, which were exclusively places for the art-culture system, have often turned into contact zones for diverse people and collections to encounter in innovative and democratising ways (Clifford 1988, 1997, 2013). In this vein, the chapters in the second part of this volume argue how marginalised people's art practices appropriate and resist the global art world in the marginalising-centring dynamism.

Even in the global academic world of anthropology, movements, encounters, centring and marginalising have been occurring. As in the global world in general, the West has been centred from the beginning of the history of the global academic world of anthropology in the early 20th century. Because writing has been the most important process in anthropology, the fact that English has played a role in the common language has unmistakable significance. In other words, the academic worlds of the English-speaking countries, especially the UK and the US, have been centred in the global academic world of anthropology. While it is quite typical that for non-native speakers the use of English is accompanied by some difficulty, both as a matter of language as well as the challenges associated with converting ways of thinking, it is also true that the global academic world in English is open to whoever uses the language in academic writings and presentations. In a sense, like museums, this could work as a contact zone for anthropologists of diverse linguistic, national, cultural, social, economic and political backgrounds, whose encounters may innovate the global academic world and even the academic worlds of English-speaking countries. All the contributors of this volume are in a marginal positionality with regard to the global academic world of anthropology in terms of languages and scholarly careers. We hope our volume based on our encounter at the 18th IUAES Conference in Brazil will work as an academic contact zone, and our hybridity will make some contribution to the study of arts in the margins of world encounters.

New forms of art and ethnography in museums and development

If "margins", as suggested above, can be sites not only of exclusion, but also of resistance, it is important to ask in what ways that can be possible. To this question there are many potential answers. As the essays in this volume suggest, one of the main means through which art can act as resistance not only to the state of marginalisation itself, but to the conditions that have created that situation, is precisely what might be termed "aesthetic resistance" — creating forms, objects and performances that challenge the "canon" and represent embodied forms of imagination materialised in ways that are significantly different from the conventionally defined qualities of art. Essentially, this is what is meant by the term "polycentric aesthetics". That there is not one centre from which aesthetic values flow, and which retains the right of definition but many, each one of which is valid in its own terms. In other contexts, art can be activist: quite self-consciously opposing economic structures (typically capitalist ones), the negative impacts of globalisation, particular political formations or practices which are deemed to be oppressive or unjust (e. g. Raunig 2007). This latter stance often links the arts to the question of "development" and the role that they may play in advancing humane and sustainable forms of such development. At yet another level questions of both cultural appropriation and of the role of museums arise. The problem of potential or actual cultural appropriation is a complex one. The arts have always borrowed from one another across cultures. But the question of when artistic appropriation becomes akin to "biopiracy"—the illegitimate taking without acknowledgement or compensation the biological, intellectual or artistic property of others—is a vexed one. In a globalised world where access to knowledge about alternative art forms is easily available through the internet, publications, documentary films, and travelling exhibitions, that is hard to resolve. Situations in which indigenous artists have few legal or other resources to defend the originality and integrity of their productions, are particularly vulnerable to exploitation and appropriation, and this is an issue that should be constantly kept in mind when discussing the arts presented in this volume and parallel cases from around the world (Anderson and Geismar 2017; Brown 1998; Geismar 2013).

But keeping this in mind, the two questions of the relationship of arts from the margins of global encounters to, on the one hand "development", and on the other representation in museums both locally and internationally, can be fruitfully explored in relation to the empirical and interpretative contents of the book.

The arts and development

Classical paradigms in the field of development studies have been heavily economistic. Even the subject of the sociology of development has tended to emphasise social structure (issues such as class, caste and gender) at the expense of discussions of culture as actually practiced. That would include areas such as religion, and most certainly the arts. Slowly however, a paradigm shift has begun to occur. We see that not only in academic writing on the subject in the areas of a more holistic approach to development studies (Clammer 2015), in the anthropology of development, and comparative cultural studies, particularly those interested in manifestations of "popular culture". We also see that in publications by mainstream multilateral institutions such as the United Nations Development Program (UNDP) and the United Nations Educational, Scientific and Cultural Organization (UNESCO). These two have made a concerted effort to not only highlight the role of culture in development, but to concretise this through encouraging the recognition and stimulation of what they have termed the "creative economy", or local cultural industries including crafts, studio art, theatre, dance, music and film making. These cultural industries are not only important aspects of culture worth preserving and publicising, but they are also powerful routes to poverty alleviation and to the creation of self-respect (UNESCO/UNCTAD 2008; UNESCO/UNDP 2013).

It is not only scholars but also UN agencies and in many cases NGOs who are pursuing this route: many governments are beginning to do the same. A visitor to Delhi for example who is interested in the large range of Indian indigenous arts, can find a large government-run dedicated centre, a virtual shopping mall in fact, on the periphery of the major Connaught Place shopping area, with many floors of paintings, carpets, furniture, brass-work, wood carving, textiles, pottery, and local herbal products, teas and fashions. Similar centres can be found in other major Indian cities and represent concerted efforts to market art forms (and to preserve and stimulate them) that are otherwise inaccessible to the average visitor without travel to provincial towns or remote villages.

Quite apart from this bureaucratic stimulation and marketing of local art forms, has been the rapid expansion of the market for "tribal art" in India, a phenomenon perhaps parallel to the virtual invention (as a marketable and museum-enabled form) of Aboriginal art in Australia. Such art is now widely shown in dedicated art museums, sold in specialised galleries and is easily available for purchase at outlets in the cities, including in such venues as the Craft Museum in central New Delhi, and various crafts fairs. The advent of the internet has made access to images of a huge range of art forms instantly possible, and many on-line outlets now exist through which such art can be bought, whether through what are in effect virtual galleries or through NGOs that have set up marketing networks for the sale of arts and crafts that they have themselves stimulated. A number of such organisations now exist for marketing the art of the marginalised and the handicapped in Africa and elsewhere.

This expansion, however, also raises the question of "tourist art": the production of art forms thought by their creators to appeal to the tourist market, a phenomenon apparent wherever such tourism occurs. This raises a number of interesting questions implied by many of the case studies in this book: not only of appropriation, but also of authenticity. Such work is clearly indigenous but produced for a largely foreign market. Should this be read as an example of local entrepreneurship, as promoting exactly the kind of artistic activities that UNESCO among others recommends, or as an aesthetic sell-out, producing ersatz work of low artistic quality for purely commercial reasons? Such a question cannot be easily answered as it involves a complex constellation of aesthetic judgements, local and global economics, the rights and autonomy of local artistic communities and social policy. Nevertheless, it hovers at the edges of the situations analysed in many of the essays in this book, and of any discussion of "art from the margins", and links the discussion here to both older debates about "ethnic" and tourist arts initiated principally by Nelson Graburn (Graburn 1976), and which have re-appeared more recently in debates about the position of art in postcolonial situations, in which the power of the global economy still influences and distorts what is possible politically, economically and artistically in formally independent nations (Phillips and Steiner 1999).

Incorporating such approaches, which build on the kinds of art forms discussed in this volume (specifically in Chapter 8), extend the scope of anthropology itself in fresh and important directions. These include a dialogue between the anthropology of art and the anthropology of development, and by doing so drawing attention to the central role of culture in any holistic approach to development, promoting the idea of what might be called "aesthetic democracy"—the genuine co-existence of alternative forms and systems of artistic production and appreciation, and promoting empowerment, re-skilling and the active preservation of cultural forms, not as monuments, but as living expressions of artistic creativity. Such approaches not only link up with contemporary discourses of sustainability (not only economically, but equally because a good case can be made for the position that cultural diversity is as important as biodiversity for the future of our planet), but with post-colonial discourses as well. Post-colonial theorising about culture has been heavily literary and has overwhelmingly focused on the written word: visual cultures and performance have been given much less attention. But as the cultural critic and scholar of "Third Cinema", Rey Chow has cogently put it:

"What is needed, after the ethical polemic of Said's *Orientalism* is understood, is the much more difficult task of investigating how visuality operates in the postcolonial politics of non-Western cultures besides the subjugation to passive spectacle that critics of orientalism argue." (Chow 1995, 13).

The chapters in this book are in large part, answers to that question. The notion of "exhibition" also raises the question of public representation, and in particular the role of the art gallery or museum in showing the forms of art discussed in this book, an issue that again some of the chapters address.

It has long been recognised that museums are highly political spaces: what they show (or fail to show), how what is shown is presented, and how it is explained or justified, are critical questions, often concealing deeply ideological questions. As the Indian scholar and theatre director Rustom Bharucha rightly argues, museums can all too easily "freeze" a dynamic reality and in so doing produce an ahistorical and distorted view of the culture and artefacts being represented (Bharucha 2002). They ideally have positive educational roles, and even democratic ones by making available aspects of history and culture either largely unknown or the preserve of the elites, and in the context of this book, of making accessible the arts of cultures that have fallen for the most part outside of the mainstream of art history and criticism (Karp et al. 1992; Sylvester 2009). Recognising these dangers, many museums now very consciously attempt to present the art of the "margins" in its proper cultural and historical context and to give such art equal status with conventionally recognised "high art".

Good examples include the Bharat Bhavan in Bhopal, India, a gallery that shows side-by-side modern and contemporary Indian painting and the tribal arts of India, the juxtaposition creating a fascinating dialogue between the two traditions. Very close by, also in Bhopal, is the Indira Gandhi Rashtriya Manav Sangrahalya, which is a museum devoted entirely to "tribal arts". Around the world numerous other examples can be found: in Paris, France, the Musee du quai Branly (which contrasts interestingly with the main ethnographic museum in Paris, the Musee de L'Homme), in El Salvador the Museo AJA de Culturas y Artes Populares para la Ciudadania Global y Planetaria (the AHA Museum of Folk Arts for Global and Planetary Citizenship) (Desmond and Benavides 2013), or in New Caledonia the architecturally remarkable Tjibaou Cultural Centre designed by Renzo Piano for the indigenous Kanak people.

In commenting on the issues raised by such museums, Arun and Gita Wolf in discussing the work of the Indira Gandhi museum in Bhopal introduce the concept of "symbolic inversion". That means the viewing of the world from the aesthetic perspective of the "margins" by those artists who in their words "remain outsiders and are seldom invited to participate in dialogues around culture and representation" (Wolf and Wolf 2015, 144). In their book, based on an analysis of the tribal arts in the museum in question, they argue that new and hybrid art forms can and do emerge from multicultural milieus in which different art forms are brought into contact with one another, and that museums have a critical role in mediating an inclusive and authentic pluralism. This points them towards developing what they term an "innovative curation pedagogy" in which "crafts" are seen as authentic art forms, and in which the pluralism of which they have spoken is practised. At the same time, it is recognised that in the context of a globalised world in which tribal artists are often excluded or situated on the periphery, "the challenge becomes to face rather than ignore this dispossession while trying to find more egalitarian ways of conducting dialogues" (Wolf and Wolf 2015, 12). When this is done well, museums of the art of the "periphery" can sow the seeds of the rejuvenation of those art forms and can create conversations around and between cultures.

The fundamentally political nature of museums, intersecting with their formal cultural and artistic roles, has of necessity to be included in any discussion of the presentation of art from the "margins" (Karp and Lavine 1991; Karp et al. 2006). This in turn has implications for art education (Hanley et al. 2013): if "Third World" art students are expected to be exposed to the art of the West, it is only reasonable that Western art students should be exposed to the art of the "rest". They would indeed receive great stimulation from their exposure to "alternative" aesthetic systems and expressions at the same time as art students anywhere are exposed to critical pedagogies and a heightened awareness of the social and political contexts of art production and consumption, including that of "minorities" in the so-called advanced countries.

References

Abramovitz, Mimi. 2014. "17 Economic Crises, Neoliberalism, and the US Welfare State: Trends, Outcomes and Political Struggle." *Global Social Work: Crossing Borders, Blurring Boundaries*, edited by Noble, Carolyn, Helle Strauss and Brian Littlechild, 225–240. Sydney: Sydney University Press.

Anderson, Jane L. and Haidy Geisma, eds. 2017. *The Routledge Companion to Cultural Property*. London and New York: Routledge.

Appadurai, Arjun. 1986. *The Social Life of Things: Commodities in Cultural Perspective*. Cambridge: Cambridge University Press.

Bakke, Gretchen and Marina Peterson, eds. 2018. *Between Matter and Method: Encounters in Anthropology and Art*. London: Bloomsbury.

Basu, Paul, ed. 2017. *The Inbetweenness of Things: Materializing Mediation and Movement between Worlds*. London: Bloomsbury.

Becker, Howard S. 1984. *Art World*. Berkeley: University of California Press.

Bell, Joshua A. 2017. "A Bundle of Relations: Collections, Collecting, and Communities." *Annual Review of Anthropology* 46: 241–259.

Benjamin, Walter. 1968 [1936]. "The Work of Art in the Age of Mechanical Reproduction." In *Illuminations*, edited by Hannah Arendt, 217–251. Translated by Jarry Zohn. New York: Schocken Books.

Benjamin, Walter. 1978 [1934]. "The Author as Producer." In *Reflections*, edited by Demetz, Peter and Edmund Jephcott, 220-238. New York: Harcourt Brace.

Bharucha, Rustom. 2002. "The New Asian Museum." In *The Third Text Reader on Art, Culture and Theory*, edited by Rasheed Areen, Sean Cubitt and Ziauddin Sardar, 290–300. London and New York: Continuum.

Biddle, Jennifer. 2018. "Remote Avant Garde: Tjanpi Desert Weavers." In *Senses and Sensation: Critical and Primary Sources. Vol. 4. Art and Design*, edited by David Howes, 179–195. London: Bloomsbury Academic.

Binsbergen, Wim van and Peter Geschiere, eds. 2005. *Commodification: Things, Agency, and Identities (The Social Life of Things Revisited)*. Münster: LIT Verlag.

Bishop, Claire. 2012. *Artificial Hells: Participatory Art and the Spectatorships*. New York: Verso.

Blanes, Ruy, Alex Flynn, Maïté Maskens and Jonas Tinius. 2016. "Micro-Utopias: Anthropological Perspectives on Art, Relationality, and Creativity." *Cadernos de Arte e Antropologia* 5 (4): 5–20.

Bourriaud, Nicolas. 2002. *Relational Aesthetics*. Translated by Simon Pleasance and Froze Woods with participation of Mathieu Copeland. Dijon: Presses du réel.

Brown, Michael F. 1998. "Can Culture be Copyrighted?" *Current Anthropology* 39 (2): 193–222.

Bucher, Annemarie, Sonam Choki and Dominique Lämmli. 2017a. "Tigers and Splashes: An Action-Oriented Art and Art Education Exchange Between Bhutan and Switzerland." In *Alternative Art and Anthropology: Global Encounters*, edited by Arnd Schneider, 163–181. London: Bloomsbury.

Bucher, Annemarie, Sonam Choki and Dominique Lämmli. 2017b. "Remains and Gains: A Conversation Between Sonam Choki, Dominique Lämmli, and Annemarie Bucher on Expectations, Challenges, Benefits, and Learning Processes." In *Alternative Art and Anthropology: Global Encounters*, edited by Arnd Schneider, 183–188. London: Bloomsbury.

Butler, Judith. 1999. *Gender Trouble: Feminism and Subversion of Identity*. New York, London: Routledge.

Chow, Rey. 1995. *Primitive Passions: Visuality, Sexuality, Ethnography and Contemporary Chinese Cinema*. New York: Columbia University Press.

Clammer, John. 2015. *Art, Culture and International Development: Humanizing Social Transformation*. Abingdon and New York: Routledge.

Clifford, James. 1988. *The Predicament of Culture: Twentieth-Century Ethnography, Literature, and Art*. Cambridge, Massachusetts, London: Harvard University Press.

Clifford, James. 1997. *Routes: Travel and Translation in the Late Twentieth Century*. Cambridge, Massachusetts, London: Harvard University Press.

Clifford, James. 2013. *Returns: Becoming Indigenous in the Twenty-First Century*. Cambridge, Massachusetts, London: Harvard University Press.

Clifford, James and George Marcus, eds. 1986. *Writing Culture: The Poetics and Politics of Ethnography.* Berkeley: University of California Press.

Chua, Liana and Mark Elliott. 2013. "Introduction: Adventures in the Art Nexus." In *Distributed Objects: Meaning and Mattering after Alfred Gell,* edited by Chua, Liana and Mark Elliot, 1–24. New York, Oxford: Berghahn Books.

Coote, Jeremy and Anthony Shelton, eds. 1992. *Anthropology, Art, and Aesthetics.* Oxford: Oxford University Press.

Danto, Arthur. 1964. "The Artworld." *Journal of Philosophy* 61: 571–84.

Danto, Arthur. 1988. "Artifact and Art." In *ART/ARTIFACT: African Art in Anthropology Collections,* Exhibition Catalogue, 206–208. New York: Center for African Art.

Danto, Arthur. 1992. *Beyond the Brillo Box: The Visual Arts in Post-Historical Perspective.* New York: Farrar Straus Giroux.

Descola, Philippe. 2018. "The Making of Images." In *An Anthropology of Contemporary Art: Practices, Markets, and Collectors,* edited by Thomas Fillitz and Pau van der Grijp, 25–40. London: Bloomsbury.

Desmond, Cheryl T. and Marta Benavides. 2013. "Kindling the Imagination: The Twenty-Third Century Movement (Movimento Siglo XXIII) and the AHA Museum of Folk Arts and Cultures for Planetary and Global Citizenship." In *Culturally Relevant Arts Education for Social Justice,* edited by Mary Stone Hanley, George W. Noblit, Gilda L. Sheppard and Tom Barone, 36–46. New York and Abingdon: Routledge.

Errington, Shelly. 1998. *The Death of Authentic Art and Other Tales of Progress.* Berkeley: University of California Press.

Ferguson, James. 2009. "The Uses of Neoliberalism." *Antipode* 41, no. s1: 166–184.

Fillitz, Thomas and Paul van der Grijp, eds. 2018. *An Anthropology of Contemporary Art: Practices, Markets, and Collectors.* London et al.: Bloomsbury.

Firth, Raymond. 1992. "Art and Anthropology." In *Anthropology, Art and Aesthetics,* edited by Coote, Jeremy and Anthony Shelton, 15–39. Oxford: Clarendon Press.

Foster, Hal. 1995. "The Artist as Ethnographer." In *The Traffic in Culture: Refiguring Art and Anthropology,* edited by Georg E. Marcus and Fred R. Myers, 302–309. Berkeley, Los Angeles, London: University of California Press.

Geismar, Haidy. 2013. *Treasured Possessions: Indigenous Interventions into Cultural and Intellectual Property.* Durham, NC: Duke University Press.

Gell, Alfred. 1998. *Art and Agency: An Anthropological Theory.* Oxford: Clarendon Press.

Gell, Alfred. 1999 [1992]. "The Technology of Enchantment and the Enchantment of Technology." In *The Art of Anthropology: Essays and Diagrams,* edited by Alfred Gell, 159–186. London: Brunswick, NJ: Athlone.

Gell, Alfred. 1999 [1996]. "Vogel's Net: Traps as Artworks and Artworks as Traps." In *The Art of Anthropology: Essays and Diagrams,* edited by Alfred Gell, 187–214. London: Brunswick, NJ: Athlone.

Gell, Alfred. 2013 [1985]. "The Network of Standard Stoppages". In *Distributed Object: Meaning and Mattering Alfred Gell,* edited by Liana Chua and Mark Elliott, 88–113. New York and Oxford: Berghahn Books.

Graburn, Nelson H.H. 1976. *Ethnic and Tourist Arts: Cultural Expressions from the Fourth World.* Berkeley and London: University of California Press.

Hanley, Mary Stone, George W. Noblit, Gilda L. Sheppard and Tom Barone, eds. 2013. *Culturally Relevant Arts Education for Social Justice: A Way Out of No Way.* London and New York: Routledge.

Harney, Elizabeth and Ruth B. Phillips, eds. 2018. *Mapping Modernisms: Art, Indigeneity, Colonialism.* Durham: Duke University Press.

Helguera, Pablo. 2011. *Education for Socially Engaged Art: A Materials and Techniques Handbook.* Taipei: Jorge Pinto Books.

Henare, Amiria, Martin Holbraad and Sari Wastell, eds. 2007. *Thinking Through Things: Theorising Artefacts Ethnographically.* London, New York: Routledge.

Hook, Philip. 2014. *Breakfast at Sotheby's: An A–Z of the Art World.* London: Penguin Books Ltd.

Hook, Philip. 2017. *Rogues' Gallery: A History of Art and its Dealers.* London: Profile Books.

hooks, bell. 1990. "Marginality as a Space of Resistance." In *Out There: Marginalization in Contemporary Culture*, edited by Russell Ferguson, Martha Grever, Trinh T. Minh-Ha, Felix Gonzalez-Torres and Cornel West, 341–343. Cambridge Mass.: MIT Press.

Ingold, Tim. 2013. *Making: Anthropology, Archaeology, Art and Architecture.* London, New York: Routledge.

Karp, Ivan, Christine Mullen Kreamer and Steven D. Lavine, eds. 1992. *Museums and Communities: The Politics of Public Culture.* Washington DC and London: Smithsonian Institution Press.

Karp, Ivan, Corinne A. Kratz, Lynn Swaja and Tomas Ybarra-Frausto, eds. 2006. *Museum Frictions: Public Cultures/Global Transformations.* Durham, NC: Duke University Press.

Karp, Ivan and Steven D. Lavine, eds. 1991. *Exhibiting Cultures: The Poetics and Politics of Museum Display.* Washington: Smithsonian Institution Press.

Kawada, Junzo. 2007. "Shitubo to Kitai to: Shin-Hakubutsukan ga Teikisurumono [Disappointment and Expectation: What the New Museum Raises]." In *Tokusyu, Pari no Bikkuribako: Ke-Buranri Bijutsukan ni Iko [Special Issue, A Jack-in-the-Box in Paris: Let's Go to Quai Branly Museum]. Geijutsu Shintyo* 58 (3): 88–94.

Kisin, Eugenia and Fred R. Myers. 2019. "The Anthropology of Art, After the End of Art: Contesting the Art-Culture System." *Annual Review of Anthropology* 48: 317–334.

Küchler, Susanne and Timothy Carroll. 2020. *A Return to the Object: Alfred Gell, Art, and Social Theory.* London, New York: Routledge.

Leach, James. 2007. "Differentiation and Encompassment: A Critique of Alfred Gell's Theory of Creativity." In *Thinking Through Things*, edited by Amiria Henare, Martin Holbraad and Sari Wastell, 167–188. London: Routledge.

Lévi-Strauss, Claude. 1966. *The Savage Mind.* Chicago: University of Chicago Press.

Marcus, George E. and Fred R. Myers. 1995. "Traffic in Art and Culture: An Introduction." In *The Traffic in Culture: Refiguring Art and Anthropology*, edited by Georg E. Marcus and Fred R. Myers, 1–51. Berkeley, Los Angeles, London: University of California Press.

Martin, Stéphane. 2007. "Sutefan Marutan Kantyo ni Kiku [An Interview with the President Stephane Martin]." *Tokusyu: Pari no Bikkuribako, Ke-Buranri*

Bijutsukan ni Iko [Special Issue: A Jack-in-the-Box in Paris, Let's Go to Quai Branly Museum]. *Geijutsu Shintyo* 58 (3): 82–83.

Minami, Yusuke. 2014. "The Context of Non-Art in Art." In *The Power of Images: The National Museum of Ethnology Collection*, edited by the Organizing Committee of "The Power of Images", 228–230. Osaka: National Museum of Ethnology.

Miyazu, Daisuke. 2014. *Gendai Ahto Keizaigaku* [Economics of Contemporary Art]. Tokyo: Koubunsha.

Morphy, Howard. 1994. "The Anthropogy of Art." In *Companian Encyclopedia of Anthropology*, edited by Tim Ingold, 255–260. London, New York: Routledge.

Morphy, Howard. 2007. *Becoming Art: Exploring Cross-Cultural Categories*. Oxford, New York: Berg.

Morphy, Howard. 2010. "Art as Action, Art as Evidence." In *The Oxford Handbook of Material Culture Studies*, edited by Dan Hicks and Mary C. Beaudry, 265–290. Oxford: Oxford University Press.

Morphy, Howard and Morgan Perkins, eds. 2006. *The Anthropology of Art: A Reader*. Malden, MA, Oxford, Carlont, Victoria: Blackwell Publishing.

Murphy, Peter and Edwardo de la Fuente. 2014b. "Introduction: Aesthetic Capitalism." In *Aesthetic Capitalism*, edited by Peter Murphy and Edwardo de la Fuente, 1–9. Leiden, Boston: Brill.

Myers, Fred R. 2002. *Painting Culture: The Making of an Aboriginal High Art*. Durham, London: Duke University Press.

Nagaya, Mitzue. 2014. "The Power of Images: From the Art Museum's Viewpoint." In *The Power of Images: The National Museum of Ethnology Collection*, edited by the Organizing Committee of "The Power of Images", 31–35. Osaka: National Museum of Ethnology.

Naukkarinen, Ossi and Yuriko Saito. 2012. "Introduction." *Special Issue, Artification. Contemporary Aesthetics*, Volume 4. Accessed August 20, 2019. https://www.contempaesthetics.org/newvolume/pages/journal.php?volume=49.

Ogino, Masahiro. 2009. "Tenji heno Kenri" [The Right to Exhibit Things]." In *Tenji no Seijigaku* [Politics of Exhibition], edited by Kawaguchi Yukiya, 41–59. Tokyo: Suiseisha.

Osborne, Robin and Jeremy Tanner, eds. 2007. *Art's Agency and Art History*. Malden, MA Oxford, Carlton, Victoria: Blackwell Publishing.

Phillips, Ruth B. and Christopher Burghard Steiner. 1999. *Unpacking Culture: Art and Commodity in Colonial and Postcolonial Worlds*. Berkeley and London: University of California Press.

Pinney, Christopher and Nicholas Thomas, eds. 2001. *Beyond Aesthetics: Art and the Technology of Enchantment*. Oxford: Berg Publishers.

Price, Sally. 1989. *Primitive Art in Civilized Places*. Chicago: University of Chicago Press.

Raunig, Gerald. 2007. *Art and Revolution: Transversal Activism in the Long Twentieth Century*. Translated by Aileen Derieg. Los Angeles: Semiotext(e).

Rubin, William, ed. 1984. *"Primitivism" in Modern Art: Affinity of the Tribal and the Modern*. 2vols. New York: Museum of Modern Art.

Sansi, Roger. 2015. *Art, Anthropology and the Gift*. London: Bloomsbury.

Sansi, Roger. 2017. "The Recursivity of the Gift in Art and Anthropology." In *Between Matter and Method: Encounter in Anthropology and Art*, edited by Gretchen Bakke and Marina Peterson, 117–130. London et al.: Bloomsbury.

Schneider, Arnd, ed. 2017. *Alternative Art and Anthropology: Global Encounters.* London: Bloomsbury.

Schneider, Arnd and Christopher Wright, eds. 2006. *Contemporary Art and Anthropology*. Oxford: Berg Publishers.

Schneider, Arnd and Christopher Wright, eds. 2010. *Between Art and Anthropology: Contemporary Ethnographic Practice.* Oxford: Berg Publishers.

Schneider, Arnd and Christopher Wright, eds. 2014. *Anthropology and Art Practice*. London, Oxford: Bloomsbury.

Shimada, Kotaro. 2018. "Tenrankai ni Miru Bijutsu to Jinruigakuteki Shikou no Tenkai [The Movement of Art and Anthropological Thoughts in Exhibitions]." *Tokusyu, Ahto to Jinruigaku: Tagenkasuru Sekai no Egakikata [Special Issue, How to Depict the Multiplying World: Art and Anthropology]*. *Bijutsu Techo* 70 (1067): 52–57.

Smith, Terry. 2009. *What is Contemporary Art?* Chicago: Chicago University Press.

Standing, Guy. 2014. "The Precariat." *Contexts* 13 (4): 10–12.

Strathern, Marilyn. 1988. *The Gender of the Gift: Problems with Women and Problems with Society in Melanesia.* Berkeley: University of California Press.

Suwarno, Wisetrotomo. 2010. "Introduction." In *Modern Indonesian Art: From Raden Saleh to the Present Day*, second revised edition, edited by Koes Karnadi, translated by Garret Kam, 14–22. Denpasar: Koes Artbooks.

Svašek, Maruška. 2007. *Anthropology, Art and Cultural Production*. London: Pluto Press.

Sylvester, Christine. 2009. *Art/Museum: International Relations Where We Least Expect It*. New York and Abingdon: Routledge.

Tilley, Christopher, Webb Keane, Susanne Kuechler, Mike Rowlands and Patricia Spyer, eds. 2006. *The Sage Handbook of Material Culture*. London: Sage.

Tsing, Anna Lowenhaupt. 1993. *In the Realm of the Diamond Queen: Marginality in an Out-of-the-Way Place*. Princeton: Princeton University Press.

Tsing, Anna Lowenhaupt. 1994. "From the Margins." *Cultural Anthropology* 9 (3): 279–297.

Tsing, Anna Lowenhaupt. 2015. *The Mushroom at the Ende of the World: On the Possibility of Life in Capitalist Ruins*. Princeton, Oxford: Princeton University Press.

UNESCO/UNCTAD. 2008. *Creative Economy*. Paris and Geneva: UNESCO Press and UNCTAD Publications.

UNESCO/UNDP. 2013. *Creative Economy Report 2013: Widening Local Development Pathways*. Paris and New York: UNESCO and UNDP.

Wolf, Arun and Gita Wolf eds. 2015. *Between Memory and Museum: A Dialogue with Folk and Tribal Arts*. Delhi, Chennai and London: Tara Books.

Yoshida, Kenji. 2007. "Chikyujin no Isan: Ke Buranri Bijutsukan 27 Sen [Global Human Heritage: 27 Items from the Quai Branly Art Museum]." *Tokusyu: Pari no Bikkuribako, Ke-Buranri Bijutsukan ni Iko [Special Issue: A Jack-in-the-Box in Paris, Let's Go to Quai Branly Museum]*. *Geijutsu Shintyo* 58 (3): 24–55.

Part I.
Re-Creating Art Conventions in the Margins of World Encounters

Chapter 1

Dress as art: portrait of an ikat weaver in Eastern Indonesia

Willemijn de Jong
University of Zurich, Switzerland

Abstract

After tracking textiles as art in Indonesian textile studies, the author argues that highly accomplished weavers on the island of Flores, Indonesia, create a unique form of art through their richly decorated *ikat* sarongs. One of the locally well-known weavers of a main cultural centre and weaving village in Central Flores is portrayed through her sarongs, particularly figurative ones. Theoretically, de Jong refers to Alfred Gell's anthropological theory of art and agency (1998) and the postcolonial approach by Niessen, Leshkowich and Jones (2003) with regard to the globalisation of Asian dress and orientalism. She further engages with Schneider's concept of alternative art (2017). Based on these authors, it is proposed that the textiles presented obtain their artistic quality through the entanglement of local, national and transnational social encounters. In these interactions they are imbued with agency through technical skills, aesthetics and intentionality regarding the ikat designs. By explicitly including creative, high-quality ikat clothing in the global art system and by relating them to counter-orientalism and modernity, a rethinking of the Eastern Indonesian cultural heritage of ikat textiles is suggested.

Key words: textile art, ikat sarongs, globalisation, counter-orientalism, Flores

In textile studies, ikat clothing from Eastern Indonesia, similarly to batik from Java, is often analysed in regard to tradition, and in retrospection. To get fresh insights into handmade clothing today, it seems fruitful to look at them in the context of contemporary fashion and art without losing sight of historical processes (Clifford 1988). In some earlier publications I focused on fashion (de Jong 2020; Kunz and de Jong 2016), but in this chapter I will focus on art, acknowledging that we cannot make a strict separation between the fields of fashion and art (Steele 2012).¹ My aim is to achieve a deeper understanding of textile art in Indonesia that takes women as textile artists seriously and draws attention to the marginality of regional textile art as folklore.

Generally, Indonesian arts are seen to have developed in specific social and ritual contexts (e. g. Aragon and Leach 2008, 615). Politically they have always been regulated, locally or translocally. For example, during the dictatorial era of President Suharto (1966–1998), textiles of outer-island minorities were categorised, homogenised and hierarchised as static regional arts. But in fact, "Indonesian regional arts engage fluid and polysemic ideas about social hierarchies, group identities, and cosmology" (Aragon and Leach 2008, 620). That also applies to regional textile arts.

In his article "Indonesian Textiles from Dress to Art", Michael C. Howard denies the artistic character of handmade clothing by making a categorical distinction between cloths "to be worn" on the one hand, and textiles "to be hung as works of art" (Howard 2007, 38, 52) on the other. As examples of clothes to be worn, he shows that a new batik movement emerged in the 1960s. Some years later the long-sleeved batik shirt was introduced as an official dress. New styles of regional or local dress decorated with local patterns and tailored according to European styles were also created.

As examples of textile arts, Howard (2007) highlights painted pieces of bark cloth (*maro*) from Papua and sacred ikat textiles (*paramba*) of the Toraja. He categorises them, drawing on Nelson Graburn, as "commercial fine arts" (Graburn 1976, 6), that means pieces made for sale but with culturally embedded aesthetic and formal standards. Moreover, Howard distinguishes high-quality narrative ikat textiles (*hinggi*) of East Sumba that are used as wall hangings following Graburn as "reintegrated arts": art objects based on "tradition" but with "new forms" regarding ideas, materials or techniques (Ibid, 7). In all the three cases, the making of the cloths has been revived, or recently created.² Howard attests that in post-Suharto Indonesia, "independent-traditional" weavers continue to weave quality textiles. In general, local elites, next to national elites and foreign markets, revive interest in high-quality, figuratively patterned textiles for display, exemplified by the work of some elite batik producers. Howard stresses that men came to dominate batik art even

---

[1] An earlier version of this article has been published in German in 2011 with the title „Kleidung als Kunst: Porträt einer Ikatdesignerin in Eastern Indonesia" in the journal *FKW///Zeitschrift für Geschlechterforschung und visuelle Kultur* 52. Accessed August 13, 2019. http://www.fkw.journal.de/index.php/fkw. It has been reworked and reprinted with the permission of the publisher.

[2] Similarly, the blankets (*pua kumbu*) of the Iban Dayak have been reinterpreted (Low 2009).

though it was formerly largely a female domain. Finally, he concludes that Indonesia's textile art is marginal in national and international art markets.

How can we get a deeper understanding of textile art in Indonesia, and one that pays homage to women textile artists as well? How can the marginality of regional textile art be explained and countered? These are the questions that I address in this chapter. First, I will briefly look at how handmade textiles are characterised in Indonesian textile studies. Then I will portray the accomplished weaver Elisabeth Pango, called Mama Ango, through an analysis of her ikat tube skirts, or sarongs. Ikat is a tie-and-dye technique to create complex designs. Mama Ango lives in a regionally well-known weaving village in Central Flores, Eastern Indonesia, a junction of early world trade and since the 1970s of global travels for pleasure. I will look at her ikat sarongs with a perspective particularly inspired by the art anthropologists Alfred Gell (1998) and Arnd Schneider (2017) and by studies on Asian dress by Sandra Niessen, Anna Marie Leshkowich and Carla Jones (2003).

My argument in this chapter is that the intricately patterned textiles made by skilful, usually female weavers in Eastern Indonesia have a high quality through an entanglement of local, national and transnational processes and social interactions. Particularly through their technology and motivic intentionality, following Gell, ikat textiles as clothing can enact a unique artistic agency and their aesthetic is efficacious as well. Mama Ango's sarongs are a telling example. But there are also forces at work that impede the art character of these textiles, and that have to be countered to overcome the marginality of regional textile arts.

Handmade cloths as art in Indonesian textile studies

In Eastern Indonesia, handwoven textiles are used as prestigious festive dress, gifts and other objects of display in rituals. They have often been considered as art, be they worn or not. This is reflected in many publications, often even in the titles (see e. g. chronologically Hein 1890; Jasper and Pirngadie 1912; Rouffaer and Juynboll 1914; Steinmann 1941; Langewis and Wagner 1964; Breguet and Martin 1983; Orinbao 1992; Fisher 1999). A detailed exploration is not possible here, but the following main indications should suffice.

In 1890, the Austrian painter and art historian Alois Hein published a first influential study about the "decorative arts" of the Dayak in Borneo, later called Iban (Hein 1890). The term "decorative art", in contrast to "fine art", has been used since the Renaissance to describe the artefacts that are used. Hein attested that women who make *ikat* textiles have an "irrepressible drive for art" (Ibid, 153) through which they produce their own motifs and transform foreign motifs originating from early Arabian, Indian and Chinese influences. As his study is often referenced in early textile works, I assume that it laid the foundation of a discourse of Indonesian textiles as art.

Another well-known textile publication with an explicit art approach is *Decorative Art in Indonesian Textiles* (Langewis and Wagner 1964). The authors present more than two hundred cloths, mostly from the Royal Tropical Institute in Amsterdam from the 19th up to the beginning of the 20th century. Of the 41 ikat cloths of which the warp is tied, 11 are from Sumba and one from Flores, which shows how popular textiles were from Sumba—and how unknown textiles were from Flores—at that time. Interestingly, they do not distinguish any function of the textiles, but it seems that most of them were pieces of clothing. Their goal is to show the rich variety of ornamentations depending on the decorative technique but also to stress which ones are most important from an ornamental-aesthetical point of view. The authors remark that in Flores, similarly to in Sumba, one finds cloths with combinations of autochthonous and copied ornaments. Moreover, they distinguish cloths with large central fields ornamented with motifs derived from the famous Indian *patola* silk cloths that were imported by the Dutch during colonial times (Ibid, 23). Innovatively, they point to the individual artistry of the weaver with the conclusion that "the ornamental and aesthetical value of a work of art is determined by the 'creative surplus' and the craftsmanship of the person making it" (Ibid, 40). Their approach is also echoed in the edited volume with the title *Decorative Arts of Sumba* (Fisher 1999).

We can thus trace a genealogy of talking about "art" with regard to Indonesian textiles that has its source in Dutch colonial history. This contrasts with the discourse of "craft" in the British colonial and postcolonial context. But practices of marginalisation through traditionalisation and ethnicisation were similar and can impede the artistic quality of regional textiles, as I will show later. Aarti Kawlra has argued that the "cartographic paradigm of 'craft'" was part of the process of "traditionalization" of the colony (Kawlra 2014), as a contrast to Britain's modernisation. She remarks: "Colonial administrators and art officials appropriated artisanal production in India by spatially marking and fixing products and producers in the very process of mapping and documenting them as 'traditional crafts' of the colony" (Kawlra 2014, 6). Traditionalisation thus also means attributing a static and ahistoric quality to certain products and producers, as well as the social groups (gender, caste, ethnic group) with which they were identified. Different visual representations of the colony's products, through museums, expositions, fairs, etc., show "this official ossification and validation of artisanal production within an imagined, authenticating past" (Ibid, 7). Innovations and imitations allegedly testified a quality decline of the craft products. And the producers have been marginalised as "'living' repositories of an unchanged, even if fuzzy, technocultural past" (Ibid, 8). Such practices continue until today, according to Kawlra, for example when the production of a certain type of silk sari is marked by a geographical indication. Aimed to empower producer groups, the result is that materials, processes and producers are fixed to specific places of production, which is in contradiction to the creative local dynamics.

Considering the Indonesian textile arts, these publications show that the textiles have always been produced against the backdrop of global knowledge encounters and social interactions. In most surveys, as well as in regional publications of the last decades, the textiles are just coined as art whether they are dress, wall hangings or have other functions. The artistry of the handmade textiles, however, is hardly analysed based on any concept or proposition explicitly referencing the anthropology of art, or any other theory of art or aesthetics. Also, aspects that could jeopardise the view of these textiles as art are not explored. This also applies to the textiles of Flores and the Solor islands that only gained wider scholarly recognition from the 1970s onwards (Watters 1977; Barnes 1989; Orinbao 1992; Hamilton 1994).

Textiles as efficacious works of art

This chapter proposes a renewed orientation towards art in the study of Indonesian regional textiles as a step to overcome their marginality compared to other forms of art. This may further contribute to a higher appreciation and prestige of these artefacts in Indonesia and beyond, and increase the recognition of the makers, especially the women.

Increasing recognition of the textile makers may also lead to an improvement in the economic situation of their families. The weavers in the main textile areas of Flores (Ende, Lio, Sikka) are important income earners in their families, as their husbands often do agricultural work for daily use. But the prices for ikat textiles are not high compared to the long process required for making them, even when chemical dyes are used, which is mostly the case today.[3] At the same time, the needs for cash are extensive, especially to give children a good education. That is why many families are living at a subsistence minimum.

Like Susanne Küchler and other anthropologists, I generally presume that textiles entail agency through their materiality such as surface, textures and motifs, which again constitute social relationships and ways of life (Küchler

---

[3] During the 1990s a weaver earned the equivalent of one kilo of rice each day (de Jong 1998, 213–224). This is now a little less than one US dollar. When the weavers can regularly sell to tourists or to Chinese traders, they can earn up to three times more. A government teacher earns about six times more, and, moreover, is also entitled to an old age pension.

and Miller 2005; de Jong 2016a). My approach to ikat dress as art draws on the anthropological theory of art by Alfred Gell (Gell 1998; 1999 [1992]; 1999 [1996]). His approach has been influential and was vigorously debated during recent decades (Pinney and Thomas 2001; Mrazek and Pitelka 2008; Chua and Eliott 2013). To my knowledge, there are hardly textile studies that draw on Gell's art theory.[4] Ikat dress in Flores should be included into the global art system, similarly as Sandra Niessen and others advocate the inclusion of batik textiles into the global fashion system (Niessen et al. 2003; Niessen 2003a; 2003b; 2016). Particularly, handmade dress by weavers in allegedly peripheral regions should not be ethnicised or culturalised, and thus marginalised as folklore. A study of the sarongs of Mama Ango is pertinent, as they can be identified as striking pieces of art. But let me first present the basic ideas of Gell's art theory.

Gell embarks from a genuine social-anthropologically-based assumption that art is a system of social action, consisting of art objects, artists, recipients and things that are represented in the works of art (Gell 1998). Provocatively, he remarks: "In place of symbolic communication, I place all emphasis on *agency, intention, causation, result, and transformation*. I view art as a system of action, intended to change the world rather than encode symbolic propositions about it" (Ibid, 6). He does not define an art object starting from allegedly universal aesthetic criteria, as these are mostly created in a Western context. An object obtains its artistic value through a matrix of social relationships of persons and objects in which it is embedded. Subsequently, he calls his art theory a "theory of the art nexus" (Ibid, 12–27). As an example, Gell mentions *malangan* carvings from New Ireland, Papua New Guinea. They function as repositories of the "life-force" of deceased persons. They are accumulated during death rituals and are considered as the result of social activities during the whole life of that person. The technical procedures, through which the carvings gain more and more life force, are heating, burning and painting of the raw piece of wood by the carver who is inspired by the ancestors (Ibid, 225–226). In the same vein, Gell does not distinguish between an artistic "performance" and "artefacts". An artefact is "a congealed residue of performance and agency in object-form" (Ibid, 68).

For my analysis of handmade textiles and art that follows, I identified three criteria in Gell's works that are most useful. A first criterion to determine an artefact as art is its kind of manufacture. In a much-cited earlier article, he discussed the enchantment that certain objects effect due to the knowledge, skill and technical precision of work. In other words, the artistic quality of an

---

[4] Traude Gavin proposed an analysis based on Gell's approach at the end of her study on Iban ritual cloth (Gavin 2003). Samantha Hauw analysed the impressive colors of Chinese Miao textiles following Gell (Hauw 2009).

artefact is the "social technology" of "enchantment" (Ibid, 74) that we experience through such an object by its hardly comprehensible, and therefore often as magically conceived origin (Gell 1999 [1992], 166).

A second important criterion to assess an object of art is its complex "intentionality", as Gell calls it. He defines an art object as a vehicle of complex ideas with meanings that are often difficult to decipher (Gell 1999 [1996], 211). The technically and intentionally multiple character with regard to the agency of an object of art is clearly expressed in the following quote: "Where indexes [material entities from which cognitive interpretations result] are very recognizably works of art, made with technical expertise and imagination of a high order (…), then we are dealing with a canonical form of artistic agency which deserves special discussion" (Gell 1998, 68).

As a third criterion, I would like to draw attention to the aspect of aesthetics. Basically, Gell's endeavour is not a project of "indigenous aesthetics" (see also the introduction to this volume). Instead, his anthropological theory focuses on social contexts of art production, circulation and reception. He criticises art analyses that depart from non-Western aesthetics, as this would be a cultural and not a social approach. He concedes, however, that works of art sometimes are intended to be objects of aesthetic appreciation and are also thus perceived (Ibid, 66). Indonesian textiles are often both objects of clothing and objects of art, as I argue. Local people praise technicality, discuss the intentionality of motifs, and attribute an aesthetic quality to handwoven textiles. Therefore, within the specific social context of the local art nexus, the aesthetic quality is analysed here as well.

In his book *Arts and Agency*, Gell begins his discussion of the anthropology of art with "decorative art", which many "classical" studies about arts have dealt with. Moreover, many artists worldwide in this realm are women, including textile makers. Gell was well aware of a gender bias in the literature, also in his own work, but he saw the need to rectify that:

> "There is another reason for commencing the substantive discussion of 'the anthropology of art' with a consideration of decorative art, and that is the elimination of a form of gender bias which is prevalent in much of the anthropology-of-art literature (this work included) (…). Many, even most, decorative artists world-wide are women (…)" (Ibid, 73).

Gell particularly deals with the inherent agency in decorative patterns, with part-to-part and part-to-whole relationships, their animation through motions (reflection, translation, rotation, glide reflection); and with the interesting, never-finished exchange between the complex patterns of the decorated objects and the recipient, which dominates any aesthetic response, as well as patterns as protection and obstacles. In the ethnographic cases that Gell illustrates, pattern construction often is a form of art that shows knowledge and mastery, or generally "efficacy, the capacity to accomplish tasks, not 'beauty'" (Ibid, 94). Textile patterns in Flores serve multiple aims—knowledge and mastery as well as aesthetics—as I will show.

Mama Ango and her efficacious works of textile art

Mama Ango was born in 1947. She is one of about two dozen of the most accomplished weavers[5] who live and work in the cultural centre of Nggela in the south Lio area in Central Flores.[6] In this village of a little more than one thousand inhabitants, women in most of the households practice weaving to make a living. Mama Ango lived with her husband, a subsistence farmer, in a small, auxiliary ceremonial house made of bricks and bamboo. In addition to the usually simple furniture, the family-owned some stately wardrobes and a TV set. Mama Ango could buy these items because during the times of regular tourist visits in the 1980s, she could sell her clothes at the highest prices. As tourism declined in the area, but not in West Flores, this became more difficult. Mama Ango had to store many of her valuable textiles in her wardrobe. However, in October 2018 a terrible disaster happened, shortly after I met her that year. During a fire incident in the village centre, her house burnt down, together with 33 other houses (23 of which were ceremonial houses). All the belongings, including the precious textiles Mama Ango worked on, were lost. Until a new house can be build, she and her husband live in a small provisional house from sheet metal.

Mama Ango started to tie, dye and weave after attending primary school (de Jong 2016b, 118). Her mother had only mastered the simplest ikat designs, so she learned the more complicated ones from a neighbour. But after some time, she created many geometrical and figurative motifs anew by herself. About her learning process and her creativity she narrated:

> "With regard to doing ikat, I began with the horse motif [of the *lawo wenda*]. I found it easy, from the start. It seemed that I had talent. It was a gift from above (*karunia*). (…) When I was about thirteen, I began with

---

[5] Women usually make textiles in Flores, but there are also single men who practice the art of ikat.

[6] The weaving region in the southern Lio area counts about twenty villages. Nggela is one of the most important cultural centres with 1,019 inhabitants, 338 households, 214 peasants, and 248 weavers in 2016 (information by the village secretary). The system of handwoven clothes consists of thirty textile types, each with a name of its own, among which are twenty types of sarongs with different patterns (de Jong 1994).

a second and a third ikat pattern (...). After that I learnt for myself, just by looking at the patterns on the sarongs the women were wearing. (...) Whenever I begin to put the warp on the tying frame, I still have other thoughts. But during arranging the yarn in small bundles on the frame I get an image of the sarong that I will make. Before that I don't know yet. I never follow the motifs of other weavers, and I always make variations of the motifs. I only make the *lawo luka semba* as in former times" (Interview 8 July 2013).[7]

Today, Mama Ango is considered as one of the best weavers in the village. Over a period of more than thirty years, I have cooperated with her and other weavers, and also purchased textiles in that context.[8]

Technological agency: the manufacture of ikat textiles and the transformation of motifs

At first glimpse, the efficacy of Mama Ango's textile works depend on her technological virtuosity, especially her special skills in tying.[9]

Mama Ango does not tie too many threads per ikat bundle (*gami*), and not too many layers (*lapis*) at once. She also cleverly calculates the proportions of the motifs and their overall shape on the surface of the sarong. Then she dyes the tied yarn (*bue lele*) with several chemical dyes (*sumba*) as dark as possible, to look like she had used the natural dyes indigo (*nggili*) for blue to black and *morinda citrifolia* (*mengkudu/ kembo*) for different shades of red (de Jong 2016c). After that she accurately fixes the pattern with several bamboo sticks (*tu'e*), and she carefully weaves (*seda*) the three pattern sections of the sarong with a backstrap loom while sitting on the floor.[10] Finally, she sews the three parts together into a sarong of about 165 cm long, depending on the pattern design.[11] This complicated procedure cannot be dealt with in detail here but makes clear what Gell from a technological perspective considers as characteristic for art works in non-Western societies: a radical transformation of materials, yarn and dye stuffs in this case, into intricately patterned and sewn

---

[7] Translations of the quotations of Mama Ango from Bahasa Indonesia into English by the author.
[8] Since 1985, I have made regular cultural visits to the region and conducted about two years of anthropological fieldwork in 1987/88 and 1990/91.
[9] The tying of two sarongs, that are mostly made together, with complicated motifs takes up to one month.
[10] For pictures of weaving tools in Flores, see Hamilton 1994, 228–229 and de Jong 1998, 161, 199.
[11] The sarong is mostly worn tied around the waist or put over one or both shoulders.

weavings using simple tools; thus, prestigious objects are manufactured that can be sold for quite a high price in the market (Gell 1999 [1992]).

Figure 1.1 Mama Ango is tying a *lawo gamba* at her ikat frame.

Photograph by Willemijn de Jong, Nggela, Flores, 2011.

Mama Ango's technical knowledge and skills are also visible in her mastery of a broad range of different types of ikat designs.

Figure 1.2 Mama Ango shows several types of sarongs: *lawo pundi, lawo luka semba, lawo gamba.*

Photograph by Sabine Wunderlin, Nggela, Flores, 2009.

She mostly produces her ikat designs with synthetic, but sometimes with natural, dyes. Firstly, she makes a now-classic, formerly ritual dress (*lawo luka semba*) with a stylised pattern with eight-pointed flowers in the central field, similar to the pattern of the most known type of Indian *patola* cloth. This female sarong has the same main motifs as the male *luka semba* shoulder cloth (de Jong 2016a). These textiles are among the few cloth types with motifs that should not be changed; otherwise, the weaver could experience harm caused by the ancestors. The dress nevertheless shows her signature. Secondly, she creates rich varieties of geometrical designs, which few weavers are able to do. Thirdly, she manufactures designs on the pictorial sarong, called *lawo gamba*, which technically are still more difficult, and also rarer, and figurative designs on shoulder cloths (*luka tege*).

I will now look into the geometrical and figurative sarongs that can be freely invented. Geometrical patterns are the most familiar ones in the Ende-Lio area, especially the horizontally banded ones and those in the centre fields of the sarongs. More individual creativity is contained in sarongs designed with vertical rows and with motifs over the whole surface. Mama Ango calls the richly decorated sarong with nine vertical rows, each with another motif that she made in 1999, the "sarong with nine motifs" (*lawo sembilan motif*). It is a unique example of her ornamental creativity (de Jong and Kunz 2016, 119). Certain stars and lozenges resemble *patola* motifs that were freely reinterpreted on the local ikat sarongs. Moreover, she gets inspiration by looking at the patterns in a booklet with plaiting designs, also used for house walls.[12] She selects motifs she prefers and transforms and composes them in her own way on the ikat frame. Some years ago, she started to create fine lozenge motifs over the whole surface, calling them alternatively "batik" or "banana slices" (*jaba muku*) (de Jong and Kunz 2016, 87). The composition of the motifs gives this recent type of sarong a new flair.

The figurative sarongs (*lawo gamba*) originated in the 1970s in the Lio region (de Jong 2020). Before that, stylised anthropomorphic, zoomorphic and jewellery-like motifs sometimes appeared on shoulder cloths and sarongs. Mama Ango told:

> "Mama Gamba was the first weaver who made the national eagle motif, called *Garuda*, a large tree with gold jewellery and the house lizard. The motifs were different from the ones today. Now there are more motifs." (Interview 23 July 2010).

---

[12] Seri Kacapakan Khusus: Seni Anyaman (Series Special Skills: Plaiting Art). Departemen. Pendidikan dan Kebudayaan, INPRES No. 6, 1974.

One can distinguish two types of *lawo gamba*: those with mythical and ritual motifs, and those with motifs derived from everyday life. Mama Ango has created *lawo gamba* more and more since the 1990s, combining different motifs (de Jong and Kunz, 158, 159, 160). She is a great master in transposing model figures on the yarn at the ikat frame. In doing so, she does not care about naturalistic proportions. An impressive piece is the *lawo gamba Garuda* she made in 2016 with the eagle as the main motif.

For the motifs of this type of sarong, Mama Ango gets inspiration from pictures in all kinds of schoolbooks, from pictures of objects in everyday life (such as on match boxes, bank notes, and images such as the national mythical bird emblem (*Garuda*) on governmental flyers or in booklets), and from her own phantasy. As already hinted at, she sometimes "photocopies", as she says, certain motifs from sarongs of other women. She is able to tie small motifs and those that she already knows by heart. Regarding the *Garuda* sarong, Mama Ango interestingly recounted:

> "When you were here formerly, I was already thinking that I must tie a sarong with the *Garuda*, especially to sell but also to wear. But at the time of Suharto, people were afraid. They only looked at a sarong with such a motif [but did not buy one]. Now I have made the *lawo Garuda* two times, each time I tied two sarongs together, on a small tying frame. The first time, I made one for me and one for my daughter Flo, so that she will care for me when I am old. (…) The picture of the motif is from a booklet of the government (…). Quite some weavers tie that motif now, so I also did. I also want to tie the *Garuda* on a large tying frame. But if that motif is too big, it is not nice. It is coarse when it is too big. (…) The motif is difficult to make." (Interview 12 October 2017).

When we compare her older figurative sarongs with newer ones, it is striking that the motifs and patterns show an interesting formal transformation. The motifs achieve more technical precision and clearness. Particular combinations of motifs become more diverse and complex. Certain motifs are continuously slightly changed and also partly diminished. That means that the process of tying is more difficult and takes more time as the motifs become more complex. Moreover, the overall structure is increasingly vertically arranged, with ornamental borderlines. But recently she dissolved this strict composition, as seen in the sarong made in 2016.

Dress as art 15

Figure 1.3 *Lawo gamba* made by Mama Ango in 2016 with motifs of the ritual sacrifice, the sacred snake, gold jewellery, the national eagle emblem and the photographer.

Photograph by Sabine Wunderlin, 2017.

As an interesting example of how Mama Ango continuously transforms her motifs is the gold jewellery (Figure 1.3, de Jong and Kunz 2016, 159). This motif is composed of a chain with one or two decorated gold plates (*gebe rajo*) and several vulva-shaped golden earrings (*ome mbulu*) of different sizes, sometimes linked with one or two small dancers. As a whole, the gold jewellery is an imagined motif combination, the parts of which occur in reality in different contexts. Chains with gold plates decorate high-ranking elderly women at the ritual of the renewal of the roofs of certain ceremonial houses. The earrings circulate as part of bridewealth and are worn at the rain dance ritual by high-ranking younger women. "I make them all by heart. I once looked at the rain dance, and at the gold jewellery at the neck of the dancers", Mama Ango commented (Interview 23 July 2020). On her sarongs, the gold jewellery motifs are technically created in a specially differentiated and imaginative way. Thus, their agency is fully displayed.

Intentional agency: rituals, everyday life, and the foreign gaze

As far as their content is concerned, the motifs and motif combinations on the sarongs of Mama Ango, especially on the figurative sarongs, excel by "complex intentions" (Gell 1999 [1996], 211). They illustrate mythological ritual sacrifices of the rice mother, ritual objects such as the gold jewellery just mentioned, ceremonial houses and pictures alluding to working activities (e. g. domestic and agricultural work, fish vending), and scenes that show heroes from earlier overseas origins, for example in pictures of ships. The ritual motifs enact crucial local and regional cultural ideas or knowledge practices[13] and desires for fertility, prosperity and wealth (cf. also de Jong 2020).

One example of a complex and partly enigmatic idea, which the sarongs embody, is the motif of the ritual sacrifice of a young woman by one of her brothers. It is the most important motif of many pictorial sarongs and is derived from a myth that is widespread from Southeast Asia to Japan. The rice and other plants grow from the buried parts of the young woman's body, and she arises anew as the divine rice mother locally called Ine Mbu Ine Pare. The Catholic priest and ethnographer P. Sareng Orinbao initiated this motif, assuming its marketable potential. In an earlier article, I dealt with this motif more in detail (de Jong 2020). Mama Ango once found a picture from Orinbao's book (Orinbao 1969) with drawings of the rice mother and used it as a template for her sarongs. By their multi-layered meanings, such motifs have an artistic potential in the sense of Gell, and at the same time they are part of a politics of belonging and also marketing.

---

[13] Following Marilyn Strathern, I define knowledge practices as knowledge of the world and knowledge of the practices and methods that build knowledge of the world (Strathern 2005, 184).

A second, particularly illustrative example of a multiple but not really comprehensible intentionality is the foreign person (*orang asing*), the tourist (*turis*), or the photographer (*tukang potret*) on many of Mama Ango's figurative sarongs (Figure 1.3, de Jong and Kunz 2016, 158). The model is a picture of a man from a schoolbook who is taking a photo of a dinosaur and his tracks. Mama Ango translates the figure in a small size, in several variations, kneeling or standing. She places him semi-randomly at different places in the textile space—mostly on the margins of the sarong's scenes. On a sarong made in 2011, he is even shown in two different contexts: photographing the rice mother scene and photographing some animals. He represents, as I would argue, the foreign gaze or a foreign perspective—a kind of reversal, or at least a distancing of local views. By including the foreign perspective, Mama Ango enhances the significance of her motifs and her ikat art at large in that she testifies that they are worth being photographed by foreigners. Moreover, she makes a rupture with her local lifeworld, which is, as elsewhere, full of tensions. Her ikat work fascinatingly shows not a closed conception of a local lifeworld but a collage of different translocal and transnational perspectives of the present, with selected aspects of daily life and localised adaptations of myths and rituals.

Aesthetic agency: "sweet" motifs and colours

Mama Ango has aesthetic ideas that are strongly influenced by local as well as by personal taste. The main features of the local aesthetics of the ikat sarongs concern the motifs, their composition on the surface of the cloths, and the special ground colour, dark blue or dark redbrown, that is valued as "quiet". Generally, the white or yellow-orange motifs should not be too big, and the surface of the textile should not show any empty areas. The main motifs are horizontally or vertically arranged, placed in the centre field or over the whole surface of the sarong. The simplest motifs, such as zigzag lines of the horizontally arranged patterns, may have originated in the 14th century or even later (cf. Hamilton 1994). More sophisticated geometric and animal figures were inspired by the silk and cotton trade cloths from India since the first millennium AD and particularly with the Dutch "incursions" from the 16th to the 20th centuries (Hamilton 1994; Maxwell 2014 [1990]). The most complicated, rather naturalistic motifs have emerged since the 1970s and 1980s, when the weavers began to search for new images from all kinds of pictorial materials, influenced by international tourism and subsequent efforts of the Catholic church and also of the government support of making artistic and fashionable ikat textiles (de Jong 2020).

In this respect, Mama Ango follows the local aesthetics, but at the same time she is highly innovative regarding the motifs and patterns. She always tries to create new motifs according to her own ideas, be they geometrical or figurative. She also continually searches for new templates. She even used to ask me to bring her new pictures to enlarge her motif stock. The "sweetness" of the motifs is an important criterion for her. She thinks, for example, that animals such as Komodo monitor lizards that attract tourists to the small islands to the west of Flores, are too coarse, or not "sweet" enough *(manis/mi)*, to be depicted on sarongs. She only creates them on shoulder cloths. Once she explained the selection of motifs like this:

> "I need pictures for my motifs. After I have seen another *lawo gamba* I can make the motifs by heart. I also make own variations in the spare space on the tying frame. (…) When I see good pictures, I keep them. I got the Ine Mbu picture from a book that other people had thrown away, the Komodo dragon from a bag of cement. A small ceremonial house must always be there, so that foreign people feel attracted to come to Flores. If I want to make new motifs, I take coarse ones for the shoulder cloth and sweet ones for the sarong. If you have pictures, please bring them with you" (Interview 25 September 2009).

When people in the village discuss the highest quality ikat work, they often praise her and two other local weavers. Their works are called artistic (*nggiku* in the Lio language and *seni* in Bahasa Indonesia). In contrast to Mama Ango, the other two weavers inherit their "magic", or enchanting, ikat competences, as the interlocutors and as Gell would say, from their clan descent in the maternal line. Accomplished weavers like Mama Ango often fear that while weaving (but not while dyeing, cf. Hoskins 1989, 2008), their ikat motifs can be destroyed by the witchcraft of other weavers. Therefore, they often work in a hidden setting, or try to protect their weaving work from the views of others.

Acquisitions of the most expensive sarongs of Mama Ango and other accomplished weavers by solvent dealers from nearby towns and from Bali, as well as by collectors for private and museum collections, confirm the artistic quality of their diverse and fanciful ikat textiles. As we have seen, selected ikat cloths have been considered as art in many publications on Indonesian textile studies, but often without further theoretical foundation. Along with Gell, I agree that the artistic quality of artefacts—in this case ikat sarongs—cannot be based on universal aesthetic criteria (Gell 1998). It rather bears on a connection of enchanting mastery and complex intentionality of motif designs that cannot always be fully reconstructed, including the intention to enlarge the spectrum of local aesthetics by creating new motifs and patterns.

Ikat sarongs as art: impeding and favourable knowledge practices

As the analysis drawing on Gell shows, we can aptly consider Mama Ango's ikat clothing as art. But why is it not usual to look at textiles in this way (cf. Howard 2007)? I will now argue that looking at textiles in other ways than as art has to do with knowledge practices about Asian dress. Firstly, ethnicisation and gendering of this kind of clothing by the makers and by the nation-state impede that ikat sarongs are considered as art. Secondly, the practice of internal orientalism of the nation-state can be detrimental to the art character of ikat clothing. And thirdly, ideas about traditional and contemporary art are constricting. The first two issues are convincingly problematised in the postcolonial debate on fashion Asian dress (Jones and Leshkowich 2003) and can also be applied to the art context. In this debate, performative practices of self-fashioning by making, wearing, buying or selling clothes are central. I suggest that related to these performative practices, knowledge practices play an important role as well.

Let us first look at ideas of ethnicisation and gendering, implicated in dress. Self-fashioning as a part of self-making in Asian contexts is inevitably linked to self-orientalism or self-exoticism, meaning "producing and consuming an exoticised image of one's own cultural identity" (Jones and Leshkowich 2003, 28). This, they say, is an unconscious strategy to get discursive control over the negative narrative of Western orientalism. At the same time, it is linked with a devaluation and feminisation of Asian clothing, for example of Indonesian sarongs. In the pattern designs of Mama Ango, we see creative performative practices of self-fashioning. They can be understood as an answer to external global and regional influences through trade, tourism, religion (Catholicism in this case), and politics. Not uninfluential was the contact with the anthropologist, as Mama Ango once remarked. Moreover, Mama Ango's self-fashioning can be looked at as an indirect answer to important political changes at the end of the 1990s, when President Suharto resigned. These developments have also stimulated local processes of cultural revitalisation and reinterpretation in Flores beyond individual practices (Erb 2007).

Mama Ango's self-fashioning shows transmitted motivic representations of group memberships (regional, ethnic, village-wise, educational), in addition to idiosyncratic motifs. This kind of self-fashioning draws collective and personal boundaries. These representations are strongly gender-specific, for example in the female motif of the sacrifice of the young woman who becomes a rice mother, the earrings, the male motif of the hero, and the fish vendor. The ikat designs represent a social and cultural universe, inspired by myths, rituals and everyday life. The origin of such clothing is immediately visible for people with the same local background and is often ethnically interpreted. For Western eyes, the intentionality of such an iconography is inaccessible. It is strange and exotic. Only with in-depth local and regional knowledge can it be familiar. One can say that Mama Ango cultivates a self-orientalism for a Western public that can be detrimental to seeing her ikat sarongs as art objects. But the universe of her ikat designs is not a closed one. It is open for variations, and new elements are integrated if they are "sweet" enough according to her taste. National elements are present, too: for example, the hero from the banknote and recently the Garuda emblem.

Secondly, the practice of internal orientalism of the nation-state can impede the art character of ikat clothing as well. Particularly in Asian peripheries, women and their dress practices are often represented as exotic Others and backward, in contrast to the allegedly civilised, development-oriented nation-state citizens. At the same time, the unity of the heterogeneous nation-state is often constituted by folkloristic ethnicisations, and the cultural richness is played down. In an article about clothing, nationality and urban Indonesia, Jones reminds us that it is not unusual for postcolonial citizens "to embrace a form of self-Orientalizing that represents the national collective through women's 'traditional' dress in ways that make both the particular outfit and the connection between women's bodies and the national body appear to be natural and timeless" (Jones 2003, 186). The ethnicisation and traditionalisation takes place both for an Indonesian public to fix the coherence of the modern nation, and for a foreign public with the aim of international commercialisation. At first glance, Mama Ango's work with her specific ikat designs is in line with a certain form of internal orientalism and ethnicisation of clothing. For both kinds of public, Indonesian and foreign, tourism plays an important role. This contributes to the fact that cultural artefacts, such as houses, rituals and dances, and also regional or local arts, achieve a new, also partly folkloristic meaning. Next to national ceremonies, tourism events offer a favourable space of the traditionalising of the handwoven dress. Thus, similarly as in the Indian case of "crafts" mentioned before, a governmental tendency to reify handwoven textile work regarding tradition, gender and ethnicity is taking place. These forces are partly but not always at the expense of the dynamic creative and artistic potential of the local in Indonesia. For example, Mama Ango's creed is a continuous variation of motifs and types of sarongs, also based on the imagined demands of the market: "I have to take into account what tourists like, and they like *lawo gamba*". And because we sometimes talk about textiles and museums, she is convinced: "In a museum, people would very much attend to *lawo gamba*" (Interview 14 July 2011). At another visit she makes clear:

> "Each *lawo gamba* is different. That is what I want because I have to earn money for living. It is now difficult to get money. Bapak [her husband] works on the field for food. I myself want to make a different sarong each time, also a different *lawo gamba*" (Interview 16 June 2015).

Thirdly, basic knowledge practices in the global art world play a role in the misrecognition of regional handmade dress as art. This continues to be the case despite current efforts of cooperation between "alternative artists" and anthropologists (Schneider 2017). Only very selectively, and based on specific networks, have Indonesian regional textiles begun to find a place in national or global art (Low 2009). Even recent studies and conversations show that both artists and anthropologists often create a subtle, mostly implicit but consequential binary between so-called "traditional arts" (or "folk arts") and "contemporary arts" (see the introduction to this volume). This is even the case when regional artefacts are part of, or a point of departure from, art exhibitions—or when they are included in projects of transcultural art research and art collaboration (Schneider 2017). Moreover, rural weavers are affected by the "global hierarchy of value" (Herzfeld 2004, 2–5) that goes along with economic and cultural globalisation. That means that due to their origin in the countryside, producers of artefacts are socially and economically classified lower than urban designers and artists. Their creations, although those creations amply bear witness of their independence, high technical skills, originality and innovativeness, can nevertheless easily be traditionalised and devalued.

Nevertheless, coming back to Mama Ango, when taking a closer look at the motifs of her sarongs, their ethnicisation and traditionalisation visibly rupture. Namely, we can detect counter-orientalist practices that favour the view of her ikat clothing as art. The term "counter-orientalism" was coined for the conscious strategy to struggle against orientalism, with the makers of the Japanese suit as an example (Kondo 1997). Another example deals with male designers in Hong Kong who critically reflect cultural debates in their society through their creations (Skov 2003). In the alienating motif of the photographer on the figurative sarongs of Mama Ango, we can indeed locate a counter-orientalising practice of the weaver. Mama Ango anticipates the foreign gaze, and she appropriates it. Hardly any other weavers I know try to find out which figurative motifs are attractive for Western visitors and make transnational links, as Mama Ango does. She makes herself a subject to the foreign gaze, but only to a certain extent. Her ikat work shows in a particular way her selection of exotic elements that constitute her own creative world while enabling the livelihood of her family and the purchase of some consumer objects as well.

Mama Ango does something structurally similar to Asian designers and artists on global stages such as in Hong Kong or Jakarta: With her kind of cultural production, she creates a reflexive distancing from a culture that dominates in her local context (Spielmann 2017). This even contains a neutralising aspect of gender (degendering), or gender ambivalence, because depending on the foreign visitors, she denotes the photographer as male or female. Thus, the identification with the textile is easier, and the desire to buy is stimulated, according to Mama Ango. Designers in Hong Kong would make a "critical form of art" by their counter-orientalism (Skov 2003, 239). In the case of Mama Ango, a similar practice is at stake. It reinforces the complexity of intentionality and thus contributes to the artistic potential of her ikat clothing. Mama Ango, one can suggest, creates in her ikat designs, especially in the figurative ones, a new and open view of a local, regional, national and transnational life-world. In other words, she makes visual collages of multiple perspectives that can be interpreted in different ways. The visual collages of her sarongs enact a form of efficacious and reflexive dress art, less radical than, for example, the T-shirt art in the Pacific (Colchester 2003), but nevertheless with a touch of irony.

Decolonising regional textile arts

Ikat textiles in Central Flores are a product of many local and translocal encounters of textile knowledge and related social interactions due to trade, tourism, religion and politics. They are created in the margins of Indonesian's current flows of wealth. But these margins are also a site of creativity, i. e. a centre of a specific network of social relationships that enabled centuries-old cultural inventions that are continuously changing. These inventions include communal ceremonies and kin-oriented rituals and feasts with their specific material expressions. In such a context, through a multitude of relations with persons and things, weavers like Mama Ango could achieve the knowledge and skills to create textiles of enchanting technicality and complex intentionalities. As small-scale entrepreneurs, they are involved in multifarious networks with other producers and a plethora of consumers who include relatives and receivers of their textile gifts and non-related local, regional and international dealers and other interested buyers. Moreover, they or their daughters proudly display the textile creations at rituals, feasts and other occasions. Besides their personal efficacy, or mastery, the most knowledgeable and skilful weavers want to show that they innovatively build on a specific, efficacious aesthetic legacy of handwoven clothing of their community and textile area. Especially Indian *patola* silk textiles regularly traded by the Dutch in colonial times were a source of inspiration regarding motifs, patterns and design. And since the second half of the 1970s, new imaginations and pictures have been induced by development efforts of the regional Catholic church and the government, related to the growing importance of international tourism. These current and former social encounters and relationships enable certain textiles to become considered works of art.

As we have seen, ikat sarongs can easily be orientalised: in a self-fashioning way, and by the governmental image regimes of traditionalising and ethnicising ideas about female clothing. At the same time, closely reading their motifs rich with ideas and creating distance from orientalising or colonising devaluations, helps discover expressions of counter-orientalism and art in ikat dress. If one draws on Gell (1998), specific ikat creations become unique works of art. This is particularly the case if one looks at them in the frame of a co-constitution or interaction of an "enchanting" technology that enables the making of unusual motifs on the one hand and complex intentionalities regarding the motifs and their combinations on the other (Gell 1999 [1992]; 1999 [1996]). One of these intentions is to enlarge the spectrum of local aesthetics with innovative patterns. Many textiles are fascinating, dynamic visual collages from newly created local, national and transnational elements. These aspects should be stressed against reifying practices of traditionalisation, gendering and ethnicisation.

Not only further theoretical debates against dichotomous conceptions of "traditional" and "contemporary" art are needed. More systematic public displays of marginalised art forms in interplay with mainstream art are also necessary, as are increased efforts to bring these various art forms into interaction with each other in educational and developmental institutions. These efforts require a decolonising stance regarding the nexus of regional textile arts, their social practices and knowledge practices.

Eventually, when handmade clothing, such as the sarongs of Mama Ango, are considered as art, it should be possible to include them into the art world of Indonesia and beyond as objects on equal footing with contemporary art. Thus, the diversity of the Indonesian and greater art world could significantly be enriched. Such an inclusion may also lead to more equality in the power relations related to global art. At the same time, it would be important that the specific social relationships that form the art nexus of Indonesian handmade textiles are kept alive. That would implicate that the social relations of giving these textiles as gifts and/or the demand for high-quality handmade textiles for ceremonies, feasts and collections would remain intact. Under such conditions, the economic value of high-quality regional textiles would be increased, the precarious situation of the makers improved, and their artistic work further encouraged. The spaces of textile making in the margins could then become efficacious sites of both creativity and power.

References

Aragon, Lorraine and James Leach. 2008. "Arts and Owners: Intellectual Property Law and the Politics of Scale in Indonesian Arts." *American Ethnologist* 35 (4): 607–631.

Barnes, Ruth. 1989. *The Ikat Textiles of Lamalera: A Study of an Eastern Indonesian Weaving Tradition.* Leiden: Brill.

Breguet, Georges et Jacques Martin. 1983. *Art textile traditionennel d'Indonésie*. Lausanne: Musée des arts décoratifs.

Chua, Liana and Mark Elliott, eds. 2013. *Distributed Objects: Meaning and Mattering after Alfred Gell*. New York, Oxford.

Clifford, James. 1988. "On Collecting Art and Culture." In *The Predicament of Culture*, 215–251. Cambridge, MA: Harvard University Press.

Colchester, Chloe. 2003. *Clothing the Pacific*. Oxford: Berg.

de Jong, Willemijn. 1994. "Cloth Production and Change in a Lio Village." In *The Gift of the Cotton Maiden. Textiles of Flores and the Solor Islands*, edited by Roy Hamilton, 210–227. Los Angeles: UCLA Museum of Cultural History.

de Jong, Willemijn. 1998. *Geschlechtersymmetrie in einer Brautpreisgesellschaft. Die Stoffproduzentinnen der Lio in Indonesien* (Gender Symmetry in a Bridewealth Society. The Cloth Producers of the Lio in Indonesia). Berlin: Reimer Verlag.

de Jong, Willemijn. 2016a. "The Shoulder Cloth *luka semba*: Being (Trans)Local in Flores." In *Striking Patterns. Global Traces in Local Ikat Fashion*, edited by Willemijn de Jong and Richard Kunz, Museum der Kulturen Basel, 104–114. Berlin: Hatje Cantz.

de Jong, Willemijn. 2016b. "Six Weavers." In *Striking Patterns. Global Traces in Local Ikat Fashion*, edited by Willemijn de Jong and Richard Kunz, Museum der Kulturen Basel, 115–127. Berlin: Hatje Cantz.

de Jong, Willemijn. 2016c. "Red Threads in Flores." In *The Common Thread. The Warp and Weft of Thinking*, edited by Vanessa von Gliszczynski, Eva Ch. Raabe and Mona Suhrbier, 50–61. Berlin: Kerber Verlag.

de Jong, Willemijn. 2020. "Ikat Patterns in Flores and the Global Fashion Trajectory." In *Fashionable Traditions: Asian Handmade Textiles in Motion*, edited by Ayami Nakatani, 19–40. Lanham, Maryland: Lexington Books.

de Jong, Willemijn and Richard Kunz. 2016. *Striking Patterns. Global Traces in Local Ikat Fashion*. Berlin: Hatje Cantz.

Erb, Maribeth. 2007. "Adat Revivalism in Western Flores: Culture, Religion, and Land." In *The Revival of Tradition in Indonesian Politics: The Deployment of Adat from Colonialism to Indigenism*, edited by Jamie S. Davidson and David Henley, 247–274. London and New York: Routledge.

Fisher, Alison, ed. 1999. *Decorative Arts of Sumba*. Amsterdam, Singapore: Pepin Press.

Gavin, Traude. 2003. *Iban Ritual Textiles*. Leidern: KITLV Press.

Gell, Alfred. 1998. *Art and Agency: An Anthropological Theory*. Oxford: Clarendon Press.

Gell, Alfred. 1999 [1992]. "The Technology of Enchantment and the Enchantment of Technology." In *The Art of Anthropology: Essays and Diagrams*, edited by Eric Hirsch, 159–186. London: Brunswick, NJ: Athlone.

Gell, Alfred. 1999 [1996]. Vogel's Net: Traps as Artworks and Artworks as Traps. In *The Art of Anthropology: Essays and Diagrams*, edited by Eric Hirsh, 187–214. London: Brunswick, NJ: Athlone.

Graburn, Nelson H.H. 1976. "Introduction: Arts of the Fourth World." In *Ethnic and Tourist Arts: Cultural Expressions from the Fourth World*, edited by Nelson H.H. Graburn, 1–32. Berkeley, Los Angeles: University of California Press.

Hamilton, Roy W., ed. 1994. *The Gift of the Cotton Maiden. Textiles of Flores and the Solor Islands*. Los Angeles: UCLA Museum of Cultural History.

Hauw, Samantha. 2009. "Words Like a Charm: Cultural Tourism, Colour and its Efficacy in Chinese Miao Traditional Dress." In *Asian Material Culture*, edited by Marianne Hulsbosch, Elizabeth Bedford and Marthe Chaiklin, 141–162. Amsterdam: Amsterdam University Press.

Hein, Alois Raimund. 1890. *Die bildenden Künste bei den Dayaks auf Borneo. Ein Beitrag zur allgemeinen Kunstgeschichte*. Wien: Alfred Hölder.

Herzfeld, Michael. 2004. *The Body Impolitic: Artisans and Artifice in the Global Hierarchy of Value*. Chicago: University of Chicago Press.

Hoskins, Janet. 1989. "Why do Ladies Sing the Blues? Indigo, Cloth Production and Gender Symbolism in Kodi." In *Cloth and Human Experience*, edited by Annette Weiner, and Jane Schneider, 141–173. Washington, London: Smithsonian Institution Press.

Hoskins, Janet. 2008. "In the Realm of the Indigo Queen: Dyeing, Exchange Magic, and the Elusive Tourist Dollar on Sumba." In *What's the Use of Art? Asian Visual and Material Culture in Context*, edited by Jan Mrazek and Morgan Pitelka, 100–126. Honolulu: University of Hawai'i Press.

Howard, Michael C. 2007. "Indonesian Textiles from Dress to Art." In *Arts, Popular Culture and Social Change in the New Indonesia*, edited by Michael Leaf, Michael, Seminar Proceedings, 33–57. Vancouver: University of British Columbia.

Jasper, J.E. and Mas Pirngadie. 1912. *De inlandsche kunstnijverheid in Nederlands-Indië. Bd. II. De weefkunst*. Den Haag: Mouton.

Jones, Carla. 2003. "Dress for *Sukses*: Fashioning Femininity and Nationality in Urban Indonesia." In *Re-Orienting Fashion: The Globalization of Asian Dress*, edited by Sandra Niessen, Ann Marie Leshkowich, and Carla Jones, 185–214. Oxford, New York: Berg.

Jones, Carla and Ann Marie Leshkowich. 2003. "Introduction: The Globalization of Asian Dress: Re-Orienting Fashion or Re-Orientalizing Asia?" In *Re-Orienting Fashion: The Globalization of Asian Dress*, edited by Sandra Niessen, Ann Marie Leshkowich and Carla Jones, 1–48. Oxford, New York: Berg.

Kawlra, Aarti. 2014. "Duplicating the Local: GI and the Politics of 'Place' in Kanchipuram." *NMML Occasional Paper: Perspective in Indian Development, New Series 29*. Nehru Memorial Museum and Library. 32 p.

Kondo, Dorinne. 1997. *About Face: Performing Race in Fashion and Theater*. London and New York: Routledge.

Küchler, Susanne and Daniel Miller, eds. 2005. *Clothing as Material Culture*. Oxford and New York: Berg.

Kunz, Richard and Willemijn de Jong. 2016. "Introduction." In *Striking Patterns. Global Traces in Local Ikat Fashion*, edited by Willemijn de Jong and Richard Kunz, Museum der Kulturen Basel, 7–16. Berlin: Hatje Cantz.

Langewis, Laurens and Frits A. Wagner. 1964. *Decorative Art in Indonesian Textiles*. Amsterdam: Uitgeverij C-P.J. van der Peet.

Low, Audrey. 2009. "Tension on the Back-strap Loom." In *Asian Material Culture*, edited by Marianne Hulsbosch, Elizabeth Bedford, and Marthe Chaiklin, 193–229. Amsterdam: Amsterdam University Press.

Maxwell, Robyn. 2014 [1990]. *Textiles of Southeast Asia: Tradition, Trade and Transformation*. Clarendon, Vermont: Tuttle Publishing.

Mrazek, Jan and Morgan Pitelka, eds. 2008. *What's the Use of Art? Asian Visual and Material Culture in Context*. Honolulu: University of Hawai'i Press.

Niessen, Sandra. 2003a. "Three Scenarios from Batak Clothing History: Designing Participation in the Global Fashion Trajectory." In *Re-Orienting Fashion: The Globalization of Asian Dress*, edited by Sandra Niessen, Ann Marie Leshkowich and Carla Jones, 49–78. Oxford, New York: Berg.

Niessen, Sandra. 2003b. "Afterword: Re-Orienting Fashion Theory." In *Re-Orienting Fashion: The Globalization of Asian Dress*, edited by Sandra Niessen, Ann Marie Leshkowich and Carla Jones, 243–266. Oxford, New York: Berg.

Niessen, Sandra. 2016. "Afterword: Fashion's Fallacy." In: *Modern Fashion Traditions: Negotiating Tradition and Modernity through Fashion*, edited by Jansen, M. Angela and Jennifer Craik, 209–217. New York, London: Bloomsbury Publishing.

Niessen, Sandra, Ann Marie Leshkowich and Carla Jones, eds. 2003. *Re-Orienting Fashion: The Globalization of Asian Dress*. Oxford, New York: Berg.

Orinbao, Sareng P. [Pater Piet Petu SVD]. 1969. *Nusa Nipa: Nama Pribumi Nusa Flores (Warisan Purba)*. Ende: Nusa Indah.

Orinbao, Sareng P. [Pater Piet Petu SVD]. 1992. *Seni Tenun Suatu Segi Kebudayaan Orang Flores*. Nita, Flores: Seminari Tinggi St. Paulus Ledalero.

Pinney, Christopher and Nicholas Thomas, eds. 2001. *Beyond Aesthetics: Art and the Technologies of Enchantment*. Oxford, New York: Berghahn.

Rouffaer, G.P. and H.H. Juynboll. 1914. *De batik-kunst in Nederlands-Indië en haar geschiedenis*. Utrecht: Oosthoek.

Schneider, Arnd, ed. 2017. *Alternative Art and Anthropology. Global Encounters*. London: Bloomsbury.

Skov, Lise. 2003. "Fashion–Nation: A Japanese Globalization Experience and a Hong Kong Dilemma." In *Re-Orienting Fashion: The Globalization of Asian Dress*, edited by Sandra Niessen, Ann Marie Leshkowich, and Carla Jones, 215–242. Oxford, New York: Berg.

Spielmann, Yvonne. 2017. *Contemporary Indonesian Art: Artists, Art Spaces, and Collectors*. Singapore: NUS Press.

Steele, Valerie. 2012. "Fashion." In *Fashion and Art*, edited by Adam Geczy and Vicky Karaminas, 13–27. London, New York: Berg.

Steinmann, Alfred. 1941. *Die Ornamentik der Ikat-Gewebe*. Ciba-Rundschau 51: 1876–1882.

Strathern, Marilyn. 2005. *Kinship, Law and the Unexpected: Relatives Are Always a Surprise*. Cambridge: Cambridge University Press.

Watters, Kent. 1977. "Flores." In *Textile Traditions of Indonesia*, edited by Mary Hunt Kahlenberg, 87–93. Los Angeles: Los Angeles County Museum of Art.

Chapter 2
The enchantment of *topeng*: thinking art through Balinese masks

Maria Bonome Pederneiras

Museu Nacional/Universidade Federal do Rio de Janeiro, Brazil

Abstract

Masks feature prominently in Western theoretical constructions and have been part of their imaginary since ancient history. In anthropology, masks are present in important scholarly works in which questions about crucial anthropological categories such as "personhood", "performance", "agency" and "art" are raised. The author analyses traditional Balinese performances with masks, called *topeng*, through the perspective of art proposed by Alfred Gell (1992), as a specific form of technology which he coined the "technology of enchantment". Based on this approach, she extends the analysis by considering the processes of mask manufacturing and training for the masked performances through which the Balinese artists pursue *taksu*—a special moment in which the mask becomes alive. After further exploration of this concept, it became clear that *taksu* is achieved when the artistic expression reaches a level of unprecedented technical excellence. If *topeng* is considered as a "technology of enchantment", *taksu*—as the moment of efficacy of this specific technology—can be looked at as an "enchantment of technology", Pederneiras suggests. This chapter thus also aims to reflect on the "effects" that *topeng* processes can have on the conception of "art": it finally raises questions of how we can make an anthropological analysis, if we use that long-honoured concept in non-Western contexts.

Keywords: maskmaking, *topeng*, *taksu*, technology, Bali

Masks have wide-reaching influence throughout Western thought and culture. They feature prominently in Western theoretical constructions and have been part of its imaginary world since ancient history—whether in analytical psychology, theatrical theories or mythological analyses, not to mention their importance in the carnivals (from Venice to Rio de Janeiro).

In anthropology masks have also been a prominent subject of thought, being present in many theoretical formulations. For example, in his analysis of the origin and transformation of the notion of the person, Marcel Mauss saw the mask as an indication of the idea of character, which he later developed into the concept of *self*. He remarked: "You all know how normal and classical the notion of the Latin *persona* is: a mask, a tragic mask, a ritual mask, and the ancestral mask. It dates back to the beginnings of Latin civilization" (Mauss 1985 [1938], 13).

In alignment with the Maussian tendency to relativise and defamiliarise personhood, the anthropologist Alfred Gell proposes an understanding of art objects as persons. In his efforts to formulate different manners to analyse "art-like situations" anthropologically, Gell explicitly avoids the semiological approach that focuses on understanding *what* such objects *mean* in a certain social context. He proposes instead to investigate *how* these objects *act* in social terms. In other words, it is about thinking those objects as persons, not as symbols, and therefore, to follow their agency: "In place of symbolic communication, I place all the emphasis on *agency, intention, causation, result,* and *transformation*. I view art as a system of action, intended to change the world rather than encode symbolic propositions about it" (Gell 1998, 6).

Taking all of this into account, we can see why masks are such a relevant theme. They raise questions about crucial anthropological categories, like that of personhood, performance, agency and art. As we move towards this chapter's main theme—*topeng*, a traditional Balinese theatre-dance performance with masks—the different grades of personhood that can emerge from human-object interactions will become clearer and clearer, as will the manner in which such interactions index socio-political agencies.[1]

---

[1] This chapter is the result of my fieldwork in Bali, in 2013. There, I stayed in the village of Batuan, in the region of Gianyar, with a family of artists from the *Tri Pusaka Sakti* foundation. The foundation, led by renowned performer I Made Djimat, his children and grandchildren, was not only my home throughout the fieldwork, but also my main access to most of the Balinese performances I experienced while there, since I was able to follow the family's shows throughout the island, both in ceremonial situations and in touristic shows.
I was also frequently able to observe the dance classes and rehearsals that took place in the foundation—not only *topeng* classes, but also *legong* (an exclusively female dance) and *baris* (the warrior dance) lessons. Besides that, I also took some *topeng* dance classes taught by Djimat and some mask-manufacturing classes taught by his neighbour, I Dewa Gede Mandra, who manufactured ceremonial masks, including *topeng* masks.

About *topeng* and its *taksu*

"*Topeng*" means "mask" in Indonesian or, in ancient Javanese, "something pressed against the face", and is the term used by the Balinese to refer to both the performance with the masks and the mask as an object. It dates from approximately 800 AD and it is one of the most important and ancient types of traditional Balinese performances. It is a dance-theatre with masks accompanied by the *gamelan* orchestra in which, as already mentioned, the ancient chronicles in palm-leaf manuscripts called *Babad* are narrated. Among the most frequent stories performed by the *topeng* are the *Babad Dalen*, stories of the glorious past of the Balinese and Javanese kingdoms, as well as stories concerning the ancestral heritage of the island's highest caste families.

Topeng masks are very popular in Bali, well known by everyone, from children to the elderly, as are the musical themes that go with their dance. With only small variations of the main masks characters and their musical themes, the traditional *topeng* leaves little room for what we would understand as "new", or "original" elements. That may be one of the reasons why, during a performance (especially in ceremonial contexts, when they are longer), the audience frequently gets distracted, talking or even sleeping during the show. However, it was not unusual to be surprised by sudden intense reactions to the masked characters during these long shows. At some moments in the performance, the audience would react to the performer with shouts, laughter, or even crying and running away—the last reactions were especially common among children.

These "disturbing" moments did not always happen in the presence of the same masked characters or even in the same passages of the story. But the variation of the masked character seemed to show an aspect of the performance that displaced the masked character from the commonplace, raising questions as to what happens during this transformation and how it happened. In other words, the point is to ask, as Carlos Fausto (2011) does, how the mask can be *effective*. In his own wording: "(…) how the disguise is not taken literally but, on the contrary, gives rise to an attribution of misplaced subjectivity. How does the absent make itself present (and the present, absent)? How does the visible give place to the invisible made visible through the mask?" (Fausto 2011, 50, translation by the author).[2]

When talking about these questions with dancers, mask-makers and other *topeng* enthusiasts, it was common for them to describe this phenomenon as a moment of *taksu*. Some people from the audience would say that in these

---

[2] The original French text is: "comment le déguisement n'est pas pris à la lettre, mais, au contraire, donne lieu à une attribution de subjectivité déplacée. Comment l'absent se rend-il présent (et le présent, absent)? Comment le visible recule-t-il pour céder la place à un invisible rendu visible par le moyen du masque?" (Fausto 2011, 50)

occasions the mask is "full of energy", it "becomes alive", while some performers described the moment when they "feel the mask's feelings and wishes", changing their body, from the eyesight to their breathing rhythm. In an attempt to explain to me the concept of *taksu*, the mask dance performer and teacher I Made Djimat also described it as when the mask "comes to life" on the scene. That is, when the performer goes beyond a "simple representation" and he/she "becomes the mask". Also, according to him, it is not the performer who has *taksu*, but it is a quality that is *attributed* to a moment in the performance.

The Balinese artist and scholar I Wayan Dibia, in his article on *topeng*, works with a very similar conception of *taksu*, one that also allows us to approach it with an idea of the mask's "efficacy", in the sense used by Fausto (2011). Dibia explains: "The presence of *taksu* will not only alter the artistic quality of the performance, it will also transform the actor into the character he or she plays. [...] It is through the presence of *taksu* that the performance can be 'elevated' above the mundane performance" (Dibia 2004, 10).

As I further explored the concept of *taksu*, it became clearer that this would be a moment that could be experienced not only through *topeng* performances, but in any activity in which, by being entirely engaged in that moment, one reaches a level of unprecedented technical excellence and thus, of "true happiness", as described by the *topeng* dancer Sangtu Adi. Therefore, *taksu* was pursued not only by performers, but also by mask-makers, sculptors and artists in general while practicing their craft.

Considering this condition and the questions it raised about the mask's efficacy during the performance, I looked for analytical ways to allow me to explore the various dimensions of *topeng*, including both its technical processes (mask production and dance teaching) and its insertion in ceremonial contexts.[3]

Therefore, in this ethnographic essay I intend to analyse *topeng* through the perspective of art in the sense proposed by Alfred Gell (1992), that is, as a specific form of technology, a "technology of enchantment". In this approach, I will extend the analysis to the processes of mask manufacturing and training for the masked performance, understanding both as components "of a vast and often unrecognized technical system, essential to the reproduction of human societies, which I will be calling the technology of enchantment" (Gell 1992, 43).

---

[3] By "ceremonies" I refer exclusively to those of the Hindu-Balinese. Bali is a mainly Hindu province in Indonesia, but it has a considerable variety of religions, including Islam, Christianism and Buddhism. Also, the Hindu-Balinese religion is known by its particular incorporation of aspects of Indian Hinduism and Balinese animist entities. Although *topeng* is common in non-ceremonial situations as well, the ceremonies will be the focus of my analysis here.

Once looking at *topeng* as a "technology of enchantment", we can think of *taksu*, known as the moment of efficacy of *topeng*, as an "enchantment of technology": "It seems to me that the efficacy of art objects as components of the technology of enchantment [...] is itself the result of the enchantment of technology". That is to say, the technical processes "are construed magically so that, by enchanting us, they make the products of these technical processes seem enchanted vessels of magical power" (Gell 1992, 46).

Through this exploration of the technical and magical processes of *topeng*, I intend to avoid the weight of conceptions such as "art" and "representation", which could flatten the analyses of the enchanted experience of watching a masked dancer in a Balinese ceremony. Thus, the goal here is not to (re)define these concepts (as "art" and "representation") but to widen and stretch them through *topeng* and its *taksu*.

Topeng as art and technology

As we enter a Hindu-Balinese temple during a ceremony (in celebration of its anniversary, for example), we may see a reserved place in which offerings are neatly disposed. This place, called *jero*, is where altars are arranged and offerings are made, particularly great arrangements of food, flowers, incense, and coins. Near them, usually seated in structures apart, the priests and priestesses pray and bless the ceremony. Going outside to the temple courtyard (called *jaba*), we see the *gamelan* orchestra[4] set up, ready to accompany the other shows that are also a part of the ceremonies (many of which often happen at the same time).

The Balinese ceremonies can include a variety of traditional performances. There is, for example, the *wayang kulit*, a shadow puppet show that tells the stories of the classic Indian epics *Mahabharata* and *Ramayana*.[5] We can also observe the *wayang wong*, a mask performance originated around the 17th to 18th centuries, inspired by the *wayang kulit* (Slattum 2011), that also tells the stories of the Indian epic *Ramayana*.[6] Moreover, there is the *barong* and the *calonarang*, one of Bali's most popular mask performances, which represents entities like *Rangda* (also called *Dewi Durga*, the 'witch queen') and *Barong*, an

---

[4] Here, gamelan orchestra refers to the traditional set of instruments that accompany performances like the *topeng*. The orchestra is mainly composed of *gamelans* (a type of metallophones played by mallets), accompanied by drums and gongs. They may also feature bamboo flutes, string instruments, voices, etc.

[5] According to Rubin and Sedana (2007, 16), the *wayang kulit* is one of the oldest documented theatrical forms in Bali.

[6] Most of the masks used in this kind of performance refer to animals, which lead authors like Judy Slattum to understand them as one of the evidences of the articulation between Bali's pre-Hindu Buddhist religion, considered animist, and Indian Hinduism (Slattum 2011).

animistic entity known as protector of the villages of Bali. And finally, the mask performance that we are dealing with here, the *topeng*.

The *topeng* performance

In the midst of prayers, offerings, puppet shows and abundant incense, the *gamelan* begins to play, announcing the beginning of the *topeng* performance. Seated in the courtyard (*jaba*), we can see the first masked character coming out from inside the temple, or from behind an arranged curtain. The first character to appear, opening the show, is determined by the story to be told on that day. He could be the *topeng Dalen* (the king), or the *topeng Tua* (the old man and usually the king's counsellor), or even the *topeng Patih Manis* (the prime minister).

Other characters, each wearing different full masks (*tapel bungkulan*),[7] enter and leave the scene dancing to their own music theme in a variety of personalities—the calmness and delicacy of some (such as the *topeng Dalem*) contrasting with the brutality and anxiety of others (as that of *topeng Lucu*, another kind of prime minister).

These main characters are accompanied by two characters with half masks (*tapel sibakan*) responsible for narrating the story: the brothers *topeng Penasar* and *topeng Wijil* (the older and the younger, respectively) are servants of the King and, by singing and dancing, those two add some punctual touches of humour to the drama.

At the end of the story, the so-called *bondres* enter in scene. One by one, these characters with half masks, which are not characters from the story and do not have a pre-determined choreography or music, amuse the audience by satirising popular figures, such as the flirty girl, the grumpy old man and the ignorant (but rich) foreigner. Not even the priest is left out and can be satirised as a womaniser, for example. With crooked teeth, deformed noses, and other "freakish" physical traits ludicrous enough to make the audience laugh, these figures quickly pass through the scene as the *topeng* heading towards the end.

The last mask to appear is essential for the performance's closing: *Sidhakarya* enters screaming and laughing, making offerings and "blessing" during the whole ceremony.[8] Although it is a full mask, it is possible to speak through

---

[7] By "full masks" I mean those that cover the whole face, not allowing the performer to speak. All the main characters in *topeng* are full masks. I refer to masks that cover only half the face, leaving the performer free to speak, as "half masks".

[8] The origin of this mask is found in the myth that tells the story of a priest named Keling who, due to a lack of communication, was prevented by the prime minister from entering

Sidhakarya's mask because of an opening in its mouth. This mask also does not necessarily belong to either the main story performed or the group of *bondres*, but without it the *topeng* is not considered as finished, regardless of the story that is told.

Figure 2.1 *Topeng Sidhakarya*, performed by I Made Djimat in an anniversary ceremony.

Photograph by Maria Bonome Pederneiras.

the ceremony to which he had been invited by the king to assist. Angrily, he cursed the ceremony, leaving crops devastated and people ill. The king was then advised to go after Keling to apologise and appointed him as the official priest of the ceremony. Keling accepted the apologies and successfully remedied the problems that he had created. For that, the king gave him the high title of *Brahmin Sidhakarya* and made a mask of his image. The term *Sidhakarya* consists of two words: "*sidha*" meaning "successful,", and "*karya*", "religious labor", or "celebration". Such a character marks the transition from secular to religious in *topeng* performances (Rubin and Sedana 2007).

This format of performance, with its variations,[9] is found in virtually every Hindu-Balinese ceremony, from New Year's celebrations and temple anniversaries, to weddings, funerals and birth ceremonies. But they can also be found in other contexts, such as in shows aimed at tourists, set up in hotels and theatre stages. In this article, as I mentioned earlier, I will focus only on ceremonial contexts.[10]

I Wayan Dibia, in his article "*Topeng*: The Masked Dance Theatre of Bali" (2004), points out that *topeng*'s structure—the interactions between the story's characters (whole masks) and everyday plots brought by the *bondres*—allows the performance to play simultaneously with past and present. This would be evidence of the *topeng*'s "didactic" aspect, which enables it both to convey through the story some of the main concepts of "Balinese philosophy" and to contextualise them in the present (Dibia 2004).

This important "didactic" aspect of *topeng* could be perceived during the dance classes, when stories were explained to young pupils in order to help them understand the character of the mask they were dancing with, including their values and personality. When building the comic masks' characters, these values also come up, as they are distorted and made fun of. Besides, learning traditional dances like *topeng*, *legong* and *baris* (see footnote 1) is considered a matter of great importance in Balinese education. This can be perceived in the big dance competitions promoted by schools, in which the result may impact the student's school record. I Nyoman Budi Artha, Djimat's son, proudly told me about his victories in the past and how that helped him to have a good curriculum vitae and, therefore, to get a good job.

The importance attributed to the technical knowledge of *topeng* dance instead of just the knowledge *about* the *topeng* performance made me ask whether it is possible to recognise the presence of this "Balinese philosophy" (Dibia 2004) beyond discourse, that is, not only in the content of their stories but also in their movements and in the very materiality of their masks. In other

---

[9] Besides the variety of chronicles performed, the *topeng* also has different styles of performing it. They mainly are: the *topeng pajegan*, performed by a single actor-dancer; the *topeng panca*, usually performed by five actors-dancers; the *topeng prembom*, a more recent type of performance (created in 1942 with the collaboration of a group of artists from Gianyar and Badung) as a mix of characters with masks and others without (combining elements of *topeng* with the ones of the Bali-Arja opera); and the *topeng bondres*, created around the 1980s, composed only of the comic characters already described here (Dibia 2004).

[10] This discrimination is not only because I had more opportunities to observe ceremonial performances (Djimat was invited to an average of five times per week), but also because of the mainly Balinese audience in those events, a very important factor that made the presence of *taksu* more visible to me.

words, to investigate not just what can be taught about *topeng*, both as mask and performance, but also what *topeng* can teach.

During his classes, while teaching the choreography of *topeng Dalen* (mask of the king), I Made Djimat said that the king is "the most powerful man" and therefore his movements should be "sweet, like a woman's", because the king is very gentle and is always smiling. This matches the expression of the mask, which smiles sweetly. In his choreography, *Dalen* is delicate, with small, discreet movements, almost static.

Interestingly, there is a close resemblance between the quality of the dance of *topeng Dalen* and the description made by Clifford Geertz of the Balinese king and his role in the *Negara*, "the classical state of pre-colonial Indonesia" (Geertz 1980, 4). The king is described as "[the] still point of the turning world; for, insofar as he was an actor in court ceremonies, his job was to project an enormous calm at the centre of an enormous activity by becoming palpably immobile" (Geertz 1980, 130). Thus, according to Geertz, the stillness was an important feature in governance, and the "king's ability to project himself (or, better, his kingship) as the stationary axis of the world rested on his ability to discipline his emotions and his behaviour with meticulous rigor" (Ibid.). Looking at this description, one can see the resemblance with *topeng Dalen* dance and expression: a gently smiling mask, dancing with delicate movements, practically still.

Taking into account Geertz's proposition that Balinese ideas about the world and modes of behaviour are fused into "a lexicon of sensory symbols", such as dances and masks (Geertz 1980, 103), this resemblance between *topeng Dalen's* dance and the king's role in the ceremonies would allow us to extend the idea of *topeng's* "didactics" (Dibia 2004) beyond the story told, applying it to the composition, as well as to the gestures and personality of each *topeng* mask. That may enlighten the importance of knowing how to dance the *topeng*, since it is through the performance that some aspects of Balinese socio-political knowledge are apprehended—not in the sense of *representing* these ideas, but as "arguments" that reinforce and compose them. Or, in Geertz's formulation, "that is, theatre to present an ontology and, by presenting it, to make it happen—make it actual." (Geertz 1980, 104).

In other words, *topeng* implies these socio-political aspects. and vice versa, since it is also through the performance that these terms are produced, as I argued above. Allied with Gell's (1998) conceptions, one could recognise *topeng* as a social actor in the Balinese ceremonial context. Thus, one could argue that *topeng* acts as an index, inducing inferences or reactions through the abduction of Balinese socio-political values (Ibid.).

However, some limits of Gell's theory of agency may arise when analysing *topeng* masks. As already pointed out by other authors (see e. g. Ingold 2007;

Miller 2005), his distinction between primary and secondary agents (Gell, 1998, 36–38), is still attached to a conception of agency based on a more conventional understanding of social action as a primarily *human* attribute. That is, non-human agency cannot be conceived without assuming a primary human source. But, as we can see in the case of *topeng*, there are non-exclusively human forces taking part in the mask's agency—for example, the spirit of the wood and the *taksu* itself. Nevertheless, in my view, Gell's (1992) conception of "enchantment of technology" as a magical efficacy leaves open the possibility to take these other forces into account.

Figure 2.2 *Topeng Dalen* (mask of the king) performed by I Made Djimat in a funeral ceremony.

Photograph by Maria Bonome Pederneiras.

Taksu as enchantment of technology

The first time I heard about *taksu* in a conversation with Ida Bagus Anum, a mask-maker from the village of Mas. He explained to me that we can experience *taksu* in any activity in which we are fully engaged, and that this was his goal while sculpting a *topeng* mask—even though he had reached it only rarely, it was worth trying. Anum confessed this while he proudly went to get a mask with which he had reached this experience: transforming the wood into the mask it asked to be.

One of the points that most caught my attention and, therefore, will be central in this analysis is that *taksu* seems to be directly related to an activity, or craft.

It is reached through the search for technical improvement and, therefore, in the material working process: a craftsman seeking to improve his sculpture; a mask-maker seeking to improve his masks; a *topeng* performer seeking to improve his performance with the mask, etc.

During my mask manufacturing classes with I Dewa Gede Mandra,[11] I could observe their great technique. Seated on a straw mat, the mask-maker holds the wood with their feet while sculpting with just a few instruments. It also caught my attention how, looking at the rough wood stump, they could perceive its "excesses" and accurately remove them—knowing how much and in which direction to carve. Most of the time, Rico, who taught me to sculp, would only look at the wood stump and mark where I should keep carving with a pencil. Sometimes, he would comment on how the wood "was not helping"— when it was not soft enough, or kept getting dry, making it hard to carve it "kindly".

Thus, we could say that the mask-maker's technique of "working together" with the wood is also a means for him to attain and experience *taksu*: recognising the indications it gives about the direction of carving; recognising its limits, for instance, how thick a mask can be without breaking as soon as it is used against the face.

Alfred Gell (1992) proposed considering "art" from an anthropological perspective as a specific type of technology, an enchanting one. "Technology is enchanting because it is enchanted, because it is the outcome of some process of barely comprehensible virtuosity, that exemplifies an idea of magical efficacy that people struggle to realize in other domains" (Thomas 1998, viii). In other words, "the technology of enchantment is founded on the enchantment of technology" (Gell 1992, 44), and its magical efficacy stems from the excellence in the technical processes they objectively embody. Gell concludes that "art, as a separate kind of technical activity, only carries further, through a kind of involution, the enchantment which is immanent in all kinds of technical activity" (Ibid, 44).

In convergence with Gell's (1992) ideas, we can approach the concept of *taksu* as an "immanent enchantment" attained through technical excellence. That is to say, consider it as *topeng*'s "enchantment of technology", including both the mask as an object and the masked performance. Thus, one can also look at *topeng* through the experience of *taksu* as "art" (in the sense proposed by Gell, i.e., as a technology of enchantment). This seems close to how Balinese

---

[11] The classes were at his house, and although he was the main teacher, I also learned with Rico, another mask-maker that worked with him there and who taught me most of the sculping skills.

audiences evaluate the performance—not *only* by what it tells or "represents" in its context (a way of expressing Balinese values and ethics) but also by *how* it is told, through the enchanting and magical experience of *taksu*.

Figure 2.3 I Dewa Gede Mandra, in his house, finishing a *Jauk Manis* mask by nailing the eyebrow with a bamboo nail.

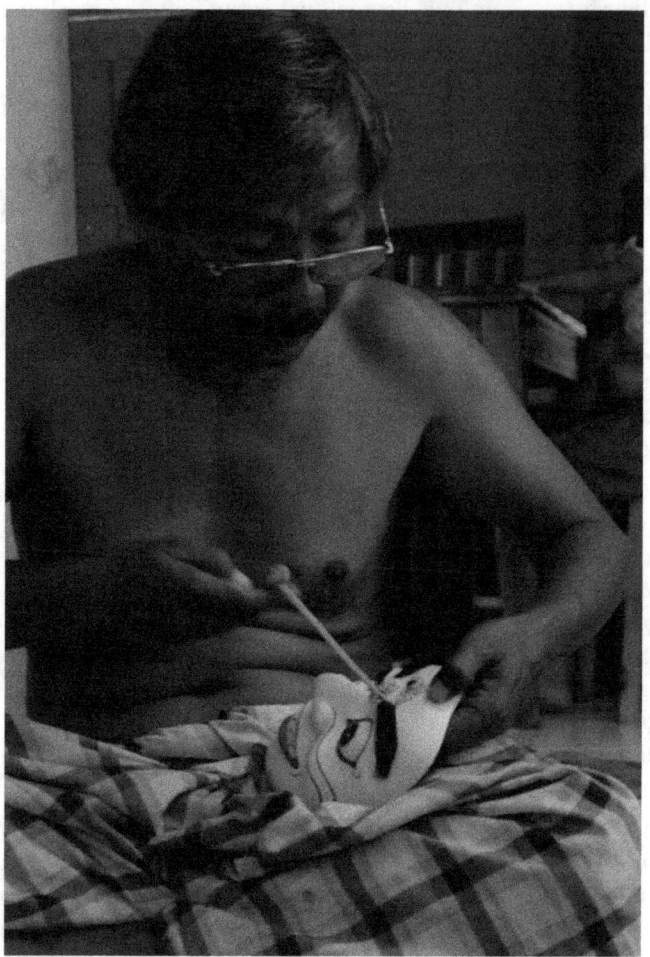

Photograph by Maria Bonome Pederneiras.

More specifically, in the case of the *topeng* performance, this "enchantment" could be understood as the moment in which there is a subjectivation of the mask, as its "effectiveness" (Fausto 2011). But, as has been pointed out by both mask-makers and performers, *taksu* is not easily achieved. It is instead the result of a technical improvement. In other words, *taksu* does not happen as soon as the mask is put on; nor does it stem exclusively from the performer or from the mask. In fact, *taksu*, as we shall see now, is all about collective efforts.

In the *topeng* dance classes, it was common practice to first learn the character choreography and how to dance it along with the music.[12] Masks were only introduced after that.[13] When I asked I Made, why we put on the mask only after learning the dance, he told me that first the dance should be well established and only then should the "touch of the mask" be introduced and that, after learning the steps, the mask would indicate how to dance them. These would become clearer through some indications made during the lessons: for example, when I Made Djimat advised to mimic the masks' facial expression even while wearing them, such as smiling gently when dancing the *topeng Dalen*. According to him, this would be one way of knowing how to "listen to the mask", changing our sensation during the dance, our rhythm and even our own breathing, in order to understand the character's choreography.

Thus, for both the mask-maker and the performer, the means to achieve *taksu* are in some way homologous: it happens through the technical process of working together with the mask in order to create a new subjectivity. In other words, if, for the mask-maker, *taksu* is achieved through the effort of making the mask that the wood has asked to be, for the performer it is achieved by dancing in the way that the mask asked to dance. Here, the homology between the mask-maker's and the performer's efforts to attain *taksu* is "a fundamental scheme transfer" (Gell 1992, 56) indispensable to achieving magical efficacy. That is also the reason for the very efficacy of *topeng* as an enchanting technology and, consequently, as art.

Moreover, similarly to Rico's statement that sometimes the wood "is not helping" (because it is too dry, or it has been wrongly cut off from the tree),[14] the performers from I Made Djimat's family more than once praised a mask for being "good to be danced", often referring to the specific mask-maker who

---

[12] The lessons were with songs recorded on a CD. But during the *topeng* performance, with the live orchestra, the dancer and the musicians create these nuances together, one accompanying the other. Most of the time, this "improvisation" is guided by physical signs the dancer performs while dancing the choreography or through musical signs made by the musicians.

[13] I cannot state that this is a methodological pattern of Balinese masked dance classes in general. I am basing these analyses specifically on Djimat's methodology.

[14] Most *topeng* masks are made with the wood of a sacred tree called *pule*. Usually only one piece of the tree is removed, since cutting it is dangerous, and a ceremony is held to ask tree's spirit for permission to use the wood (Slattum 2011). Unfortunately, during my stay in the field, I did not witness such a ceremony, but they were commonly mentioned by the mask-makers.

made it. Djimat, for instance, showed an explicit predilection for the masks of I Wayan Tangguh, a well-known mask-maker from the village of Mas. Through these statements we can see that the agency of objects (like wooden masks) is taken as of primary importance to achieve the magical efficacy, *taksu*, that will enchant the *topeng* technology. At this point, the distinction made by Gell (1998, 36–38) between primary and secondary agents in a way that objects' actions are emanations of a human agency seems insufficient to capture those relations of "co-working" between wood and mask-maker, and mask and *topeng* performer.

Conclusion

To think of *topeng* as art is not a great novelty, nor does it seem to disagree with many analyses on the subject. Like other Balinese performances, *topeng* is recognised as an important inspiration for so-called "Western theatre" (e. g. see Artaud 1958).[15] Besides, Balinese masks are very prominent in the international art market, and they draw much attention from tourists. With Gell, however, we gain explicit and highly valuable insights into the efficacy of the notion of art from a contemporary anthropological perspective.

With the intent of overcoming Western-centred analyses of art, Gell argues that an anthropological approach should adopt an "aesthetic atheism". Instead of focusing on the finished object itself and letting its fabrication process and its agency in the background—which Gell would have described as an aesthetic approach—one should turn to the "art in action", that is, to its creation process, involving a complex web of interactions, agencies and virtuous techniques. As Pedro Cesarino argues, Gell's position is not about denying an object's ability to "produce aesthetic potency" but to say that an anthropological approach "should not take that premise as a starting point" (Cesarino 2017, 5 translation by the author). Thus, by focusing on the technical processes involved in the production of art objects as well as not reducing the range of effects incited by such objects to "aesthetic reactions", Gell aims to find an anthropological approach that does not neutralise the magical and religious powers that constitute art-like situations (Gell 1998, 157).

---

[15] In his book *The Theater and its Double,* Artaud (1958) works with the idea of Balinese performance as the essence of what would be the "true theater". This "essence" is what Western theater would have lost mainly for what he considered to be a "psychologisation" of the drama. Other theatrical authors, such as the directors Peter Brook and Ariane Mnouchkine also bring Balinese dance theater as a major source of inspiration.

It is worth mentioning that there are some relevant criticisms of Gell's idea of the aesthetic (e. g. see Morphy 2009). Most of what Gell has defined in his theory, through his critique of the aesthetic approach, is in fact what most anthropologists would recognise as constituting an aesthetic dimension. On the other hand, there are others who defend Gell's position, arguing that it was not meant to reject the notion of aesthetics *per se*, but the reification of aesthetics as a category artificially separated from the socio-relational matrix from which it emerges (see Rampley 2005).[16]

In this chapter I analysed both the mask and the performance of *topeng* as a "technology of enchantment", in alignment with Gell's proposals (1992). In this perspective, I extended the analysis towards *topeng*'s production and considered it an agent involved in an inherently social system of technique and intentionality. The aim here was to raise some questions about personhood and the agency of humans and non-humans.

By thinking *taksu* as an "enchantment of technology" (Gell 1992), it was possible to extend the analysis to the mask's magic, perceived through both processes of carving the wood and performing the *topeng* in ceremonial contexts. Achieving *taksu* is thought of as the moment of "efficacy" (inspired by Fausto 2011, 50) of the whole system of techniques that make up the *topeng* performance. Thus, the conception of *topeng* as an "art-like situation" is intrinsically linked to these moments of virtuous technique known as *taksu*. For, as Dibia would say: "making the mask come to life in fact is the key to the success of the Topeng performance" (Dibia 2004, 10).

The analyses developed here were guided by the question of how far the idea of *topeng* as an enchanted social technology and as an agent in ceremonial contexts can lead us. Moreover, this chapter reflects on what kind of "effects" these perspectives have on the conception of "art" and how can it help us build a fair analysis using this concept in non-Western contexts.

Finally, inspired by Aristóteles Barcelos Neto's reflections on the concept of art among the indigenous Wauja and their *Apapaatai* masks (Neto 2008, 34), I did not intend to (re)define the concept of art throughout this analysis of *topeng* and its *taksu*. My goal was instead to avoid the flattening effects of the weight of this concept on ethnographic efforts of understanding ways of

---

[16] That discussion does not fit this chapter's purpose, but as far as it concerns the analysis of *topeng*, the undetermined and flexible aspects of Gell's conception of "art" (and therefore of "aesthetics") make it more appropriate in contexts where art-like situations do not stem from specific institutions (as they do in Western societies) but are entangled in interactions and mediations pervading social life, as I argued to be the case of *topeng* in Balinese ceremonies.

thinking and acting that do not properly fit into the Western model. After all, like Gell, I believe that part of the fascination generated by facing a work of art such as *topeng* is, to some extent, "because we are essentially at a loss to explain how such an object comes to exist in the world" (Gell 1992, 62).

References

Artaud, Antonin. 1958. *The Theatre and Its Double*. New York: Grove Weidenfeld.

Cesarino, Letícia. 2017. "Anthropology and the South-South Encounter: On 'Culture' in Brazil-Africa Relatios." *American Anthropologist* 119 (2): 333-341.

Dibia, I Wayan. 2004. "*Topeng*, a Masked Dance Theatre of Bali." *SPAFA Journal* 14 (1): 5–20.

Fausto, Carlos. 2011. "Le masque de l'animiste." *Gradhiva* 13 (1): 48–67.

Geertz, Clifford. 1980. *Negara: The Theatre State in Nineteenth-Century Bali*. New Jersey: Princeton University Press.

Gell, Alfred. 1992. "The Technology of Enchantment and the Enchantment of Technology." In *Anthropology, Art and Aesthetics*, edited by J. Coote and A. Shelton, 40–66. Oxford: Clarendon.

Gell, Alfred. 1998. *Art and Agency: An Anthropological Theory*. Oxford, New York: Clarendon Press.

Ingold, Tim. 2007. "Materials against Materiality." *Archaeological Dialogues* 14 (1): 1–16.

Mauss, Marcel. 1985 [1938]. *The Category of Person: Anthropology, Philosophy and History*. London: Cambridge University Press.

Miller, Daniel. 2005. "Materiality: An Introduction." In *Materiality*, edited by Daniel Miller, 1–50. Durham, NC: Duke University Press.

Morphy, Howard. 2009. "Art as a Mode of Action: Some Problems with Gell's *Art and Agency*." *Journal of Material Culture* 14 (1): 5–27.

Neto, Aristóteles Barcelos. 2008. *Apapaatai: Rituais de Máscaras no Alto Xingu*. São Paulo: Editora da Universidade de São Paulo/Fapesp.

Rampley, Matthew. 2005. "Art History and Cultural Difference: Alfred Gell's Anthropology of Art." *Art History* 28 (4): 524–551.

Rubin, Leon and Nyoman Sedana. 2007. *Performance in Bali*. Abingdon and New York: Routledge.

Slattum, Judy. 2011. *Balinese Masks: Spirits of an Ancient Drama*. Singapore: Tuttle Publishing.

Thomas, Nicholas. 1998. "Foreword." in *Art and Agency*, Alfred Gell, vii–xiii. Oxford: Clarendon.

Chapter 3

Aboriginal art, transits and transitions: exhibitions in Japan and the US

Sachiko Kubota

Ashiya University, Japan

Abstract

The general acceptance and image of Aboriginal people in Australia have changed a great deal over the years. Aborigines have been seen as savages without civilisation and they were socially marginalised. Since the 1970s, however, their image started to change and by the 1990s, they were seen as the people with the oldest living culture with a strong spiritual tie to the land. Kubota analyses two historical "transits" concerning Aboriginal arts. The first transit happened when these arts moved beyond the Australian national border to the US. They were highly accepted as arts there, which changed the situation of the Aboriginal people at home tremendously. The second transit took place when Aboriginal art came to Japan. Two Aboriginal exhibitions, one in 1965 and the other in 2016, were both very successful and were accepted quite differently compared to Australia. These two exhibitions are examined to understand what kind of transitions of Aboriginal art happened in Japan by the physical transfers of the artworks. Finally, by analysing historical transits that occurred to Aboriginal paintings, the author discusses how transits can affect the arts in a more general sense.

Key words: Aboriginal painting, exhibition, primitivism, transit, transition

This chapter focuses on the arts of Aboriginal people in Australia, who have experienced changes in their representation in recent years. This especially concerns their paintings. Aboriginal people and their works have been marginalised by the historical and political conditions in Australia, in so far as they were not recognised as having artistic agency for a long time. They were seen as culturally backward and were placed in the margins of society. Indeed, the discrimination Aboriginals still face stems from a long colonial history. I will examine the relationship between marginalisation and art by focusing on the changes in representation in Aboriginal art. I argue that Aboriginal paintings played a significant role in the alteration of the widespread image of "savage"

Aboriginal people. By the end of the twentieth century, in the mainstream Australian society they were seen as modern artistic people with their own unique traditions (Kubota 2007). To discuss this topic, I refer to Svašek's theory on the anthropology of art (Svašek 2007).

Svašek pays special attention to the "processual" nature of art production instead of considering art as a universal category. Art and aesthetics should be analysed in "concrete, specific socio-historical contexts from a dynamic point of view" (Svašek 2007, 15). One of the main topics discussed in her book is why some objects are considered art and others are not. To consider why some objects are categorised as art in a particular period and place, she proposes to use the concepts of "transit" and "transition". She defines "transit" as the movement of objects over time and across social and geographic boundaries, and "transition" as the way in which meaning, value, and the status of those objects change during the process. Svašek writes that "the processes of transit and transition are always shaped by the different relations between institutions or individuals who produce, consume, give, take, buy, sell, use, or display artefacts" (Svašek 2007, 5).

By means of the concepts of transit and transition, I examine how Aboriginal artworks transited from Australia to the United States (US) and to Japan in certain historical periods and what kind of transition occurred. Through the examination of these cases of transit, the dynamic and concrete dimensions of change in the representations of Aboriginal people will be made clear. For the first case of transit from Australia to the US, which happened in the 1940s, I will refer to the work by Geissler (Geissler 2019). To examine the transit from Australia to Japan, I focus on two exhibitions, one was held in 1965 (Matsuyama 2008) and the other was in 2016–17 (Weber and Nicholas 2010; Maeda et al. 2016).

I argue that the changes, or transitions, occurred when the objects moved geographically from one place to another, as suggested by Svašek. I will examine what happened when Aboriginal artworks first moved across the local border and then across the national one. When objects transit the border, they get into different social and political contexts, which gives them an utterly new representation. Predictably, this new representation will be reintroduced into the original place and changes the representation at home. I first talk about the historical changes that happened to Aboriginal arts, and then I will examine the difference that occurred because of the intersubjectivities of materials and audiences. After that, I look at two cases of representation of Aboriginal arts in Japan and examine them comparatively.

Perception, representation, and hegemony before the Aboriginal Referendum

Indigenous populations around the world have often been treated similarly, as uncivilised, inferior and primitive, and they are made invisible. This is also the case with the Aboriginal people in Australia. They migrated to the Australian continent approximately 50,000 years ago and lived as hunters and gatherers until the beginning of English colonisation in 1788. Many, especially those in the south, experienced harsh and violent encounters with colonisers. A significant number of people were killed by brutal acts and also by the diseases brought by the colonisers. The Aboriginal population declined from an estimated 300,000 in 1788 to 60,000 by the beginning of the 20th century. The colonisers saw them as people who were unable to adapt to modern life, as they were too primitive and would die out sooner or later (Broome 2010). Their treatment started to change in the 20th century. The government recognised the miserable situation of the Indigenous people as a social problem, and Christian missionaries expanded their activities to the northern part of the continent around that time (Harris 2013).

In 1967, a national referendum was held, and Aboriginal people were included as members of the Australian nation, which meant that, theoretically, they had the same rights as mainstream Australians. The government took various measures to improve the status of the Aboriginal people, for example through the Aboriginal Land Right Act in the Northern Territory in 1976 (Broome 2010).

The trajectory from Aboriginal artefacts to souvenirs and primitive artworks

When Christian missionaries started their religious activities, it was a common strategy to introduce arts and crafts activities. Missionaries built townships to settle down, Christianise and assimilate the Aboriginal people to a Western lifestyle. These missionaries stayed in the remote townships and tried to make the communities self-sustaining. For example, in the Earnabella Presbyterian Mission, established in 1937 at the northern edge of South Australia, a craft room was set up in 1948 with various crafts, such as mural paintings, carpets and batik cloth production. From the beginning of the 20th century, missionaries had also started their activities in the north. There, they encouraged Indigenous people to produce arts and crafts, such as ritual poles, bark paintings, carvings, baskets and shell necklaces for the souvenir market. These items were unique and exotic, but still seen as savage. Nevertheless, they were suitable as souvenirs representing Australia.

Particularly, bark paintings began to attract public attention. The anthropologist Sir Baldwin Spencer was the first person who made a collection for the Museum of Victoria in Melbourne in 1912. This collection included a sheet of painted bark originally used for a roof hatch. Bark paintings gradually increased in popularity. They were made from the sheets of bark from eucalyptus trees, which were gathered in the bush, dried, flattened and painted using ochres. The paintings were based on Aboriginal mythology, sacred places or spiritual beings (Morphy 1991). Another anthropologist, Donald Thompson, visited Eastern Arnhem Land and collected bark paintings in the 1930s. Some of the missionaries in the area also showed interest and put effort into circulating and merchandising them. For commercial purposes, a special technique was developed to prevent the cracking of the bark. It was tied with two vertical sticks at both ends (Williams 1976). Anthropologists collected bark paintings mainly as ethnographic specimens, but some of them like Spencer valued them as artworks (McLean 2011).

In the 1930s, most of the major museums and galleries in Australia expressed no interest in collecting Aboriginal arts and crafts. They did not value Aboriginal productions as art and saw them just as ethnographic objects or mere souvenirs. Only a handful of people were interested in Aboriginal bark paintings as art. One of them was the orthopaedic surgeon Dr. Stuart Scougall. He travelled several times to Arnhem Land to collect bark paintings as well as burial poles. He was a friend of Tony Tuckson, director of the Art Gallery of New South Wales, and strongly recommended him to collect these artistic artefacts for the gallery. Scougall also took Tuckson to Arnhem Land in 1958 and 1959 and financed the acquisition of burial poles. Later, Scougall donated 200 bark paintings to the Art Gallery (Morphy 2007). Ms Dorothy Bennett, Scougall's secretary, was also present on the trip in 1958. I will come back to her.

In 1941, the exhibition *Art of Australia 1788–1941* was organised by the Museum of Modern Art (MoMA) in New York (McLean 2014). This exhibition was based on the exhibition *Australian Aboriginal Art and Its Application* held at the place of the large retailer David Jones in Sydney earlier in that year. It was the very first exhibition of bark paintings in the US. It treated Aboriginal paintings from an evolutionist viewpoint, with a few counterbalancing views. Nevertheless, in the US the artworks were accepted favourably and seen as an essential contribution to modern art, far more than in Australia.

In the post-war period, in the late 1940s and 1950s, becoming an ally with the US was crucially important for Australia, especially for national security purposes. This was symbolically represented by the formation of the ANZUS Treaty, a 1951 military alliance between the US, New Zealand and Australia. To improve the relationship with the US, the ANTA (Australian National Travel Association) took various measures to attract American tourists to visit Australia. Furthermore, a series of exhibitions were planned and held in various cities in the US following the policy to increase American interest to visit Australia (Geissler 2019).

In 1945 and 1946, the anthropologist Charles Mountford held a series of lectures in several cities in the US and raised awareness for Aboriginal art. He also published the book *Australian Aboriginal Paintings* for the UNESCO as a part of *The World Art Series* in 1954. More than 1.8 million copies of the book were sold by 1959.

A series of exhibitions on Aboriginal bark paintings followed after that. In 1953, the Australian Commission of the UNESCO sponsored a travelling exhibition of Arnhem Land bark paintings to five venues. In the same year, the exhibition *The Arts Festival of the Olympic Games Melbourne*, organised by the Victoria Museum, toured. In 1965, the exhibition *Aboriginal Bark Paintings: Cahill and Chaseling Collections—National Museum of Victoria* was displayed at Houston, Texas. In 1965 as well, the exhibition *Bark Paintings from Arnhem Land* was held at the University of Kansas. Another exhibition, titled the *Australian Aboriginal Art: Lui A. Allen Collection*, was held at the University of Santa Barbara in 1970, and in 1972 at the Field Museum in Chicago (Geissler 2019).

When Aboriginal bark paintings transited the border of the country, they experienced their first transition to "primitive arts". The American art world was fascinated by "primitive art" when the Aboriginal bark paintings exhibitions were brought to the US. Therefore, they gained a high status.

"Primitivism" is an aesthetic appreciation of foreign artefacts that emerged at the end of the 19th century in Europe. It was defined as efforts to utilise primitive people's cultural expressions to change European art. It entirely depended on the European perspective in selecting what is "primitive" (Shinohara 2017). The fascination of early modern European artists with what was then called "primitive art", including "tribal art" from Africa, the South Pacific, and Indonesia, as well as prehistoric and early European art, is well documented (Errington 1998). They had a profound impact on modern Western art. The famous story of the discovery of "African tribal art" by Picasso around 1906 had an important influence on his work and was a significant factor in leading him to cubism. Primitivism also means the search for a more simple and basic way of life. A classic example was the artist Paul Gauguin, who moved from Paris to Tahiti in the South Pacific in 1891. He borrowed ideas and experiences from the Pacific region, where people were seen as primitive.

In New York, the Museum of Modern Art (MoMA) was established in 1929. It became one of the most authoritative modern museums, and it continues to be very influential in the global art scene. Okubo argues that the MoMA took part in making modern art movements and discourses, especially in the making of 20th-century modernism. She also points out that the MoMA's mission was a self-realisation by making a narrative of 20th-century modernism. The MoMA exhibited primitive art and modern art on the same basis for the first time in history, including the following exhibitions: *American Sources of Modern Art (Aztec, Maya, Incan)* in 1933; *African Negro Art* in 1935; *Indian Art of United States* in 1941; and *Art of Australia 1788–1941* which I mentioned earlier (McLean 2014).[1] These were exceptional exhibitions for a modern art museum at that time. But interestingly, by doing so the MoMA emphasised the continuation and the affinity between modern art and primitive art, and thus showed the universal aesthetic value of primitive art (Okubo 2009).

The change of Aboriginal representation in Australia

Let us now look at the situation in Australia. After the 1967 Referendum and the passing of the Racial Discrimination Act in 1975, the Australian government had to take measures to improve the livelihood and economic independence of Aboriginal people. For that purpose, several attempts were made to secure their financial base. One of the attempts that seemed promising was the promotion of the arts and crafts industry, which had started and operated in various places since the time of missionary activities. In 1971, the Australian government set up the Aboriginal Arts and Crafts Pty. Ltd., and in 1973 the Aboriginal Art Board. Their purpose was to promote Aboriginal arts and crafts activities and develop them into a profitable industry. They employed art advisers and dispatched them to remote Aboriginal communities. The advisers monitored the quality of the artworks and distributed them. The Aboriginal Art Board also helped to develop the industry through fiscal spending (Kubota 2011).

In Central Australia, unlike in the north, there were no traditional items such as bark paintings to sell. Before World War II, there were various attempts to promote carvings, batiks, weavings and ceramics. But only carvings and batiks had some success. In 1971 in Papunya, one of the Aboriginal communities in the Western Desert of Central Australia, several men started to paint murals on scrapped pieces of board. A schoolteacher who saw the pieces stimulated the manufacture of them, and later canvas and acrylic paints were introduced. Around the same time, the Australian Council of Arts set up the Aboriginal Arts and Crafts Pty. Ltd., and the schoolteacher became an art adviser in the community and a promoter of these paintings (Bardon and Bardon 2004). They consisted of iconographic symbols of lines, concentric circles, U shapes and various other symbolic marks painted with dots. Each iconographic symbol represented water holes, rivers, campsites, mythological beings and their travel routes, as well as different vital places—the dreaming stories of the area. Gradually, these unique paintings became popular, and other people in the vast

---

[1] MoMA Exhibition History. Accessed January 27, 2021. https://www.moma.org/calendar/exhibitions/history.

area of the Western Desert started to adopt this style (Perkins and Fink 2002). Thus, the art movement of the Western Desert started and spread, and, little by little, the paintings came to be highly appreciated both domestically and internationally (Myers 2002; Anderson and Dussurt 1988). However, they were not seen as authentic enough because they used introduced materials, including paints and canvases. The mainstream Australian society did not recognise these Aboriginal paintings as art. And aside from a few exceptional institutions, not many prominent art galleries displayed an interest in collecting acrylic dot paintings, as they did not regard them as serious art (Kubota 2011).

In 1988 and 1989, the Aboriginal exhibition, *Dreamings: The Art of Aboriginal Australia*, was showcased in the Asia Gallery in Chicago and toured through the US. It was claimed that it attracted the largest attendance (27,000 visitors) of any exhibit ever held at the Asia Gallery. One hundred and three objects were on display, including wood sculptures, bark paintings, acrylic paintings and shields. The exhibition had a high profile, and the objects were accepted as art and illustrated in a magnificent catalogue (Keneally 1988; Myers 2002; Sutton 1988). Around that time, several other significant exhibitions took place outside Australia and were also very popular. For example, an exhibition of *Aratjara* was held in 1993 and toured through Europe, and the *Fluent* exhibition featured three Aboriginal artists in the Australian pavilion of the Venice Biennale in 1997. The admiration in the US and Europe influenced the recognition of the Aboriginal acrylic paintings in Australia. Gradually, major art galleries in Australia started to acquire these paintings for their collections (Kubota 2011).

In the 1990s, the style of the acrylic paintings started to diversify. Although the theme of the arts remained the same (i. e. mythological stories and land), several artists started to use different techniques. For example, some started to use various abstract styles, and others very vivid colours. The paintings now looked considerably modern and attained a high profile in the international art world. In 1994, the world's oldest auction company, Sotheby's, created an Aboriginal auction section (Kubota 2011).

Other major auction companies followed soon afterwards. Thus, a wider audience began to recognise Aboriginal arts as contemporary fine arts. Moreover, many international collectors started to collect Aboriginal arts. In the early 2000s, some of these paintings were sold at very high prices. For example, Emily Kngwarreye's work was offered for A$1,050,000 in 2007, and Rover Thomas's work was offered for A$800,000 in 2010. Because of these high prices, Aboriginal art attracted wide attention, and it became a huge industry. Thus, in Australia, arts became the most famous representation of Aboriginal people and their culture. And as their artworks attained a high profile in the international art world, it changed the public image of Aboriginal people considerably in Australia and beyond.

Two Aboriginal exhibitions in Japan

The Australian Primitive Art exhibition of 1965

The first exhibition with the title *Australian Primitive Art (Oosutoraria Genshi Bijutsu)* was held in Tokyo in 1965. It showcased a collection of Ms Dorothy Bennett. As already mentioned, she served as a secretary to Dr. Scougall, who collected bark paintings in the 1950s and donated them to the Art Gallery of New South Wales. Dorothy became interested in this art form and made her own original collection of bark paintings. The exhibition of her collection was held in the Shinjuku Station building. More than 150 items were exhibited: 103 bark paintings and 27 carvings. The exhibition was sponsored by Yomiuri Shimbun, a nationwide newspaper company. Although it was only for twelve days, from May 22 to June 3, according to Dorothy Bennett the exhibition was quite successful (Matsuyama 2008). It was an exhibition of mainly bark paintings on sheets of bark from eucalyptus trees with ochres of yellow, red, black and white. They appeared very earthy and conjured an image of people near to nature. Matsuyama accounted that the bark paintings in this exhibition were introduced as "primitive art" (Matsuyama 2008). Moreover, according to Matsuyama, in the catalogue accompanying the show Aboriginal people were introduced as one of the world's most ancient races, living a traditional tribal life in the wilderness and adhering to primitive beliefs. Since the contact with civilisation, their primitive arts had begun to disappear and were at risk of being lost. Thus, the exhibition placed Aboriginal people as people of the past who had survived to modern days but were disappearing rapidly. This exhibition was intended to be an example of artworks of primitive people.

Dorothy fondly remembered this exhibition until late in her life. Dorothy's son, Lance Bennett, helped with the exhibition and published a book entitled *Australian Native Art*. The Japanese anthropologist, Hiroko Hara, translated it and published it in the following year (Bennett 1969 [1966]). Dorothy's exhibition in 1965 was accepted and enjoyed by the Japanese people. However, it evoked no challenges or enthusiasm as in Europe. It is probable that as the knowledge about Aboriginal people was limited, their artworks were simply recognised as unique and exotic in Japan.

The exhibition was held just after the first exhibition on primitivism in the National Museum of Western Art in Tokyo in 1965. In Japan, primitivism was introduced in the 1950s. The famous Japanese artist, Taro Okamoto, spent some time in Paris to study art in the early 20th century and encountered primitivism in the Musée de l' Homme. He also studied anthropology under Marcel Mauss. He published a book on Jomon pots in 1952, on the beauty and power of the clay pots from the Japanese prehistoric era, but not directly on primitivism. Nevertheless, it was the first introduction about primitivism in Japan

(Shinohara 2017). In the 1950s, Shuzo Takiguchi also introduced the term primitivism in Japan in some articles (Shinohara 2017). In 1960, the National Museum of Western Art in Tokyo held the exhibition *Today's Focus: Primitive Art Seen through Eyes of the Present*. Based on an exploration of this exhibition in 1960, Shinohara concluded that primitivism had not directly influenced any art movement in Japan (Shinohara 2017). Rather, primitivism was passively accepted as a new European trend.

The One Road exhibition on Aboriginal art from 2016 to 2017

Another example was the *One Road* exhibition (*Wan Rodo Ten*) held from 2016 to 2017 in Japan. The timing of this exhibition occurred after changes in the profile of Aboriginal arts in Australia. The acrylic paintings, including various abstract styles, had become internationally accepted as high art. Since 1965, there were a few significant Aboriginal art exhibitions held in Japan before the *One Road* exhibition. The biggest ones are the exhibition *Crossroads—Toward a New Reality: Aboriginal Art from Australia* in 1992 and the exhibition *Utopia: The Genius of Emily Kame Knguwarreye* in 2008 (Neal 1998). The *Crossroads* exhibition was held in the National Museum of Modern Art, Kyoto, and the National Museum of Modern Art, Tokyo. The *Utopia* exhibition was held at The National Museum of Art, Osaka, and The National Art Centre, Tokyo. All of them are major cosmopolitan museums. The exhibition of Emily's works particularly evoked interest in Japan. A record-breaking number of visitors was reported. Many newspapers and TV stations covered it, and it widened the viewer's knowledge and appreciation about Aboriginal Australians. In many cases, Emily's exhibition in 2008 influenced audience to come to the *One Road*. I talked with some of the visitors of the *One Road* exhibition, and they told me that they came to see it because they liked the art of Emily.

Then in 2016, the *One Road* exhibition toured to four venues: Osaka, Chiba, Matsuyama and Kushiro (Maeda et al. 2016). The original version of this exhibition, *Yiwarra Kuju—The Canning Stock Route*, was planned and organised in Australia in 2010 as a result of the project commemorating the centenary of the construction of the Canning Stock Route (Weber and Nicholas 2010). It was a truck route stretching from north to south in Western Australia for 1,850 km from Halls Creek in Kimberley to Wiluma. It was constructed in the early 1900s along 36 wells for moving the herds of live cattle. To locate possible sites for wells, they used the knowledge of the Aboriginal people of the area, sometimes in a detrimental way. For the construction, many sacred places were destroyed.

One of the purposes of this project was to cast a light on the historical experiences of Aboriginal people. The official history always recognises the construction of the route from a colonial and postcolonial perspective, which has not cared about Aboriginal experiences and their memories. The lives of the people in that area changed tremendously because of the construction of the route. Many of the Aboriginal people in the region met non-Aboriginal people for the first time, and they experienced brutal violence in some cases. As a result, many left the area and migrated to nearby towns.

The project started in 2006, with a series of workshops organised by nine art centres around the area. About 80 artists attended and they held workshops on the route. In these workshops, Aboriginal people, originally from the district and their descendants gathered, travelled along the route, and camped together. They talked about their experiences, exchanged stories, and painted them. From that series of workshops, a total of over 100 paintings were produced. The National Museum of Australia acquired the outcome of the workshops, which resulted in an exhibition there in 2010 (Davenport et al. 2010). After that it toured to several Australian cities and closed in 2011. It was the most successful museum exhibition and attracted more than 120,000 visitors.

The exhibition, brought to Japan in 2016, also attracted a considerably broad public, considering the venues in smaller cities. The paintings in the show were bright, vivid and colourful. Many of them were abstract and did not reveal their content directly, although all of them are about important places, mythology and personal historical experiences. Moreover, they conveyed the message that history contains different Perspectives. (Maeda et al. 2016). The exhibition was highly valued by the Japanese audience.

In the interviews, many Japanese visitors expressed to me their excitement about seeing Aboriginal art. Some said that the paintings moved them deeply. Others admired the feeling of spiritual power from the paintings. Interestingly, many Japanese visitors displayed emotional responses to the paintings. Some passionately commented on how they felt freedom, extensive abundance and energy through looking at the artworks. One woman told me how her heart trembled and that she could not stop her tears. Some even connected their feelings to their personal experiences. It is rare for Japanese people to show their emotions in public, so it was an exciting experience to hear about their emotional remarks.

Compared to the 1960s, although the Japanese audience's knowledge of Aboriginal people may have increased slightly, their knowledge still remains limited. Knowledge about Australia in Japan is also minimal. Every year in the course of Oceanic studies at Kobe University, I ask Japanese students questions about their understanding of Australia. They respond with koala bears, kangaroos and the Sydney Opera House.

Most Japanese people do not know about the current situation of Aboriginal people. Thus, they do not have any concrete image about them. The explanation in the panels in the exhibition about their dreaming stories, sacred sites, knowledge about the environment and the hunting and gathering lifestyle in the bush, probably gave the Japanese public a romantic image of Aboriginal people with a unique traditional culture and with an intact connection to nature.

Conclusion

As we have seen, the images of Australian Aboriginal people have changed considerably over the years domestically and internationally. I have argued elsewhere that one of the crucial reasons for this change is the power of the arts Aboriginal people have produced (Kubota 2007, 2011). When we look back at the trajectory of Aboriginal paintings, we realise that the transformations have occurred after the objects transit the borders geographically.

As discussed, Aboriginal arts have significantly changed. The first change occurred during the mission days, from the 19th to the early 20th century, when the local products for everyday or ceremonial use were turned into merchandise for sale. Missionaries found that exotic primitive objects were suitable for souvenirs. The artefacts left their place of origin, Arnhem Land or the Central Desert, and changed into commercial products.

After that, two crucial transits took place. The first transit happened in the 1940s to 1960s, when the Aboriginal bark paintings were brought to the US. The change took place when they transited the national border. When they moved to the US, social and political circumstances differed. The visitors of the exhibitions lacked the views of Aboriginal people with social problems, and they could appreciate Aboriginal arts without this prejudice. In addition, in the US in the early 20th century, as argued by Okubo, the MoMA successfully connected modernism to primitivism and integrated them into modern art (Okubo 2009). This was the social climate in which a series of exhibitions of Aboriginal bark paintings were carried out in the 1940s and 1950s, and the success and high profile of these exhibitions gave bark paintings a status of strongly praised primitive art.

The next transit was from the 1960s to 2000s, when Aboriginal paintings crossed the border again, including two transits to Japan. In the 1970s, in the US another transition happened, when the *Dreaming* exhibition was held in 1986 (Myers 2002). The evaluation of Aboriginal arts had risen tremendously, and this trend correlated with the social circumstances around the art world at that time. When this transit took place, the transition of Aboriginal paintings from primitive art to contemporary art occurred. This particular transition was significant and meaningful for Aboriginal people, as it changed their public image strongly.

Yet the transits to Japan displayed different aspects. I focused on two exhibitions in Japan. As in the US, the acceptance of Aboriginal arts was outside the Australian social context. Thus, the public could face the arts without concrete knowledge about the social background, which made them appreciate these arts more.

In the 1965 exhibition, Japanese visitors praised Aboriginal art as exotic without any confrontation of "the other". Aboriginal people were represented as just unfamiliar people. The primitivism movement did not arise, and people only passively accepted the trend of Euro-American primitivism in Japan. Moreover, in the 2016 exhibition, the public saw Aboriginal people as unique and powerful people who have a significant and mythical connection with nature and the land. They were fascinated by the power of Aboriginal arts. The Japanese acceptance of Aboriginal paintings, though, was made possible without the concrete knowledge about the Australian social context.

However, in the Japanese case, because art has transited from its social context of origin, the Japanese audience face it without the concrete knowledge about original social context. Thus, it is probable that the transition in Japan occurred very differently as compared to the case of other countries. Maybe the most significant difference is the tradition in the arts. The emotions Japanese people expressed in the exhibition in 2016 and the impact Aboriginal art had on them have to be examined further from this perspective. It will probably show the different intersubjectivities between materials and the public from a position of transit and transition, but this is a research area needing further research.

References

Anderson, Christopher and Francoise Dussart, eds. 1988. "Dreamings in Acrylic: Western Desert Art", In *Dreamings: The Art of Aboriginal Australia*, edited by Sutton, Peter, 89–142. New York: George Braziller.

Bardon, Geoffery and James Bardon. 2004. *Papunya: A Place Made after the Story*. Melbourne: The Miegunyah Press.

Bennett, Lance. 1969 [1966]. *Osutoraria Mikaibijutsu [Australian Native Art]*, edited by Izumi, Seiichi, Translated by Hiroko Hara. Tokyo: Kodansha. (in Japanese)

Broome, Richard. 2010. *Aboriginal Australians: A History Since 1788*. Sydney: Allen & Unwin Academic.

Davenport, Carly, Monique La Fontaine and John Carty. 2010. *Yiwarra Kuju: The Canning Stock Route*. Canberra: National Museum of Australia.

Errington, Shelly. 1998. *The Death of Authentic Art and Other Tales of Progress*. Berkeley: University of California Press.

Geissler, Marie. 2019. "Cultural Tourism – Imagery of Arnhem Land Bark Paintings Informs Australian Messaging to the Post-War USA." *Arts* 8, no. 66: 1–25.

Harris, John. 2013. *One Blood—200 Years of Aboriginal Encounter with Christianity: A Story of Hope*. Bentford Square, Victoria: Australians Together.

Keneally, Thomas. 1988. "November 13 'Dreamscapes'," *The New York Times Magazine*, Section 6, 52. Accessed December 1, 2019. https://www.nytimes.com/1988/1113/magazine/dreamscapes.html.

Kubota, Sachiko. 2007. "Aborijini aato no Henbou [The Change of Aboriginal Arts]." In *Shigenka suru Bunka [Making Culture into Resource]*, edited by Yamashita, Shinji, 181–208, Tokyo: Kobundo. (in Japanese)

Kubota, Sachiko. 2011. "Aborijini Aatisuto no Tanjo [Emergence of Aboriginal Artists]." In *Gurobarizesyon to Ikirusekai [Globalisation and Life World]*, edited by Matsui, Takeshi, Katsuro Nawa and Atsushi Nobayashi, 339–387, Kyoto: Showado. (in Japanese)

Maeda, Rei, Yusuke Ogura and Ayana Watanabe, eds. 2016. *One Road—The World of Contemporary Aboriginal Arts*, Tokyo: Gendai-Kikakusha. (supervised by Sachiko Kubota, in Japanese)

Matsuyama, Toshio. 2008. "The 'Exhibition of Australian Aboriginal Art' of 1965 and its Anthropological Background." *Senri Ethnological Studies* 32 (2): 149–169, Osaka: National museum of Ethnology. (in Japanese)

McLean, Ian. 2011. "Aboriginal Art and the Artworld." In *How Aborigines Invented the Idea of Contemporary Art: Writings on Aboriginal Contemporary Art*, edited by Ian McLean, 13-75. Bribane: Power Publications Institute of Modern Art.

Morphy, Howard. 1991. *Ancestral Connections: Art and an Aboriginal Systems of Knowledge*. Chicago: Chicago University Press.

Morphy, Howard. 2007. *Becoming Art: Exploring Cross-Cultural Categories*. Oxford and New York: Berg.

Myers, Fred. 2002. *Painting Culture: The Making of an Aborigianl High Art*. Durham and London: Duke University Press.

Neal, Margo, ed. 1998. *Aborijini ga Unda Tensai Gaka: Emiri Unguware [Utopia—The Genesis of Emily Kame Knguwarre]*. Tokyo: Yomiuri Shinbun.

Okubo, Kyoko. 2009. *Purimitivisumu to Purimitivizumu: Bunka no kyoukai wo meguru dainamizumu [Primitisme and Primitivism: Dynamism of Cultural Borders.]* Tokyo: Sangen-sha. (in Japanese)

Perkins, Hetti and Hannah Fink, eds. 2002. *Papunya Tula: Genesis and Genius*. Sydney: Art Gallery of New South Wales.

Shinohara, Hanako. 2017. "Nihon niokeru Kindai Bijutu to 'Genshi Bijutu' no Kankeisei: 1960 nen 'Gendai no Me: Genshi Bijutu kara' Ten wo Jirei ni" [Modern Art and 'Primitive' Art in Japan: Exhibition, Today's Focus: Primitive Art Seen through Eyes of the Present in 1960]." *Departmental Bulletin Paper, Tsukuba University.* 41–60. (in Japanese)

Sutton, Peter, ed. 1988. *Dreamings: The Art of Aboriginal Australia*. New York: George Braziller.

Svašek, Maruška. 2007. *Anthropology, Art and Cultural Production*. London: Pluto Press.

Weber, Therese and Robert Nicholas, eds. 2010. *Yiwarra Kuju: The Canning Stock Route*. Canberra: National Museum of Australia.

Williams, Nancy. 1976. "Australian Aboriginal Art at Yirrkala: The Introduction and Development of Marketing." In *Ethnic and Tourist Arts: Cultural Expressions from the Fourth World*, edited by Nelson Graburn, 167–95. Berkeley: University of California Press.

Part II.
Appropriating and Resisting the Global Art World

Chapter 4
Life, art and commoditisation: how disabled people's works in Japan encountered gazes of the international art world[1]

Eriko Aoki
Ryukoku University, Japan

Abstract

After World War II, the French artist Jean Dubuffet proposed "L'Art Brut" as a form of genuine West European art. At the same time, in Japan Kazuo Itoga started a welfare institution for intellectually disabled people. That has led to the development of welfare institutions where the client members can be engaged in creating works. Around the turn of the century the international art-world discovered Japanese intellectually disabled people's works as those of Art Brut. This chapter aims to explore the encounter and its influence, with careful attention to the creators' lives and social milieu in the following order: first placing Art Brut within the complex tapestry of modern history to show the affinities between art and capitalism; secondly clarifying how works created by some client members of the welfare institutions in Japan were acknowledged as Art Brut works in the international art-world; thirdly reflecting upon how intellectually disabled people live in Japanese society with comparative attention to cases in Central Flores in Eastern Indonesia; fourthly shedding light on creative activities and lives pursued in some welfare institutions free from capitalist evaluation with reflection on the features of mainstream Japanese society; and fifthly delineating the different orientations of appropriating the influence of capitalist markets by three Japanese welfare institutions, and finally, concluding with some remarks from a wider historical perspective.

---

[1] My fieldwork for this research from April 2015 to March 2016 was funded by the Research Centre for Social Inclusion, Faculty of Sociology and from April 2020 to March 2021 by the Research Institute for International Society and Culture, Ryukoku University.

Keywords: Art Brut, disabled people, commoditisation, welfare institution, Japanese society

Right after World War II in Europe, the French artist named Jean Dubuffet proposed "Art Brut" as a form of genuine Western art (Dubuffet 1976; Thévoz 1975). About the same time in Japan, Kazuo Itoga, Ichiji Tamura and Taro Ikeda started "Ohmi-Gakuen", a welfare institution for intellectually disabled people, which has led the development of welfare institutions where the client members can be engaged in creating whatever works they like (Itoga 2002; Shiga prefecture n.d.; Kazuo Itoga Memorial Foundation n.d.). Since that time, while Art Brut has established itself in the art world (Danto 1964; Becker 1982), the number of institutions more or less inspired by Ohmi-Gakuen in Japan has increased. Around the turn of the century these two trajectories encountered one another. The international art world discovered Japanese intellectually disabled people's works as those of Art Brut, and some of those works have been exhibited and commoditised worldwide.

This chapter aims to explore the encounter and its influence, with careful attention to the creators' lives and social milieu. For the exploration, first I will place Art Brut within the complex tapestry of modern history to show the affinities between art and capitalism. The second section clarifies how works created by some client members of the welfare institutions in Japan were acknowledged as Art Brut works in the international art world. The third section reflects upon how intellectually disabled people live in Japanese society with comparative attention to cases in Central Flores in Eastern Indonesia, where I have conducted fieldwork since 1979. The fourth section sheds light on creative activities and lives pursued in some welfare institutions where the client members are free from capitalist evaluation. I also reflect on the features of mainstream Japanese society in terms of work and life. In the fifth section, I would like to delineate the different orientations of appropriating the influence of capitalist markets by three Japanese social welfare institutions. Finally, I will conclude with some remarks from a wider historical perspective.

Placing art brut within the complex tapestry of modern history

Jean Dubuffet questioned the conventions of the art world and advocated the concept of Art Brut. He defined it as artworks, outside of the aesthetic rules and conventions, created by those who had never been exposed to art education. For Dubuffet, this included the works of the mentally ill, people in solitude or confinement, spirit mediums and so on. As Dubuffet's definition suggests, by advocating Art Brut he intended to contest, innovate in, or even revolutionise the tradition of art and aesthetics in the modern West.[2] In this sense he had something in common with Marcel Duchamp who advocated Dadaism and the other advocators of many kinds of "ism art" in the 20th century. He was enchanted by artworks created by people living at the margins of the (art) society in the West, and he shared certain perspectives with the admirers of "primitive arts" created by colonised people living in the margins of the world from the Western perspective. Both Dubuffet and the admirers of "primitive arts" appreciated the works by those excluded from full citizenship.

Dubuffet's definition of Art Brut only covers the conditions of creators and their activities. It does not attempt to explain the features of Art Brut works themselves. The word *brut* only vaguely suggests the tendencies of the artworks. The French word *brut* means "raw", "rough", "bare", "wild", "unprocessed", "natural", "crude", "unrefined" and so on. In addition to the vagueness, Dubuffet's position appears to be contradictory because while he objected to the Western art tradition on the one hand, he simultaneously tried to place Art Brut at the core of the tradition. He held that only Art Brut was "the true art of the West". In other words, he tried to establish himself as the authority of Art Brut in the Western art world, although he contested the authority of Western art culture and institutions (Dubuffet 1976; Thévoz 1975; Kanou 2013a, 2013b). For seventy-five years after he first began advocating the notion of Art Brut, despite Dubuffet's intention, countless works other than his own collections including those from non-Western societies have been incorporated into Art Brut. Consequently, it is becoming harder to answer the question of what Art Brut is.

This difficulty occurs partly because it is also hard to answer the question of what art is. According to Morris Weitz, a philosopher of aesthetics, theories concerning the definition of art have emerged one after another in our modern time only to fail in establishing the definition or the necessary and sufficient properties of art:

> "Each age, each art-movement, each philosophy of art, tries over and over again to establish the stated ideal only to be succeeded by a new or revised theory, rooted, at least in part, in the repudiation of preceding ones" (Weitz 1956, 27).

After a brief review of several art theories, he maintains that although each theory is contending for the definition of true art, there is no common property which renders an artefact artwork, and all the properties of art theories insisted on are related to one another with "family resemblance" or series of similarities (Wittgenstein 1953). With this perspective, he argues, we can incorporate many mutually contesting art theories in a field and understand that the role of art

---

[2] In 1948 Dubuffet founded Art Brut Association. Claude Levi-Strauss and Andre Burton participated in the association (Kanou 2013a).

theories is not to define art, which is logically doomed to failure, but to concentrate our attention on "excellence in art", and accordingly, art theories turn out to be far from worthless (Weitz 1956, 35).

By applying Weitz's view, we can not only place Art Brut in the art world but also use the concept of "family resemblance" to shed light on the expanding field of Art Brut in spite of Dubuffet's prohibition. I appreciate Weitz's argument because it saves us from the vertigo of art theories emerging one over another like a never-ending revolution. However, I must critically point out that Weitz takes "excellence in art" as self-evident and he is not aware of the socio-cultural, historical, and political-economic aspects of art and aesthetics.

Historical scrutiny shows that art philosophy or aesthetics emerged in the 18th century and the concept of "art" as the object of the aesthetics was born simultaneously (Stecker 2010; Mori 2016).[3] In the late 19th century, this view was mimetically appropriated in Japan during the Western-modernisation process.[4] Needless to say, there were pictures, drawings, dance and music before the modern birth of "art", not only in the West but also in Japan. The point is that the modern view of art and the institutional agents exercising the view, such as the media, publishers, academic training, the art world, professional critics, the art market and art organisations, were all born in a certain historical time when bourgeois citizens gained power and denied God and religious belief, especially in the public sphere (Taylor 2007, 1–3). As Gell suggested, the role that "art" plays in the modern time can be compared to that religion used to play (Gell 1998, 1999). Because the "new" religion or the "art" cult lacks "something" that can be a substitute for God in the "old" monotheistic religion, especially in case of the West, that something has ever been sought for. Advocating Art Brut is also one of the quests for such true art value. Appealing to this parallel relation between religion and art, Gell develops his analysis of art. This parallel relation of enchantment, as he puts it, reminds us of another parallel relation of enchantment between religion and fashion, or between Church and shopping arcade. Walter Benjamin designates that in the mid 19th century Paris, the shopping arcades became as crowded as the Church used to be (Benjamin 1999). He points out:

> "Fashion prescribes the ritual according to which the commodity fetish demands to be worshipped. ... It couples the living body to the inorganic world. To the living, it defends the rights of the corpse. The fetishism which thus succumbs to these appeals of the inorganic is its vital nerve" (Benjamin 1999, 18–19).

---

[3] Svašek maintains that the separation of the crafts and the fine arts occurred in the fifteenth century. However, she does not give us data for that (Svašek 2007).
[4] The Western art world was also influenced by Japanese art traditions.

Benjamin also points out the simultaneous emergence of private individuals who collect enchanting items to make up their private space. They can be things from remote non-Western places, those from the nostalgic past or works of art (Benjamin 1999, 19). With his perspective, we can see the affinity among art, fashion, consumerism, commoditisation, colonialism and collecting, which are all related to the emergence of private individual selves, and all fit bourgeois citizenship in the capitalist world. It is amazing that art and capitalism are common in the sense that they have both been eager to develop by finding their own *terra incognita*. Since the bourgeois gained power and the artists lost the aristocrat patrons, artworks have been capitalistic commodities and investments (Hook 2014; Miyazu 2014). Because of the syntagmatic as well as paradigmatic affinity between art and capitalism, art and the activities concerning art can morally deviate as capitalism tends to do. James Clifford seems to warn us in dealing with art as well as culture, when he maintains as follows:

> "Modernist primitivism, with its claims to deeper humanist sympathies and a wider aesthetic sense, goes hand-in-hand with a developed market in tribal art and with definitions of artistic and cultural authenticity that are now widely contested" (Clifford 1988, 198).

Many years have passed since modernist primitivism was advocated and even since Clifford made this point. With his warning in mind, I would like to look carefully at what is happening to the lives of intellectually disabled people in contemporary Japan, whose works are now appraised as Art Brut works.

"Art Brut" in Japan

Japanese art lovers only began to pay attention to Art Brut in the early 1990s. An exhibition entitled as "*Parallel Visions: Modern Arts and Outsider Art*" held in Tokyo in 1993 opened the first chapter in terms of Art Brut history in Japan. This exhibition was part of an international travelling exhibition by the Los Angeles County Museum of Art. The word "Outsider Art" was coined by Roger Cardinal as an English translation of Art Brut in the 1970s (Hall and Metcalf 1994, xiii). In the early history of Art Brut in the 1990s in Japan, this English term was usually used in favour of Art Brut partly because the term was used in the title of the 1993 exhibition (Kanou 2013a, 2013b).

In the late 1990s, a work by a client member of Mizunoki-ryou, an institution for intellectually disabled people in Kyoto prefecture, was collected as the first Japanese piece by the Art Brut Museum Lausanne in Switzerland (Hashimoto 2013). This museum can be said to be the world centre of Art Brut because it was built on the foundation of Dubuffet's collection. In 2008, starting from Art Brut Museum Lausanne, a travelling exhibition entitled *Art Brut Japon* was held in many places in Europe and Japan in collaboration with the Borderless Art Museum NO-MA in Japan (Borderless Art Museum NO-MA n.d.). As most of the works exhibited were created by intellectually disabled people and the exhibition won significant acclaim, the term "Art Brut" subsequently came to be used widely in Japan, usually to indicate intellectually disabled people's works. As the reputation of disabled people's works spread through exhibitions and other media, this also raised the Japanese general public's awareness and acknowledgement of their works (Hattori 2003; Miyaji 2013; Hashimoto 2013; Kanou 2013a, 2013b).

As I mentioned at the beginning of this chapter, right after World War II, at about the same time Dubuffet advocated Art Brut, Itoga, Tamura and Ikeda, who are called "fathers of welfare for intellectually disabled people in Japan", started an institution named Ohmi-Gakuen in Shiga prefecture, where clay for the local pottery industry is abundant. Soon they found the client members of their institution enjoyed touching and kneading clay. Their ongoing activities with clay resulted in the creation of plastic arts. The number of similar institutions has increased since then, and today not only the ceramic arts but also many types of artworks are created in a number of institutions in Japan, especially in Shiga prefecture and also in some other regions (Hattori 2016).

Against this background, Shiga Prefectural Modern Art Museum advocates Art Brut as one of its main themes. It held an exhibition of Art Brut entitled *Sign of Life: Shiga and "Art Brut"* (Museum of Modern Art Shiga 2015). The Borderless Art Museum NO-MA is also in Shiga Prefecture. It was established in 2004 by GLOW (the Shiga prefectural corporate body for social welfare) and has exhibited Art Brut works of disabled as well as non-disabled people. Since 2006, NO-MA has conducted a joint-project with Art Brut Museum Lausanne. In 2008 they held a traveling exhibition in Japan, entitled *Art Brut Japon, Communicating Souls* as I mentioned above. After appreciating the *Art Brut Japon* exhibition, the director of the Paris municipal museum, Halle Saint Pierre, asked NO-MA to hold an exhibition entitled *Art Brut Japonais* in her museum. The exhibition was held from March 2010 to January 2011, comprised of 800 works by 63 artists, and was appreciated by 120,000 visitors over a period of ten months. The exhibition travelled in several places in Japan, and its report was published as a book. NO-MA has also conducted a variety of other activities to promote Art Brut. As a part of the activities, for example, it is engaging in research on artworks made by disabled people across Asia. NO-MA as well as Japanese "Art Brut" works have revealed their presence internationally and domestically (Borderless Art Museum NO-MA n.d.).

Interestingly the Japanese mainstream art world has historically ignored works created by disabled people and has been reluctant to accept them as works of art. Before World War II for example, the Japanese art world excluded artworks created by intellectually disabled people. Only people in the fields of welfare and medicine tried to promote those works as art. In Europe, in contrast, the artists themselves have paid attention to artworks by intellectually disabled or mentally ill people. Tadashi Hattori, curator, art critic and professor at Konan University in Japan, points out that since the Japanese art world has ignored works created by intellectually disabled people, without the contribution of people working in welfare, their works would not have won acclaim as artworks in Japan (Hattori 2003). In other words, intellectually disabled people's works in Japan have been acknowledged by the international art world without support from the domestic Japanese art world.

Thanks to the way the Japanese art world has tended to overlook their works in the past, intellectually disabled artists in Japan are currently free from its hegemony. Moreover, it is likely that many of the staff members of the institutions where attractive Art Brut works have been produced have never experienced either conventional art education or formal welfare education. This situation might mean the intellectually disabled people's lives and creative activities in these institutions are also relatively free from both welfare culture and art conventions.

In Japan, not only in Shiga but also in other regions, intellectually disabled people had been producing unique works since long before the international art agents started to pay attention to them. Even now their activities are carried out autonomously and independently from international art agents.

Usually, it is not art classes but everyday life in which art activities take place and numerous artworks are created. They are often exhibited at the galleries attached to the institutions, and at the art museums and art galleries outside the institutions. Some of the artworks are sold, namely, commoditised at art markets. It is characteristic to the Japanese Art Brut scene that more than ninety percent of the Japanese Art Brut collections for any exhibition, not only international but domestic exhibitions, are works by intellectually disabled people (Hattori 2003).

Since the 1990s, through the exhibitions of Outsider Art or Art Brut, it has become publicly recognised in Japan that the intellectually disabled are likely to be artists. As in Europe, in Japan art and artists are admired and respected by the public, especially by those in the middle and upper class. So, it is interesting to consider the question: Have the recent phenomena concerning Art Brut brought any changes to the lives of intellectually disabled people in Japan?

Intellectually disabled people in Japanese society

I met and communicated with quite a few intellectually disabled people when I visited their institutions and attended workshops with them. There were always some among them who were welcoming and invited me to share the scene of their everyday life. Except for these experiences, I seldom have opportunities to communicate with intellectually disabled people in my everyday life in Japan. It is partly because the percentage of the intellectually disabled people to the whole population is quite low (Cabinet Office of Government of Japan 2013, 2016),[5] but it is also related to the features of contemporary Japanese society. In order to clarify how they live in contemporary Japanese society in general, I would like to reflect on my experiences with intellectually disabled people throughout my life.

I have shared everyday social life with intellectually disabled people in a village called Rhepadori (pseudonym) in a mountain area on the Flores island in Eastern Indonesia, where I have conducted anthropological fieldwork since 1979. When I say "intellectually disabled", the judgement about who belongs to the category is based on my personal estimation since the official judgement is not applied in Rhepadori and its vicinity. I would like to pick up three people as examples to show how disabled people live their social lives there.

The first person I describe is Radu, who seemed to be a teenager when I started my fieldwork in 1979. I have never heard him speaking. According to my neighbours in Rhepadori, since he does not understand how to deal with seeds, he picks up and eats rice and maize seeds sown in fields. He has such a large appetite that his parents have given up trying to fully feed him. However, he has never starved because he is physically so strong that villagers like to ask him to carry heavy things and invite him to a meal in return.

The second person is Mr Hena. Villagers enjoy talking about him. According to them, he does not know how to do any form of labour, and he became like that because of the vast extents of land which he inherited from his ancestors. He lives in a village on the coast and likes to climb up to Rhepadori together with the administrative village head, who is one of his neighbours. While he does not have any official role at all, he entertains villagers by playing mimetically the role of a Dutch colonial official, or by asking them whether there are beautiful women who want to marry him. The conversation with him is a great source of enjoyment for the villagers, who are delighted to provide him with meals in return for his entertainment.

The third example is grandma Seda. She seems to have become intellectually disabled recently or may be suffering from dementia due to her old age. She does not speak as she used to do any longer. She walks around from one house to another in the village. When she feels like sleeping, she lies down in any house. When people in a household have a meal, and she happens to be there,

---

[5] According to Annual Report on Government Measures for Persons with Disabilities by Cabinet Office of Government of Japan, the percentage is 0.4 % in 2013 and 0.6% in 2016.

they share the food with her. She leaves her house in the morning and comes home in the evening every day.

It seems that in Rhepadori and its vicinity there are quite a few people with slight intellectual disability or mental disorder who are married and have children. Some people among them, who can hear and see what other people cannot, tend to play a social role of using their special sensitive power to divine providential dates for various activities, to foresee what will happen in the future, to heal the sick and so on. Rhepadori people might endure severe natural conditions, under which disabled babies and children might not be able to survive. However, whoever does survive, intellectually disabled or otherwise, can live as a full member of society with one's own name and identity. From these examples, we can see that the approach towards intellectually disabled people in Rhepadori is different in various aspects from that of contemporary Japan.

A recent tragic crime and consequent social phenomena might help to illustrate the features of the Japanese society in relation to the intellectually disabled. Before dawn on 26th of July 2016, an ex-caretaker sneaked into a welfare institution for intellectually disabled people. He then used a knife to stab 19 disabled people to death while they were asleep in their beds. In explanation for his actions, he stated that his victims were useless to society and better to be killed with mercy. The crime and the criminal are horrifying indeed. However, what happened afterwards was also shocking; quite a few opinions approving his statement were enunciated on the internet and many families of the victims chose not to announce the victims' names because they were afraid of further discrimination and verbal hate attacks. While the crime and the criminal are certainly unusual, regretfully, the consequent social phenomena seem to be, if not usual, then at least more understandable in the contemporary Japanese social context. While intellectually disabled people are alive, they are separated, even segregated from society and their social life is extremely restricted. Even after death, their identities are kept hidden from society.[6]

Atelier Yamanami is one of the institutions where intellectually disabled members are most actively producing unique works. Mr Masato Yamashita, the director of Atelier Yamanami, often speaks to the Japanese public: "please imagine how difficult your life is if you must live only in two places, at home and in an institution administratively assigned, and there you must do tedious

---

[6] There are some reports that before the 1970s intellectually disabled people lived as social members who were said to bring luck to the "house group" in rural areas in Japan (Namihira 1984).

monotonous activities, as in most institutions", "Although it is very good for many people to appreciate the works that our members made, first of all we ask you to come to know their excellent personality". Exploring the creative activities at the institutions may shed new light on the current situation of Japanese society to which Mr Yamashita makes the above-mentioned appeal.

Working and living in society

In Japan, as in many other developed countries, the administrative welfare system is applied nation-wide. By applying administrative criteria, some people are officially acknowledged as intellectually disabled, and are to be provided with services accordingly. While the Japanese welfare policy towards intellectually disabled people has been changed, it still reveals clear tendencies towards family dependency and institutional separation (Ministry of Education, Culture, Sports, Science and Technology, Japan 2010). While intellectually disabled people are born to their family and live with their own names as irreplaceable family members, it is difficult for them to live in the public sphere, which demands economic independence from others and evaluates each person according to the capitalist criteria. In order for them to be adapted to the capitalist society, the institutions usually play the role of providing a sheltered workshop for disabled people. Here, they are trained to carry out easy and simple factory work, from which they earn an income, albeit too small to live on. In these social environments, they and their identities are kept away from the public sphere.

The motto of the new social movement initiated right after World War II by the three "fathers of welfare", Itoga, Ikeda and Tamura, is "Let these children be the light of the world" (Itoga 2002). Through the process of the movement, art works, detached from capitalist evaluation, were subsequently found to be an excellent media for intellectually disabled people to communicate to the Japanese society that they are irreplaceable unique members. The "fathers" believed that intellectually disabled people's lives themselves could illuminate the world.

It is not only these three men who longed for emancipation from capitalist evaluation and promoted creative works in the institutions. Mr Yasuo Harima, the founder of Tanpopo-No-Ye, and Mr Katsuya Yamashita, the founder of Atelier Yamanami also have made all their efforts to realise the emancipation for intellectually disabled people.

Harima, an ex-journalist, resented the situation of intellectually disabled people. In 1973, together with their parents he initiated a social movement and founded a civic welfare organisation called Tanpopo-No-Ye (Harima 1975). In 1995 he initiated another social movement called the Able Art Movement in order to further promote the art activities by the client members and to enrich everybody's life by making art and society mutually engaged (Able Art Japan n.d.). Nowadays Tanpopo-No-Ye is influential both in Japan and abroad (Tanpopo-no-ye Foundation n.d.).

Similarly, Katsuya Yamashita quit his job at a sheltered workshop and started Atelier Yamanami under the motto "free work rather than routine labour" in 1986. Although he had never had any experience in building, he built a small hut for a private welfare institution with scrapped building materials and named it Atelier Yamanami. At the beginning, there were only three client members. What they did at Atelier Yamanami was: shape clay to make anything they like; draw pictures in their own way; go for walks in forests, roast chestnuts which they collected in the forests; serve tea to anybody sitting in Atelier Yamanami, including themselves, wash the teacups they served at their own pace; or simply do nothing (Nodera 1998). Now Atelier Yamanami is well equipped with reinforced concrete houses including ateliers, a gallery and a cafe. The client members, including intellectually disabled people and mentally ill people, number 88.[7] On the organisation's home page, it is written that "each member of Atelier Yamanami is engaged in his/her own activities which make him/her happy". Each client member lives in his or her own way, drawing pictures while lying on the floor, creating unique sculptures, buttoning pieces of colourful cloth while singing, touching and staring at a plastic package of ramen noodle, sitting still or laughing together, for example (Atelier Yamanami n.d.).

We can find similar situations in Tanpopo-No-Ye. One of its client members, Ms. Juri Ito, spontaneously does radio gymnastic exercises, collects plastic packagings of pills, writes a diary, and draws her favourite Chinese characters every day. She calls all of what she does in Tanpopo-No-Ye "precious work" (Nakatani 2009). Katsuya Yamashita's "free work" and Ito's "precious work" would illuminate our life, as Itoga and his fellows wished. They provide a clear contrast with our usual labour, and help us, or at least help Japanese people, to be aware that our life is embedded in a capitalist world system.

Let us see how life and work are officially designated in Japan. The Cabinet Office of Government of Japan in the "Charter of Work-Life-Balance" states that:

> "Work-Life-Balance and economic-growth are like the two wheels of a cart. Young generation's economic independence and everybody's participation in labour markets (…) with motivation and ability will

---

[7] This was the number in July 2018 (a public talk by the director of Atlier Yamanami at Ryukoku University).

raise the vitality and growing force of our country, change the flow of birthrate decline, and consequently contribute to realise the sustainable society." (Office for Work-Life Balance, Gender Equality Bureau, Cabinet Office n.d.)[8]

In this charter, in order that the vitality and the growing force of the state are raised, young people's economic independence and everybody's participation in labour markets are important. It is not work and life but work-life-balance and the state's economic-growth that make the two wheels of the cart. Economic aspects such as economic independence, participation in labour markets and economic-growth of the state are the main issues in this charter, in spite of its title, Charter of Work-Life-Balance. Under the influence of the charter, the phrase, work-life-balance, is often used not only in remarks by national and local governments and by various media, but also in daily conversations, in which work and life make two distinctive categories and emphasis is placed on the economic aspects of work. Intellectually disabled people, who may not be well equipped to contribute to the capitalist priorities of contemporary Japanese society, do not have their own place in this charter.

In contrast, as work was not related to labour markets but embedded in life and social relations in Rhepadori especially in the 1980s, the same is true for "free work" in Atelier Yamanami, "precious work" by Ms. Ito, and other creative work in quite a few institutions for intellectually disabled people in Japan. In these places, which are free from capitalist criteria of the public sphere, intellectually disabled people's work cannot be separated from their life itself.

Thanks to recognition by the international art world and staff members' efforts, many client members have been acknowledged as "artists". Accordingly, their irreplaceable personalities and proper identities can now proudly be made known to the public through the growing opportunities of outsiders' visits to the institutions, diverse media outlets, the organisations' homepages, TV programs, publications, and exhibitions.

Commoditising the works and appropriating capitalist markets

While, as we have seen, the staff members are concerned to keep the client members and their works free from the capitalist evaluation, they are also keen to improve the bad financial conditions of the client members and the institutions by appropriating the influence of capitalist art markets. Before the encounter with the international art world, intellectually disabled people were financially supported only by their family (mostly by parents), governmental welfare allowances and the tiny income from their light factory labour. Staff

---

[8] Third paragraph of "Work-Life-Balance Charter."

managed the finances of institutions by acquiring governmental subsidies and allowances, and obtaining funds from foundations, donations, and profit from charity fundraisers. While intellectually disabled people's works were sometimes sold before the Art Brut boom, the prices of the works were usually determined as little more than the cost for the raw materials. In this way, the prices were often directly linked to the size and weight of the works.

After the encounter, however, some staff members have found hope for financial improvement in the added market value of the client members' works. The orientations for the appropriation are different from one institution to another. Atelier Incurve is one of the most active institutions in selling the client members' works as legitimate contemporary arts in the art markets. Its goal is to enable the intellectually disabled members to become financially independent artists. Atelier Incurve was founded in 2002 in Osaka City. Its philosophy is ordinary happiness, and its mission is to promote the members' diverse ways of working, their life base and pride. The founder, Hiroshi Imanaka, with a slight physical disability, is a successful architect and designer. Through his work experiences, he has become well acquainted with capitalist markets including on a global scale (Atelier Incurve n.d.).

Figure 4.1 The shop corner of Good Job Centre.

Photograph by Eriko Aoki, Nara, Japan, 2020.

Tanpopo-No-Ye in Nara City is now a hub organisation of large networks, comprising corporate bodies, project groups, service organisations and local civic groups, seeking to promote job creation and social welfare for people who tend to be socially marginalised, such as the disabled, aged, women, children and so on. One of Tanpopo-No-Ye's mottos is "make art sociable and society artistic". It has developed its own strategy for appropriating the influence of capitalist market economy. Among vast ranges of mutually related activities, Tanpopo-No-Ye Art Centre, Hana Studio and Good Job Centre are important in order to understand the appropriation strategies. The art centre was opened in 2004 and at its studio many client members pursue visual arts and performing arts with their personal inspiration. Not only their works but also the patterns in their works are sold to manufacturers of fabrics, potteries, and other daily goods, by signing a contract for their intellectual property rights, which are managed by Tanpopo-No-Ye.

Figure 4.2 Artworks in process by Hideaki Yoshikawa at Atelier Yamanami.

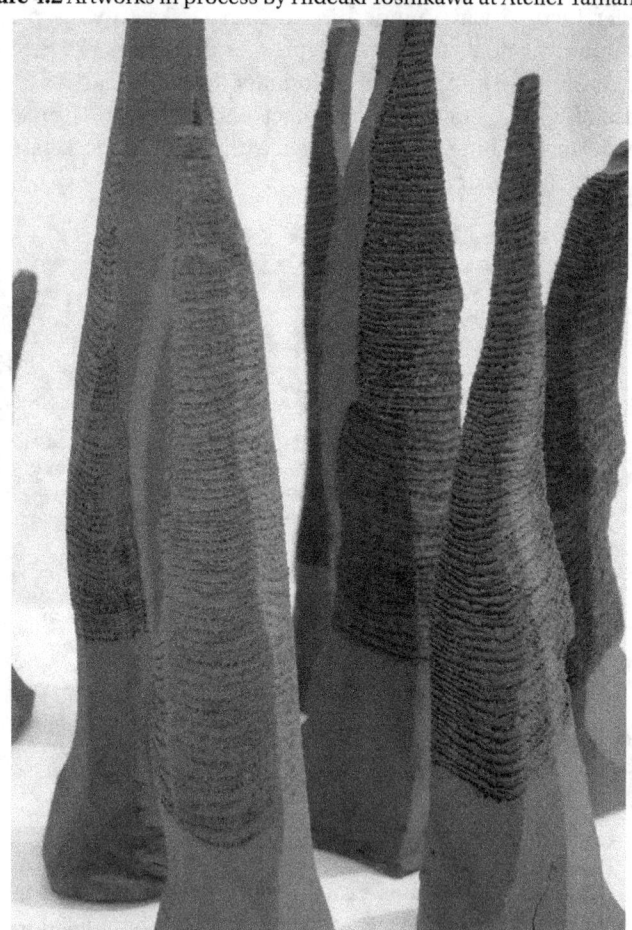

Photograph by Eriko Aoki, Shiga, Japan, 2020.

Life, art and commoditisation 73

Good Job Centre was founded in 2016 in Kashiba, a small town in Nara prefecture. It focuses on creating jobs for socially marginalised people, especially intellectually disabled people in order for them to work for an income large enough to live independently and happily in society. Good Job Centre plays leading roles in selling goods with patterns modified by professional designers based on the visual artworks made by the client members. It also aims to develop a range of different ways so that intellectually disabled people can be engaged in work. For example, it creates jobs producing handmade goods and foods, such as crafts and cookies. Because the products are handmade, they have higher market values, which may increase the client members' income (Tanpopo-no-ye Foundation n.d.).

Quite a few works from Atelier Yamanami have been sold at high prices, which has become possible due to the public appreciation of Art Brut and the encounter with the international art world. Concerning the recent appropriation of the influence of capitalist markets, Mr Yoshiaki Kasatani has played an important role. He is the creative director of a design company founded in 2004 in Osaka. He is engaged in designing for advertisements, graphics, fashion, and space composition. In 2012, he met Mr Masato Yamashita, the director of Atelier Yamanami, when he made a presentation about his institution. Since then, Mr Kasatani has been highly interested in Atelier Yamanami, the client members and the works they create. He started a project named "PR-y" in order to communicate the splendour of the works and the artists of Atelier Yamanami to the international and domestic public in many ways. PR-y designs the home page of Atelier Yamanami. Under the title *Distortion*, it has published a series of books, and founded an upper-level fashion brand which makes use of fabrics printed with drawings by the members of Atelier Yamanami (Kasatani and Walbers 2014a, 2014b; Kasatani 2016). PR-y also holds long term exhibitions and publishes films. Mr Kasatani expresses what PR-y does as follows:

> "I hope to develop and implement a multifaceted strategy to ensure that people with disabilities are seen as equal members of society. This humble effort is (…) simply about facing the distortion inherent in us and taking a new look at our own inner selves." (PR-y n.d.)

The project involves the creators in Atelier Yamanami as fellow artists, together with fashion photographers, cinematographers, upper-level fashion designers, stylists, and foreign fashion models, a *butoh* dancer, musicians, other artists, collectors, and curators. The project challenges our taken-for-granted perspectives, shakes them and tries to renew them. For example, *Distortion 2* is a book of the portrait photographs of the client members of Atelier Yamanami in fashionable dresses (PR-y n.d.). It challenges our two preoccupations at the same time. One is the tendency to think that the faces of the disabled people should not be exhibited without compassion in a publication. The other is the preoccupation that intellectually disabled people cannot be in vogue. All the works the PR-y accomplish are artistic and stylish. By successfully working for advertisement and fashion, Kasatani knows very well how the attention and emotion of the general public can be moved, how effectively and widely the global capitalist market communicates the message, and how being artistic and stylish is admired by the general public in the contemporary world. Kasatani sincerely makes his efforts to communicate the enchanting moments that the artworks and personalities of the creators in Atelier Yamanami make, by appropriating the influence of the global capitalist markets and the value codes of the contemporary global fashion markets.

The three cases outlined above tell us that the commoditisation of the works and the appropriation of the influence of the global capitalist markets is in progress, and each of the three institutions is taking different approaches to achieve its own goals. Atelier Incurve is making efforts in order for the artworks created by the client members to be acknowledged and to be sold as legitimate contemporary arts in the international and domestic markets. Tanpopo-No-Ye searches for stable and sustainable ways for the creators with intellectual disability to earn income by acquiring the intellectual property rights and extending the range of handmade production which suits intellectually disabled people. Atelier Yamanami in collaboration with PR-y makes efforts for the creators and works to be acknowledged socially by appropriating the influence and the value codes of contemporary global fashion markets.

Concluding remarks

Immediately after World War II, when the time of harsh coercion was over, Art Brut was advocated in Europe, and the institution which has led the development of welfare institutions for intellectually disabled people's free creation was founded in Japan. Both movements were to include socially those excluded so severely under the Nazi and Japanese military regimes during World War II.

In the 1990s, communism and other related political ideologies drastically lost influence, and in turn many kinds of art activities and art activisms started to flourish. Since neoliberalism has largely become the dominant global ideology after the fall of the Berlin Wall, economic concerns have been prioritised over social concerns in people's lives worldwide. In this context, what is called "the social turn" in art occurred in the 1990s. Many art projects have been carried out with the common concern about participation, collaboration and global multitude. Some art projects which criticise the existing art conventions and try to nullify the borders between art objects, artists and audiences are usually based on Marxist and Post-Marxist ideology (Bishop 2012; Helguera 2011; Sansi 2015). Simultaneously, other art projects more adaptive to the neoliberal hegemony are initiated with links to art management and "cultural policies" at different administrative levels; the international levels such as UNESCO and United Nations Development Programme, as well as the national levels, local government levels and private organisation levels (Rosewall and Shane 2018; Wesner 2018; Yoshizawa 2011; Miyazu 2014). Furthermore, there are trends which have promoted art business. Artworks have become not only capitalist commodities but also investments to many people, especially to the new-rich whose business is successful in the neoliberal global economy (Miyazu 2014). While in the 1930s Walter Benjamin made the criticism that art had come to serve commerce in Paris in the 19th century (Benjamin 1999), nowadays researchers of marketing, sociologists and even aestheticians themselves are insisting that art, artists and their aesthetic abilities should contribute to business projects (Naukkarinen and Saito 2012; Miyazu 2014; Murphy and de la Fuente 2014; Hook 2014).

Against this backdrop, the works created by intellectually disabled people in Japan came to be acknowledged as those of Art Brut in the international art world. Since then, the staff in some Japanese social welfare institutions have been extremely active and busy, on the one hand in establishing art activities free from the capitalist evaluation in order to promote social inclusion for intellectually disabled people, and on the other, in appropriating the influence of the capitalist markets to improve their financial conditions.

Although their works have acquired international and domestic acclaim, such institutions are still a minority among the social welfare institutions in Japan as a whole, and the social situation of intellectually disabled people in general has not been improved much. The criminal case in July 2016 and consequent social phenomena may illustrate that, unlike the situation in Rhepadori in Flores, Indonesia, there is yet little social space for intellectually disabled people in Japan. The Japanese state, which has been immersed in capitalist development for one and half centuries, might not be capable of changing social spaces for intellectually disabled people. Instead, all the above-mentioned efforts made in such institutions as Ohmi-Gakuen, Atelier Yamanami, Tanpopo-No-Ye and Atelier Incurve, by their staff members and related people, may be more feasible, realistic and promising in order to improve the social milieu of intellectually disabled people, and moreover Japanese society itself, in the contemporary globalising world. However, while art can provide some hope for the future, we have to remain aware of the ambivalence of art.

As we have seen in the first section, art has an affinity with capitalism, since it was born in the same modern historical era, and both are linked in a complicated but intrinsic manner. Art as well as capitalism are destined to search for new *terra incognita*. In the process of these quests, intellectually disabled people's works in Japan have been discovered as a *terra incognita*. It seems that the works created by some client members of Atelier Yamanai are appreciated in the international art markets, partly because dealers, collectors and audiences have become bored with existing artworks, and see the client members' works as new and exciting.[9] Once they become widely traded, it is possible that the art markets will gradually lose interest in them. It is also possible the likely fluctuation of art markets would disturb the peaceful life of intellectually disabled people.

A mother of an intellectually disabled man expressed her opinion from the floor at a symposium about Art Brut held in 2015: "I am really afraid this boom will finish very soon and a harsher time will come to my son, because only several years ago he was socially ignored and now is admired as an artist". When placing art in the complex tapestry of modern history, her worries are not groundless. What this mother seems to want for her son is that he can live as an accepted member of society. Whether the works he makes are considered art is not important, as long as he is not socially marginalised.

Since we are currently in the historical time of art, what intellectually disabled people make tends to be rediscovered as artworks although to the creators themselves making those works is just part of their life itself. Focusing on their life, the encounter with the art world and the consequent social phenomena would shed light on how not only art, the exclusive, alienated and enchanting category, but also our life itself is socially, historically and politically constructed. I hope that this chapter plays its role as an étude illuminating life and art under that light.

References

Able Art Japan. n.d. "About Able Art Japan." Accessed August 25, 2019. http://www.ableart.org/aaj.html.

Atelier Incurve. n.d. "about atelier incurve." Accessed August 25, 2019. http://incurve.jp/about.html.

Atelier Yamanami. n.d. "about Atelier Yamanami. Accessed August 25, 2019. http://a-yamanami.jp/about/.

Becker, Howard S. 1982. *Art Worlds*. Berkeley: University of California Press.

Benjamin, Walter. 1999. *The Arcade Project*. Translated by Howard Eiland and Kevin McLaughlin. Cambridge, Massachusetts, and London: The Belkap Press of Harvard University Press.

Bishop, Claire. 2012. *Artificial Hells: Participatory Art and the Spectatorships*. N.Y.: Verso.

---

[9] Personal communication about Jizolibido, documentary film about Atelier Yamanami directed by Kasatani in 2018 (Kasatani. dir. 2018).

Borderless Art Museum NO-MA. n.d. "home." Accessed August 25, 2019. http://www.no-ma.jp/.

Cabinet Office of Government of Japan. 2013. "Annual Report on Government Measures for Persons with Disabilities." Accessed August 25, 2019. http://www8.cao.go.jp/shougai/whitepaper/h25hakusho/gaiyou/h1_01.html.

Cabinet Office of Government of Japan. 2016. "Annual Report on Government Measures for Persons with Disabilities." Accessed August 25, 2019. http://www8.cao.go.jp/shougai/whitepaper/h28hakusho/zenbun/siryo_02.html.

Clifford, James. 1988. *The Predicament of Culture: Twentieth-Century Ethnography, Literature, and Art*. Cambridge, Massachusetts, and London: Harvard University Press.

Danto, Arthur. 1964. "The Artworld." *Journal of Philosophy* 61: 571–84.

Dubuffet, Jean. 1976. *Collection de l'Art Brut*. Lausanne: Bron SA.

Gell, Alfred. 1998. *Art and Agency: An Anthropological Theory*. Oxford: Clarendon Press.

Gell, Alfred. 1999. *The Art of Anthropology*. London & New Brunswick, NJ: The Athlone Press.

Hall, Michael D. and Eugene W. Metcalf Jr., eds. 1994. *The Artist Outsider: Creativity and the Boundaries of Culture*. Washington and London: Smithsonian Institution Press.

Harima, Yasuo. 1975. *Ikiteiru Ikiteiru* [*Living and Living*]. Nara: Fukushi Fuudozukuri Shimin Kouza. (in Japanese)

Hashimoto, Akira. 2013. "Autosaidah Ahto wo Meguru Tabi, Tokushu-goh 'Fukushi to Ahto' [A Journey for Outsider Art, special issue 'Welfare and Art']." *Shougai Hattatsu Kenkyu* 6: 27–34. (in Japanese)

Hattori, Tadashi. 2003. *Autosaidah Ahto* [*Outsider Art*]. Koubunsha (in Japanese)

Hattori, Tadashi, ed. 2016. *Shogai no aruhito no Sosakukatudo: Jissen no Genba kara* [*Creative Activities by People with Disability: From the Field of Practice*]. Kyoto: Airishuppan. (in Japanese)

Helguera, Pablo. 2011. *Education for Socially Engaged Art: A Materials and Techniques Handbook*. Taipei: Jorge Pinto Books.

Hook, Philip. 2014. *Breakfast at Sotheby's: An A-Z of the Art World*. London: Penguin Books Ltd.

Itoga, Kazuo. 2002. *Let These Children Be the Light of the World*. Translated by Takanobu Kyougoku. Higashidera Ishiba-cho: Itoga Kazuo Memorial Foundation.

Kanou, Reina. 2013a. "Ahru Buryutto: Soko ni Atta Mono no Juyoushi [Art Brut: A History of Acceptance of What Is Already There]." In *Ahru Buryutto, Ahto, Nihon* [*Art Brut, Art, Japan*], supervised by Hosaka Kenjiro and edited by Asada Wataru, 56–75. Tokyo: Heibonsha. (in Japanese)

Kanou, Reina. 2013b. "Ahru Buryutto no Genjou; 'Yunibahsaru eno Keiteki' [The Present Situation of Art Brut: Honking at 'Universality']." In *Ahru Buryutto, Ahto, Nihon* [*Art Brut, Art, Japan*], supervised by Hosaka Kenjiro and edited by Asada Wataru, 76–89. Tokyo: Heibonsha. (in Japanese)

Kasatani, Yoshiaki. 2016. *A Book About DISTORTION*. Atelier Yamanami. (in Japanese)

Kasatani, Yoshiaki. dir. 2018. *Jizolibido*. Produced by Atelier Yamanami and Rissi INC. (documentary film).

Kasatani, Yoshiaki and Rob Walbers. 2014a. *DISTORTION*. Atelier Yamanami.

Kasatani, Yoshiaki and Rob Walbers. 2014b. *DISTORTION2*. Atelier Yamanami.

Kazuo Itoga Memorial Foundation. n.d. "The Centennial for Itoga Kazuo's Birth." Accessed January 5, 2017. http://100.itogazaidan.jp/.

Ministry of Education, Culture, Sports, Science and Technology, Japan. 2010. "Chapter 4 Historical Change of Welfare Policy." Accessed August 25, 2019. http://www.mext.go.jp/b_menu/shingi/chukyo/chukyo3/siryo/attach/1295934.htm.

Miyaji, Mariko. 2013. "Nihon ni okeru Ahru Buryutto no Tenkai: Datsukyoukai no Geijutsu to Fukushi no Jissen, Tokushu-goh 'Fukushi to Ahto' [Development of Art Brut in Japan: Practice of Borderless Art and Welfare, special issue 'Welfare and Art']." *Shougai Hattatsu Kenkyu* 6: 17–25. (in Japanese)

Miyazu, Daisuke. 2014. *Gendai Ahto Keizaigaku [Economics of Centemporary Art]*. Tokyo: Koubunsha. (in Japanese)

Mori, Koji. 2016. "Bunseki Bigaku tte douiu Gakumon nandesu ka? Nihon no Wakate Bigakusha kara no Genjou Houkoku [What kind of study is analytical aesthetics? A report about the current situation by a young Japanese aesthetician]." Accessed July 30, 2017. http://synodos.jp/culture/16122. (in Japanese)

Murphy, Peter and Eduardo de la Fuente, eds. 2014. *Aesthetic Capitalism*. Leiden and Boston: Brill.

Museum of Modern Art Shiga. 2015. "Sign of Life: The Works Originated in Shiga." Accessed August 30, 2018. http://www.shigakinbi.jp/?p=18971. (in Japanese)

Nakatani, Kazuto. 2009. "Autosaidah Ahto / Ahru Buryutto wo Koete: Gendai Nihon ni okeru Shougai no Aru Hitobito no Geijutsu Katsudou [Beyond 'Outsider Art/Art Brut': Artworks Created by Disabled People in Contemporary Japan]." *Bunka Jinruigaku* 74 (2): 215–237. (in Japanese)

Namihira, Emiko. 1984. *Byouki to Chiryo no Bunka Jinruigaku [A Cultural Anthropology on Disease and Cures]*. Tokyo: Kaimeisha. (in Japanese)

Naukkarinen, Ossi and Yuriko Saito. 2012. "Introduction." *Special Issue, Artification. Contemporary Aesthetics*, Volume 4. Accessed August 20, 2019. https://www.contempaesthetics.org/newvolume/pages/journal.php?volume=49.

Nodera, Yuko. 1998. *Korobokkuru no Te: Yamanami Koubou no Tsuchi to Hito [Hands of Korobokkuru: Clay and People in Atelier Yamanami]*. Nara: Tanpopo-No-Ye. (in Japanese)

Office for Work-Life Balance, Gender Equality Bureau, Cabinet Office n.d. "Work-Life-Balance Charter, Promotion of Work-Life-Balance." Accessed August 25, 2019. http://wwwa.cao.go.jp/wlb/government/20barrier_html/20html/charter.html.

PR-y. n.d. "PR-y." Accessed June 30, 2018. https://www.pr-y.org/.

Rosewall, Ellen and Rachel Shane, eds. 2018. *Cultural Policy*. London: Bloomsbury Academic.

Sansi, Roger. 2015. *Art, Anthropology and the the Gift*. London: Bloomsbury.

Shiga Prefecture. n.d. "Omigakuen." Accessed January 5, 2017. http://www.pref.shiga.lg.jp/e/omigakuen/. (in Japanese)

Stecker, Robert. 2010. *Aesthetics and the Philosophy of Art: An Introduction*, 2nd edition. Washington, D.C.: Rowman & Littlefield Publishers.

Svašek, Maruška. 2007. *Anthropology, Art and Cultural Production*. London: Pluto Press.

Tanpopo-No-Ye Foundation. n.d. "Tanpopo-no-ye." Accessed August 25, 2019. http://tanpoponoye.org/. (in Japanese)

Taylor, Charles. 2007. *A Secular Age*. Cambridge, MA: Belknap Press.

Thévoz, Michel. 1975. *L'Art Brut*. Genéve: Skira.

Weitz, Morris. 1956. "The Role of Theory in Aesthetics." *The Journal of Aesthetics and Art Criticism* 15 (1): 27–35.

Wesner, Simone. 2018. *Artists' Voices in Cultural Policy: Careers, Myths and the Creative Profession after German Unification*. London: Palgrave Macmillan.

Wittgenstein, Ludwig. 1953. *Philosophical Investigations*. Oxford: Basil Blackwell.

Yoshizawa, Yayoi. 2011. *Geijutsu wa Sekai wo Kaeru ka: Bunkaseisan no Shakaigaku karano Sekkin* [*Can Art Change the World? an Approach from the Sociology of Cultural Production*]. Tokyo: Seikyusha. (in Japanese)

Chapter 5

Heritage and identity: contemporary art practices of Pacific peoples in New Zealand

Matori Yamamoto

Hosei University, Japan

Abstract

In this chapter, art practices of migrants in New Zealand are analysed from a perspective of heritage and identity. The migration flows from the Pacific Islands to New Zealand started after World War II. Minority groups of migrants came to live in the margins of their host country. When Oceanic artists started to create contemporary art in the 1980s and 1990s, they struggled or tackled with problems of identity, heritage and shared discriminative experiences. Their artworks were expressions of their identity related to their homelands and ancestors. What they created in visual art forms became important symbols for the Pacific peoples' communities. These artworks made the people proud of their roots and heritage. Along a different trajectory from the Western art scene, the Oceanic art world, with its markedly non-Western characteristics, has developed in ways that do not fit the paradigm of the global art-culture system and its specific characteristics. The author argues that in our time of socially engaged art, artworks play an important role as social agencies, and all the endeavours of the contemporary Oceanic artists have a potential to decolonise the arts, not only in New Zealand but also globally.

Keywords: Oceanic artist, migration, heritage, identity, social agency

The migration flows from the Pacific Islands to New Zealand started after World War II, when industrialisation took off in New Zealand. Pacific peoples primarily shifted to New Zealand with the intention to partake in labour. They were expected to remit a portion of their wages to their homelands. Their average income was lower than the standard income in New Zealand, and the burden of sending remittances led to increased difficulty in their lives. They were a minority group of migrants, living on the margins of their host country, and experienced discrimination under the government's immigration policy during the 1970s.

This chapter analyses minority art practices from the perspective of heritage and identity. When contemporary Oceanic[1] artists began their practices in the 1980s and 1990s, they adopted, applied, and integrated the Oceanic artistic heritage and traditional art into their artworks. These artworks represented their expressions of their identity to their homelands and ancestors. The visual artworks they created became symbols for Pacific peoples' community and incite pride in the roots and heritage among those in the community. As Pacific peoples' community have become more accepted in New Zealand, the increasingly complicated identities of younger contemporary Oceanic artists can be observed in the present day.[2]

Pacific peoples in New Zealand

The migration flows from the Pacific islands, primarily that of Polynesia, began after World War II. When the war ended, New Zealand was administering the Tokelau Islands, the Cook Islands, and Niue as territories, and Western Samoa as a territory under the UN trusteeship agreement. The industrialisation of New Zealand, which occurred after World War II, led to a domestic migration of the rural Maori population toward an urban environment. Nevertheless, there were still labour shortages, and the gap was filled by Polynesian migrants (Macpherson 2006, 99–102; Macpherson and Macpherson 2009, 52–53). Western Samoa became independent in 1962; however, migration continued under the immigration controls of New Zealand. Although Tonga has always been an independent country, it remained a British protectorate until 1970. There is a notable Tongan migrant community in New Zealand. Tokelau has remained under the New Zealand administration, whereas the Cook Islands and Niue are under the free-association agreement with New Zealand, and residents from these three territories can freely enter New Zealand, because they are provided with New Zealand passports. Consequently, the population

---

[1] Although "Oceanic" and "Pacific" are used interchangeably here, I have used the term "Oceanic" wherever possible. Recently, in New Zealand, the terms "Pasifika" (Polynesian pronunciation of "Pacific") and "Moana" (Polynesian word for "Ocean") are preferred.

[2] The project was funded during 2016–2019. During this period, I spent three weeks on three separate occasions staying in Auckland in March, visiting exhibitions at the Auckland Festival, conversing with young contemporary Oceanic artists and observing their art-related practices. I have also visited the country for similar purposes several times before 2016. Data were primarily collected in Auckland, where two-thirds of Pacific peoples live in New Zealand (New Zealand Ministry of Pacific Peoples n.d.) and the Tautai Contemporary Pacific Art Trust is located.

of migrants from the Cook Islands, Tokelau, and Niue is significantly higher in New Zealand, compared to that of their homelands. Migration from the Independent State of Samoa and the Kingdom of Tonga are subject to the quota systems, similar to other independent Pacific-country groups. Although there are some migrants from Melanesia, their population is limited, with the exception of a recent increase in migrants from Fiji.

According to the 2013 New Zealand census, 295,941 people—approximately 7.4% of the total population—were identified as belonging to one or more Pacific ethnic groups. Moreover, approximately half the Pacific peoples in New Zealand are Samoans. The second-largest group are Cook Islanders, closely followed by Tongans, each with a population of above 20% of all Pacific peoples in New Zealand. This group consists of a primarily young population, and the majority are aged below 25 years. Nearly two-thirds of this population were born in New Zealand. Moreover, two-thirds of the total population live in the Auckland area (Pasefika Proud 2016, 2–5). In the Manukau area in South Auckland, the Pacific groups comprise 27% of the population (Multicultural New Zealand website). Most first-generation Pacific migrants came to New Zealand as labourers, and many of them could not speak English fluently when they first arrived. In those days, there were few tertiary education systems in their homelands. In contrast, their children and grandchildren were educated in the formal New Zealand education system, and many of them have also completed university education (Macpherson 2005, 110–111).

The New Zealand government was tolerant toward migrants overstaying their visas during the 1950s and the 1960s, when the economy was booming. However, after the economic downturn in New Zealand during the 1970s, the government became strict toward migrant Pacific peoples overstaying their visas. Pacific peoples often experienced so-called "dawn raids" wherein police officers forced their way into private homes in the early morning while residents were sleeping, to check for those overstaying their visas (Anae 2012, 221–239). They arrested overstayers by force from Polynesian homes. On the streets, Polynesian-appearing persons were stopped by police officers for passport checks, irrespective of their descent.[3] Pacific and Maori leaders, church leaders, and human rights watchers condemned these "dawn raids" as racist actions. The Polynesian Panthers were organised for activism by Polynesian youth. A statistical study conducted during 1985–1986 showed that although "Pacific Island people comprised only the third of overstayers, they made up 86% of all prosecutions for overstayers" (Beaglehole 2015). Only 5% of

---

[3] Not only Maori, the indigenous people of New Zealand, but also those from Niue, the Cook Islands, and Tokelau, who were entitled to stay, were subject to the check.

citizens from the US and UK comprised another third of the overstayers that were prosecuted. The government ceased "dawn raids" in 1980.

The New Zealand immigration policy for Pacific peoples converted to the quota system after 1982, and 1,100 from Samoa, 250 from Tonga and Fiji, and 75 from Kiribati and Tuvalu are now admitted every year (New Zealand Immigration. n.d.).

As the population of Pacific peoples increased, the community enhanced its integrity. This feat was possible because they are primarily composed of Polynesians and thus have some common cultural traits, whereas each ethnic community maintains its own identity because they have their own language, customs, and ceremonies. Their identity is formed through personal relationships and interactions in daily life, such as family life, kinship network, church activities, customs, and ceremonies. Therefore, the ethnic community serves as the base of their identity, which is an extension of their homelands. On the other hand, intermarriages and schooling crosscut ethnic borderlines and increase the possibility of significant alliances (Yamamoto 2000, 71–73).

The preservation of traditional cultures in the homelands differ from one island group to another, and Samoa and Tonga are two groups where traditional culture is relatively well-maintained. During the 1970s and 1980s, the Oceanic cultures and Pasifika people were unknown among the rest of the New Zealand population. In 1993, the Auckland council established the Pasifika Festival, which is held on a yearly basis in March to celebrate Pacific peoples and their cultures. The Pasifika Festival is a notable event that attracts as many as 60,000 visitors over the course of two days (Auckland Council 2020).

We must examine the traditional art experiences of Pacific peoples in New Zealand, who are primarily of Polynesian descent. Tattooing, tapa (bark cloth) making, and weaving are notable activities among them. Polynesian tattooing declined before 1980, with the exception of Samoa, wherein tattooing had never been strictly prohibited by the missionaries. There is a fascinating story about how tattooing was revived among Tahitians, with the aid of Samoan tattooists (Kuwahara 2005). The indigenous movement in New Zealand and French Polynesia led to worldwide attention toward tattooing. Recognised traditional Samoan tattooists now spend some time during the year tattooing in New Zealand and Europe, and their customers include not only Samoans in Samoa and the Samoan diaspora worldwide, but also some Kiwi,[4] Europeans and Americans (Mallon and Galliot 2018, 133–141). They are also invited to overseas festivals. I have seen them several times at the Pasifika Festival in Auckland that is held on a yearly basis, at the Festival of Pacific Arts that is

---

[4] "Kiwi" denotes New Zealand Europeans.

conducted once every four years, and at some meetings conducted by the Pacific Arts Association. Their practices are transnational and innovative, in terms of designs and tattooed parts of the body (Ibid.).

Tapa-making and weaving are difficult in New Zealand because the materials required to produce them are difficult to obtain in cold weather. Tapa is made of beaten bark of paper mulberry, which is later dyed. The design and dyeing procedure differ from one island group to another. Traditionally, tapa was also used as clothing and a valuable item of exchange. Today, imported calico cloths have replaced the use of tapa for clothing, with the exception of specific ceremonial occasions; however, the traditional ceremonial exchange of tapa is particularly important in Tonga. Tapa made in Tonga is exported to those of Tongan migrants in New Zealand, where tapa is not produced, and is used for ceremonial exchange as well as wall decoration. Samoan fine mats are also brought from the homelands and are often circulated on ceremonial occasions in the community.

The fibre used for traditional weaving originates in plants and is thus difficult to obtain in New Zealand. On the other hand, some creative women's collectives in Auckland use new modern materials, such as yarns and plastic fibres. Due to colonial experiences, women from Tonga make crochet *ta'ovala*—a formal attire to wrap around the waist (Māhina-Tuai and Māhina 2011, 7–14)—whereas women from the Cook Islands create quilts called *tivaevae*. These traditional and semi-traditional artefacts produced by women are often reciprocated within the migrant communities and are sold in regional markets in New Zealand.

Foundation of the Contemporary Oceanic Artists in New Zealand

The practices of most contemporary Oceanic artists involve visual art, such as paintings, sculptures, installations, photos, videos, and moving pictures, as well as performing arts, such as performances, music and dancing. In this chapter, only their visual art has been discussed. Most of their practices are framed in the Western style, with the categorisation incorporating the Oceanic taste of art. They produce contemporary Oceanic art, which is distinguishable from classic Oceanic art, or tribal art as it is categorised in the Western art world. Because classic Oceanic artefacts were collected as curiosities or anthropological specimens during early contact and in the colonial era.[5] They do not usually include the names of the artists (Clifford 1988, 227), whereas the names of the individual artists are preserved in contemporary Oceanic art

---

[5] Many of them are stored in museums and art galleries or private collections in Western countries.

pieces. Clifford argued that the Western concept of art emphasises originality and singularity (Clifford 1988, 226), which are the values that contemporary Oceanic artists seek. Their art styles are primarily modern and abstract.

The artist body called Tautai has exercised a crucial influence on the development of contemporary Oceanic art in New Zealand. Tautai was not an art collective, but a loosely organised body to encourage Oceanic artists to help each other. To explain the development of Tautai, we need to start with the story of a pioneer contemporary Oceanic artist Fatu Feuʻu.

During the 1980s, several visual artists of Polynesian origin started their art practice independently; Fatu Feuʻu was one such artist. He was born in a rural village in Western Samoa in 1946. After spending a few years in the natural environment of his natal village, he moved with his family to Apia, the capital city of Western Samoa. He was fragile during his youth and was not suitable for hard work in the daily Samoan environment (Jennings 2012, 18). Therefore, he decided to become an artist, and his mother supported his ambitions. He migrated to New Zealand when he was 20 years old and dreamt of becoming an artist someday. However, he experienced a rude awakening in New Zealand, and found it impossible to be enrolled in an art school during that time. He worked at several places and had a family of his own. During the 1970s, he found his place as an industrial designer in a textile company, developing his artistic abilities there.

During the late 1980s, he decided to become a full-time artist. Although he struggled at first, he was lucky enough to meet Tony Fomison, a Kiwi artist who was interested in Polynesian artworks and helped Feuʻu. Fomison and his friends encouraged Feuʻu to attempt lithography, and he later began to paint murals (Jennings 2012, 36–41; Mallon and Pereira 1997, 16). He used various media, such as printing on canvas and walls, wood carving, and sculpture. He applied motifs from Samoan tattoo and tapa designs that were familiar to him in Samoa. Eventually, his style broadened and included Melanesian masks, and tropical flowers and leaves in his own abstract style.

In 1986, he conducted an exhibition at Samoa House (Mallon and Pereira 1997, 17), located at that time in central Auckland and owned by the Government of Western Samoa, which used it as the Consular office in Auckland. The space was intended to be used for communicating with Samoan migrants in Auckland and improving awareness of the migrant community and the Samoan government among the general public in New Zealand. The exhibition was open to Samoan migrants in Auckland, as well as to the general public, to demonstrate Samoan pride in this new field. In 1988, he left his job to become a full-time artist, and was appointed artist-in-residence at the Elam School of Fine Arts, University of Auckland.

He founded the Tautai Contemporary Pacific Arts Trust around 1986. "Tautai" means "navigator" or "pilot" in the Samoan language. In 1988, it was decided that Samoa House would provide a space for contemporary Oceanic artists to exhibit different works for a year, and Feu'u would direct the exhibition. He named it Tautai Gallery. There were already some practising Oceanic artists, such as Filipe Tohi (Tonga; sculptor), John Pule (Niue; poet and painter), Michel Tuffery (Samoa, Tahiti, and Europe; painter and sculptor), and Jim Vivieaere (Cook Islands; artist and curator). However, there was no organisation wherein they asserted their presence as a group of contemporary Oceanic artists. During the 30th anniversary celebrations in 2016, Feu'u made a speech on how he took on the challenge of fundraising for the exhibition. Although some donations came from the business sector, successful Maori artists donated a considerable amount of money. Feu'u also called on contemporary Oceanic artists to get together to communicate their own experiences and exchange information. Tautai was able to release information regarding new exhibitions and staged joint exhibitions if an individual exhibition proved to be difficult. The Tautai Contemporary Pacific Arts Trust was based on the idea of the Tautai exhibition.

There were two monumental exhibitions. First, *Te moemoea no Iotefa* (Dream of Joseph) (1990–1991), which was curated by Maori curator, Rangihiroa Panoho, exhibited museum artefacts from Oceania, products by Pasifika people, artworks of contemporary Oceanic artists, and their Palagi (Caucasians) mentors, and toured in 1990–1991 (Thomas 1996, 308). Second, *Bottled Ocean*, a collection of artworks by contemporary Polynesian artists was curated by Jim Vivieaere, and toured New Zealand in 1994–1995 (Mallon and Pereira 1997, 136–137). These exhibitions showcased the works of over twenty contemporary Oceanic artists, who later became renowned due to the exhibition. Although the exhibition was a great success, a question remained regarding to whether it was appropriate to confine these works to a singular category of contemporary Oceanic artists because each of them started their own art individually.

There was also an opportunity to showcase their works in the Pacific context. The 7th Festival of Pacific Arts was held in 1996 in Apia, Western Samoa, and this marked the time when Tautai made its official debut in the Pacific region. The Festival of Pacific Arts is conducted every four years by one of the Pacific nations or territories. The aim of the festival was to maintain the heritage and traditional cultures of each Pacific country in the process of becoming an independent nation and produce new art forms to enhance their own integrity as a nation state (Stevenson 2012, 1–5; Yamamoto 2006, 6–8). The 7th festival in Samoa included almost all forms of art—from traditional to modern forms, such as traditional and modern performing arts, drama, exhibitions of modern visual arts and museum artefacts, photography, film, tattooing, carving, and crafts. In the category of visual arts, which was introduced for the first time in the festival, there were two sections of diaspora artists: the Tautai Group of New Zealand and Overseas Samoan group, which included twelve artists in addition to Feuʻu (The Office of the 7th Pacific Festival of Arts 1996).

Figure 5.1 Installation view, the exhibition *Bottled Ocean* curated by Jim Vivieaere, City Gallery Wellington, 17 May–7 August 1994.

Image Courtesy of the City Gallery Wellington

Tautai slowly evolved from a modest organisation to a significant, loosely organised umbrella body, with the official name of Tautai Contemporary Pacific Arts Trust[6] and an office located in Auckland. Here, "contemporary" does not necessarily mean *avant garde*, but simply implies current art practices. Their art styles are modernist, and there are no realist painters or sculptors among them. Although Tautai does not exclude other art forms, its primary focus is on visual arts and contemporary performances. Tautai conducts workshops for young would-be artists at art schools and institutions, and provides the opportunity to collaborate for exhibitions, seminars, and talks. Openings of exhibitions are particularly good opportunities for them to meet. Tautai supports Oceanic artists and everything they produce, plans gatherings and events, and circulates information regarding exhibitions of artists and related occasions. Most of them produce Pacific or Oceanic works; however, this is not

---

[6] Tautai's official webpage (Tautai n.d.) tells that it started a new permanent gallery space called Tautai Gallery in July 2020.

a requirement for membership. Tautai's primary financial supporter is Creative New Zealand, the national arts development agency, and its subsidies are granted on the ethnic basis.

Heritage and identity in three cases of contemporary Oceanic artists

This section will consider three artists, the aforementioned Feu'u, Felipe Tohi, and John Pule, who are part of the first generation of contemporary Oceanic artists. They are all self-taught artists, being migrants from the islands. Feu'u and Tohi migrated after they had graduated from school, whereas Pule migrated as a child.

The style used by Feu'u was heavily influenced by his career as a textile designer. His early paintings are full of colours, particularly with his motifs of frangipani flowers of four petals. His works differ from others because he applied motifs adopted from Samoan tattooing and tapa since the beginning of his art career. He was positive about using his artistic heritage as a person of Samoan descent. Then, his design was extended to include Melanesian faces and masks. The grid style was seemingly adopted from a tapa design format. His sculpture includes Moai-like imagery. In his book, he stated, "Pacific art goes back thousands of years with Lapita pottery,[7] tapa-making, and even the star charts Polynesians used to navigate by (Jennings 2012, 122). If symbols speak to me, I use them as I hear them" (Ibid, 124). His identity that is based on Oceanic heritage goes far beyond the ethnic boundaries, extending to the prehistoric period of Austronesian migration. He started by using Samoan motifs and art styles that he knew from his experiences; however, he must have studied Oceanic heritage broadly in books and museums in New Zealand. His mentor artist, Fomison, and other Kiwi friends, who were interested in so-called tribal art, encouraged him to use his Polynesian heritage. It seems that Feu'u did not hesitate to incorporate the broadest identity to the Oceanic heritage because he was the pioneer of contemporary Oceanic artists.

Tohi migrated to New Zealand from Tonga with his mother in 1978. He was 19 years old at the time, being a boy who had always loved drawing during his growing years in Tonga. During the first years after his arrival, he was more interested in the pursuits of a young New Zealander. After working in several places, he moved to New Plymouth in 1982, and joined in the Rangimarie Arts and Crafts Centre, where he became familiar with Maori art and crafts. His talent

---

[7] Lapita pottery was discovered in archaeological sites between New Guinea and Samoa/Tonga in the Pacific during the 1500–500 BCE period. Lapita culture seemingly belongs to the Austronesian language family, a section of which is the Polynesians. Soon after the Polynesians arrived in Samoa and Tonga, this pottery-making technology disappeared. This style of pottery is a lost cultural asset for the Polynesians.

as a sculptor was discovered by Maori artists and instructors at the Centre. He spent time teaching himself how to carve, and eventually began developing his own sculpture. He later began staging his own exhibitions. Gradually, he shifted from wood carving to stone carving (Mallon and Pereira 1997, 105–110).

In an interview, he stated that he was not interested in Tongan traditional culture before he started working with Maori artists. Meeting other contemporary Oceanic artists at the exhibition *Te moemoea no Iotefa* helped him to become increasingly conscious of his identity and cultural heritage (Stevenson 2015, 10–13).

After incorporating some Tongan materials, such as sennit cords and shells, and some Tongan imagery into his artworks, he decided to learn the Tongan art of *lalava*, which is a Polynesian architectural technology used for tying or lashing two logs with coconut sennit cords (Brownson et al. 2012, 115). The Polynesians did not have access to iron nails before they encountered Europeans, and instead used *lalava* to build houses. Due to the prevalence of Western architecture, *lalava* technologies are no longer in use for most private homes. Traditional architectural technology, including *lalava*, is utilised for symbolic public or semi-public buildings in the Tonga-Samoa-Fiji triangle. The coconut sennit cords are very strong, made by hand of fibres collected by hand from dried coconut husks. Tohi provided the following explanation:

> "Lalava explores the myriad patterns used in lashing, and ideally the links to navigational and environmental knowledge (...) Lalava also represents a link to one's genealogy – to the social and cultural traditions and protocols of Tonga" (Stevenson 2015, 12–13).

He became *tufunga lalava* (*lalava* master craftsman), and in 2004, created *lalava* in Fale Maota (meeting house and residence for a high chief) in the Nofoaliʻi village in Samoa. The title Sopolemalama was bestowed upon him for this work (Stevenson 2015, 1). In the same year, he also decorated *lalava* in the Fale Pasifika (Pasifika House) at the University of Auckland (The University of Auckland n.d.). Those proficient in *lalava* technology were considered master craftsmen, but Tohi went a step further and transformed *lalava* into a modern art form, by creating various new images and colours in his own style. Moreover, he created new images using sennit cords of different colours, aluminium plates, steel, and stones. After his first experience of art involved Maori carvings, he mastered modern sculpture. At the later stage, he discovered his own heritage and eventually created his own art (Stevenson 2015).

John Pule migrated to New Zealand from Niue with his mother in 1964 when he was only two years old. He left school early and worked at different places. His early days were spent in communities of Pacific peoples, rather than in a mixed population. Although he enjoyed drawing and creating pieces of art from an early age, he was known as a writer, and specifically, a poet, before he started to work on visual arts. He came to New Zealand at a very young age. However, he felt slightly uncomfortable growing up in New Zealand, and felt that he and his people were somehow out of place. During the late 1970s, racial issues were prevalent in New Zealand, and the households of islanders were targeted by so-called "dawn raids". Those who had overstayed their visas were arrested and deported. Since Niue was under the New Zealand administration, the Niuean were entitled to hold New Zealand passports and freely migrate to New Zealand. However, Pule witnessed cases of other Pacific peoples, such as Samoans and Tongans, being subjected to harsh immigration controls. There were also nuclear issues in the South Pacific, and a movement was conducted in New Zealand against the French nuclear experiments in Mururoa.

Similar to Fatu Feu'u, Pule met Tony Fomison during the early years of his life and was influenced by him. Pule's first artistic taste originated from the Western tradition, and he was deeply interested in van Gogh. After this early encounter with art, he became active in 1991, when he met his partner Sofia Takela-Smith, a jeweller and body-ornament producer (Thomas 2010, 45–52). Pule had a chance to return to Niue in 1991, where he discovered *hiapo*, the Niuean tapa. In an essay on Pule's biography, O'Brien described the decisive moment as follows:

> "(…) a vast array of sources and influences began to coalesce—within and around the rubric of traditional Niuean hiapo. (…) happened upon a framework, within which experience, memory, and dream could be accommodated. Not only did hiapo provide a painterly structure, it also had major implications for his writing" (O'Brien 2010, 17).

Hiapo is decorated with freehand fine lines using primarily black and secondly brown colours. There are many types of geometric patterns as well as leaf and flower patterns presented in grids.

Pule explained:

> "Images on tapa are a language (…) [Tapa] is almost writing anyway, it is a pictorial language, where flatly outlined motifs are juxtaposed (…) My paintings have the same pictographic quality of tapa, I share the same relaxed grammar if you like, as well as the conceptual flexibility" (Mallon and Pereira 2002, 201).

Pule's identity is attached to Niue, particularly with *hiapo*. By comparing Pule's paintings before and after he encountered *hiapo*, the importance of this discovery becomes evident. Tohi was attracted by Tongan *lalava*, whereas Pule found Niuean *hiapo*. Both artistic heritages belong to their respective homelands. Nevertheless, they are different because *hiapo* production was ceased by 1901 (Neich and Pendergrast 1997, 71) or soon after the 1890s (Pule and Thomas 2005,

15). Pule did not have the chance to encounter *hiapo* in his daily life. During an interview, he said that his first encounter was a photo of *hiapo* in Percy Smith's ethnography, which was republished in 1983 (Thomas 2010, 52). Most existing *hiapo* are housed as classic Oceanic art in museums and art galleries in developed countries.[8] Pule stated:

> "The energy of hiapo has affected my art. It deals with identity and migration, colonization of people, destruction of indigenous practices. It conjures up past stories that live in the images – such as shark and constellations" (Pule and Thomas 2005, 20).

The ancestral connection of the three artists to an Oceanic art heritage may have provided them with special insight and inspiration, or an incarnation, in terms of developing their own original and singular forms of artistic expression. At the same time, their encounter with their heritage was made possible through their experiences of migration, which led them to question who they are and set them on a quest to discover their identity.

Fale Pasifika, a symbol of the Pacific community in Auckland, New Zealand

In 1995, the government set up the Ministry of Pacific Island Affairs to manage the growing population of Pacific peoples in New Zealand. The ministry was renamed the Ministry for Pacific Peoples in 2015. Each community was formed by ethnicity, based on language and culture, through family and kinship networks and the church organisations of their respective homelands. However, the identity of Pacific peoples was formed through interethnic church organisations, such as the Catholic Church in New Zealand and Pacific Island Presbyterian Church, the process of confronting discrimination, and the University organisations. Tautai was one such organisation for general Pacific peoples (Yamamoto 2000).

In 2004, Fale Pasifika was built at the University of Auckland. This building was planned for the compound of the Centre for Pacific Studies. In addition to being a modern compound building for offices, seminar rooms, and research facilities, the Fale Pasifika is an independent building that is used for various events, such as meetings, large lectures, and ceremonial occasions. The basic concept was proposed by a Samoan architect, Albert Refiti, and its design is similar to a huge Samoan traditional house (*fale*), with a round oval roof with posts and without walls. Since the Fale Pasifika is a modern building with air conditioning, it has a glass covering surrounding the building, thus lending it an open-air atmosphere. The University of Auckland's official webpage explains, "Our Fale Pasifika plays

---

[8] Later, Pule made many trips with anthropologist Nicholas Thomas to visit *hiapo* in museums in New Zealand, Australia, London, and Honolulu (Pule and Thomas 2005).

an important role as the touch-point between the University and Pacific communities" (The University of Auckland n.d.).

Inside the Fale Pasifika, the upper structure is connected by *lalava* by Filipe Tohi (Tonga). He used various patterns of *lalava* depicting stories of oral traditions. The use of the *lalava* means the joining and binding of the community. On the windows of the administration building in the Centre complex, John Pule painted images and symbols of his own artworks. In a video, he stated that he did not create new images, but instead put his own images and symbols together on ten windows to express his perspectives regarding education. He explained that the drawings were dedicated to cheer on the older Pasifika people (in New Zealand)—the first-generation of Pasifika migrants—instead of the younger generation.

Fatu Feu'u (Samoa) was another artist who joined in the project, and carved a big, long face on a wood sculpture and painted it using red colour. He named it Toa Pasifika (Pacific warrior) as a symbol for protecting chiefs; this artwork is located on the right side from the centre of the Fale. Toa is a guardian who protects the Fale. These three renowned contemporary Oceanic artists were joined by three other artists: Jim Vivieaere (Cook Islands), who created the decoration of frigate birds hanging up in front of the Fale, Tania Short (Cook Islands and Maori), who planned the pavement of approach, and Tomui Kaloni (Tonga), the architect who set the entrance space structure.

As explained by Refiti, Fale Pasifika became an iconic and symbolic architecture that is open for the entire community of Pacific peoples in Auckland. It is crucial that the Fale is decorated primarily with contemporary Oceanic artworks, instead of traditional artefacts. The use of contemporary artworks symbolises that the Pasifika communities are not only an extension of the island groups in Oceania, but also have their own identity within New Zealand. The practice of contemporary Oceanic artists in the Tautai group encouraged Pacific peoples and their communities in New Zealand.

As Pacific peoples' communities in Auckland have matured, more and more younger people have sought higher education. Compared with the contemporary Pacific artists of the first generation, a young would-be artist in the present day has numerous educational opportunities: the Elam School of Fine Arts at the University of Auckland; the Faculty of Art and Design at Auckland University of Technology; the Department of Creative Arts at the Manukau Institute of Technology; and the Department of Arts and Design at Whitecliffe College. Graduates of these establishments can achieve Bachelor of Arts, Master's, or even PhD degrees.

The formal art education system is based on the Western concept of art, which emphasises the originality and singularity of an artist. At the very least, art students are expected to create something new, original, and different. Although artists are allowed to incorporate some designs and motifs of traditional Oceanic art in their own work, this can only serve as a basis to help artists develop ideas and styles that differ from that of their predecessors.

For example, Dagmar Dyck, a printmaker, was born in New Zealand in 1972 to a mother of German and Tongan origin and a German father. She was raised in North Shore, Auckland and attended the Elam School of Fine Arts. While being an art teacher by profession, she is an active artist as a printmaker adopting some patterns and motifs from Tongan tapa designs. Traditional tapa is only coloured using white, brown, and black. However, her artwork uses various colours, such as orange, blue, and yellow. Tongan tapa designs differ from those on Niuean tapa. The situational difference is that Tongan tapa continue to be actively produced in Tonga.

Figure 5.2 Vaimaila Urale, "Lepo," 2017, acrylic on canvas, 3000 x 1800 mm (centre) and "Typeface: Enjoy," 2018, vinyl mural, dimensions variable (wall).

From the Solo Exhibition of Vaimaila Urale *Typeface: Enjoy*, 10 May–2 June 2018 at Enjoy Contemporary Art Space, Wellington. Image courtesy of Xander Dixon and Enjoy Contemporary Art Space.

Another example is Vaimaila Urale. Vaimaila was born in 1972 in Samoa, and soon her entire family moved to Wellington, New Zealand. She worked in a theatre group led by her sister, and then decided to become an artist herself. When I met her for the first time in 2008, she was an art student at Auckland University of Technology.

She has been working on various media in different styles, and her latest work 'Typeface' has adopted Samoan tattoo design. Making use of modern technology, she picked four symbols from the keyboard '<', '>', '/', and '\', and created patterns for *malu* (Samoan female tattoo) and Lapita designs. She has painted on canvas as well as murals on walls and pillars, using designs adapted from her heritage to match her ethnicity and gender. She has designed tattoo patterns and collaborated with tattooists.

Identity without heritage

Many younger contemporary Oceanic artists are gradually shifting away from traditional artistic heritage. They are increasingly interested in postcolonial perspectives and social issues in migrant communities. Although Michel Tuffery has been a member of Tautai since the beginning, his perspective differs from the leaders of Tautai. This difference in perspective may be attributed to the fact that he was very young when he started and experienced education in a formal art institution, whereas most Tautai members were self-made artists. He began by adopting Samoan tattoo designs in his printmaking. He went on to portray a leading role in postcolonial approaches, which have influenced the new generation.

He was born in 1966 in Wellington to a Samoan mother and a father with European, Cook Islander, and Tahitian heritage. He graduated from the Otago Polytech School of Art in 1987, awarded a MASPAC Queen Elizabeth II study grant (Museum of New Zealand/Te Papa Tongarewa n.d.), through which he visited various Oceanic countries. Prior to this, he had not felt comfortable with *fa'a Samoa* (Samoan customs), but he gained respect for the Pacific culture through his visits. "Tuffery is one of a number of New Zealand-born Pacific Islanders who reference their Pacific identity in their work while using European mediums" (Ibid.).

He became famous for his life-size cattle figure "Pisupo lua afe" (1994), which means "corned beef two thousand" in the Samoan language. This artwork was a cattle-shaped sculpture made of numerous empty corned beef tins. It expresses the irony that Samoans consumed excessive amounts of corned beef during their ceremonies, although more than thirty years had passed since the termination of colonial administration by New Zealand, and that corned beef has taken the place of pigs in ceremonial exchange in Samoa. He has criticised colonialism in Oceania, and incorporated images of Captain Cook into his artwork. The most famous artwork is "Cookie in Te Wai Pounamu meets Cook Strait". Cookie is the local term for Captain Cook. Cook is depicted as a strict and serious figure in the painting, and there are two fishes near his ears, which symbolise Tupaia, a Tahitian person who helped Cook to navigate. Tuffery has also depicted Cook in other works, some of which are tattooed on his own face. In the story he told, he identified himself as a third-generation migrant who lives in New Zealand and wanted to create something different (Mallon and Pereira 1997, 116).

John Vea was born in 1985 in New Zealand to Tongan parents. He is a PhD student whose work focuses on the conditions of migrant communities and minorities. Although he is interested in social issues, instead of writing reports or papers on them, he produces artworks with strong messages aimed toward society. His installation "Import/Export" is composed of wood-framed boxes with blocks of waves that are shaped like taro tubers. The boxes have labels to show that they originated in Tonga and other Pacific Island countries. The blocks of waves symbolise labourers from the Tonga and other Pacific communities. Although he did not experience "dawn raids" (Anae 2012), he often heard stories about "dawn raids" from his parents and relatives. The stories are vividly described because those who faced difficulties and were eventually deported were real people that were related to him. Although the "dawn raids" policy ended a long time ago, New Zealand has begun to introduce RSE (Recognised Seasonal Employer) schemes for nine Pacific countries since 2007. This scheme is aimed at short-term (up to seven months) agricultural labourers, who are required to return home every year when they reach the completion of their terms. Vea claims that although the RSE scheme is not as harsh as the "dawn raids", they are discriminatory. Vea's work appears to express anger that the majority of New Zealand perceive Pacific people only as labourers and not as human beings. He has noted that he is sensitive to issues regarding racism, and typically uses video and moving images.

Figure 5.3 John Vea, "import/export," 2008–2016 (foreground) and "Finish this week off and that's it!," 2014 (background).

From the Solo Exhibition *John Vea: Talanoa, Colloquies of the Unrecognised Worker*, at MTG Hawkes Bay, Napier, 2016. Image courtesy of David Frost, MTG Hawkes Bay.

Vea is not alone in his criticism, and many young people from Pacific communities have critical perspectives regarding how the majority of New Zealand generally perceive Pacific peoples. In 2017, an exhibition, *On the Ground*, included a video installation by Matavai Taulangau, entitled "Forestry". In the video, some labourers are seen cutting down big trees, taking off small branches, and clearing bushes. They are skilled and well-trained for the job, and the video highlights how they play a key role in the workforce of society. The labourers talk to each other in Polynesian languages, and hardly anyone seems to be aware that they are working there. It seemed to me that the creator of the video intended to attract the attention of mainstream society to the invisible labourers from the islands, advocating fair treatment for them.

Migrants' lives, as well as the social issues of migrants, in New Zealand are depicted particularly well through photography. Edith Amituanai, who is of Samoan descent, became famous for her photography of the lounge rooms of migrant Samoans in New Zealand and other places, such as Alaska and Europe. The lounge rooms in her photographs share a common Samoan atmosphere, with portraits of family members, colourful plastic leis, artificial flowers, and sofa covers made of tropical prints. Recently, she has extended her interest to young migrants from various ethnic groups in her neighbourhood (Brownson et al. 2012, 16-17).

Intermarriage has become increasingly common, and the artistic and cultural experiences of the younger generation are broader than before. Multicultural encounters are an everyday experience for young contemporary Oceanic artists in urban New Zealand, and they have become increasingly conscious of their own ethnic identities as migrants. This consciousness is not fixed but contextual, and they identify themselves with migrant communities instead of their ultimate heritage to return to their origin.

New movements in Oceanic heritage

In an interview with me, Vaimaila Urale stated, "I like the communal art style and collaboration of creating art together, believing in communicating and connecting through the power of art". She often partakes in group exhibitions, and even when she has a solo show, she invites someone to collaborate. In 2012, she mounted an exhibition *Mata* with a Maori artist, Rangituhia Hollis, at Mangere Art Centre, Auckland. They set up four pool tables with cues carved with different traditional Polynesian patterns and motifs (Hollis n.d). Visitors were able to select a favourite cue and play pool. She believes in the Oceanic philosophy of community and collaboration, an aspect that makes Pacific peoples take pride in. Although Polynesian patterns and motifs featured in their exhibition, it is important to understand that the patterns were used as indices of variations in Oceanic culture in New Zealand. Visitors could select a cue, promoting participatory art within the framework of Western concepts. She synthesises the Oceanic idea of community and collectiveness with this idea, which is minor in the Western concept of art because it makes it difficult to pinpoint the artists' originality. In many ways, her ideas around the community and collectiveness may originate in her Oceanic cultural heritage. She evaluated Oceanic art differently from Western art critics.

Graham Fletcher, who is of Samoan-European descent, represents another new direction. He earned a PhD degree at Elam in 2005 and is a painter who teaches at Otago Polytechnic. His exhibition of paintings *Lounge Room Tribalism* (2010, George Frazer Gallery, Auckland) have served to establish his style (Fletcher 2010). Each painting in the series depicts a middle-class European family's comfortable lounge room. The atmosphere in the room differs from the lounges that Amituanai depicts in her photography. Fletcher's lounge rooms, which he painted to resemble the 1950s and 1960s (Fletcher 2012,17), contain no human beings, only one or more pieces of classic Oceanic art. The statues and masks that he places in the room seem out of place in two ways. On one hand, they were taken away from their ritual context by colonialists, and most people in their original setting did not consider these pieces of art suitable for this type of lounge room. On the other hand, the owner of the room, who may have visited the tribal area in question, either for business or a holiday, is quite happy to store them in his room as guardians. Some aficionados of this art feel the *mana* of these objects sleeping in the silence of the room. This is an interesting method to examine the heritage of Oceanic art. Fletcher does not seem to be criticising Oceanic art itself, but so-called primitivists and lovers or collectors of tribal art. Although he does not strongly express his distaste, he simply conveys a sense of feeling uncomfortable. He stated, "For myself, identity was an important issue that needed addressing at that time [he is talking of his previous work], and I'm sure this was also the case for many other New Zealand-born Pacific artists of my generation" (Fletcher 2012, 49).

Conclusion

Contemporary Oceanic artists emerged in New Zealand during the 1980s after the "dawn raids", when the harsh policy aimed toward Pacific immigrants ceased. During this period, the majority of Pacific peoples living in New Zealand had better perspectives about their lives there, however, continued to experience a lack of confidence. Their lives on the margin enhanced the quest by Pasifika artists to build their identity with their heritage. The three renowned contemporary Oceanic artists have shown that their ancestral connection to an Oceanic art heritage may have led them to have special insight and inspiration, or even a type of incarnation, in terms of developing their own original and singular forms of artistic expression. Their artworks must be singular and original, in terms of the standard practices of the art community in New Zealand. They wanted to remain connected to their origin and simultaneously be recognised in their new home. Their adoption, application, and incorporation of their heritage allowed them to create their own original and singular artworks.

As the communities of the diaspora grew, the artists' situations changed. With increased intermarriages, more children were born with multiple ethnic identities, and young people now live in urban zones, where they remain in contact with European education and different ethnic cultures. For many of them, their first language is English. Nevertheless, Pacific peoples remain a minority ignored or exposed to discrimination. Many young artists are seeking methods to express their experiences as members of minority groups. Some artists remain focused on their heritage, whereas others depict the communities of their diaspora.

In the process for artists of Pacific origin to establish themselves, they have struggled or tackled with identities, heritage and shared discriminative experiences, which are inevitably collective. On a different trajectory from the Western art scene, the Oceanic art world, with its markedly non-Western characteristics, has developed in ways that do not fit the paradigm of the global art-culture system and its distinctive characteristics, as defined by Clifford (1988, 215–252). In our time of socially engaged art, artworks definitely play a role of social agencies as Gell argued (1998) and all the endeavours of the contemporary Oceanic artists can be a hope for decolonialising art not only in New Zealand but also globally.

Acknowledgements

I appreciate the financial assistance provided by the Japan Society for the Promotion of Science, without which this research would not have been possible (Title: *Anthropological Study of Contemporary Pacific Art: Art Practices of Pacific Peoples in New Zealand*. Ref. no. 15K03058). I am also grateful for the help provided by Tautai and its staff, especially the artists themselves and those in the art circles in Auckland. In this short paper, it would be impossible to mention all the artists I have met, but I truly appreciate all the information they have provided. Finally, I would like to thank the participants and the audience at the IUAES Congress 2018 session for their useful comments and questions.

References

Anae, Melani. 2012. "All Power to the People: Overstayers, Dawn Raids and the Polynesian Panthers." In *Tangata o le Moana: New Zealand and the People of the Pacific*, edited by Sean Mallon, Kolokesa Māhina-Tuai, and Damon Salesa, 220–239. Wellington: Te Papa Press.

Auckland Council, Auckland Tourism, Event and Economic Development. 2020. *History of Pasifika*. Accessed Nov. 29, 2020. https://www.aucklandnz.com/pasifika-festival-2021/history-pasifika.

Beaglehole, Ann. 2015. *Story: Emigration Regulation in Te Ara* (Encyclopaedia of New Zealand). Accessed Nov. 23, 2020, https://teara.govt.nz/en/immigration-regulation/page-1.

Brownson, Ron, Kolokesa Māhina-Tuai, Albert L. Refiti, Ema Tavola and Nina Tonga. 2012. *Home AKL: Artists of Pacific Heritage in Auckland*. Auckland: Auckland Art Gallery Toi o Tamaki.

Clifford, James. 1988. *The Predicament of Culture: Twentieth-Century Ethnography, Literature, and Art*. Cambridge MS: Harvard University Press.

Fletcher, Graham. 2010. Lounge Room Tribalism. Accessed Dec. 4, 2020. http://www.grahamfletcher.co.nz/georgefraser.html.

Fletcher, Graham. 2012. *Lounge Room Tribalism*. Auckland: Mangere Art Centre.

Gell, Alfred. 1998. *Art and Agency: An Anthropological Theory*. Oxford: Oxford University Press.

Hollis, Rangituhia. n.d. Matamata. Accessed June 27, 2019. https://rangituhia.com/2018/09/14/matamata-mangere-arts-centre-2012/.

Jennings, Shona. 2012. *Fatu Feu'u On Life and Art*. Auckland: Little Island Press.

Kuwahara, Makiko. 2005. *Tattoo: An Anthropology*. Oxford: Berg.

Macpherson, Cluny. 2006. "Pacific Peoples in Aotearoa/New Zeland: From Sojourn to Settlement." In *Migration Happens: Reasons, Effects and Opportunities of Migration in the South Pacific*, edited by Katarina Ferro and Margot Wallner, 97–126. New Brunswick: Transaction Publishers.

Macpherson, Cluny and La'avasa Macpherson. 2009. *The Warm Winds of Change: Globalisation in Contemporary Sāmoa*. Auckland: Auckland University Press.

Māhina-Tuai, Kolokesa U. and Manuesina O. Māhina. 2011. *Nimamea'a: The Fine Art of Tongan Embroidery and Crochet*. Auckland: Objectspace.

Mallon, Sean and Sébastien Galliot. 2018. *A History of Samoan Tattooing*. Honolulu: University of Hawai'i Press.

Mallon, Sean and Pandora Fulimalo Pereira. 2002. *Pacific art Niu Sila: the Pacific dimension of contemporary New Zealand arts*. Wellington: Te Papa Press.

Multicultural New Zealand: New Zealand Federation of Multicultural Councils. n.d. Official Website. Accessed September 2, 2020. https://multiculturalnz.org.nz/Counties+Manukau+Ethnic+Council.

Museum of New Zealand/Te Papa Tongarewa. n.d. *Biography of Michel Tuffery*. Accessed June 30, 2019. https://collections.tepapa.govt.nz/topic/1124.

Neich, Roger and Mick Pendergrast. 1998. *Traditional Tapa Textiles of the Pacific*. New York: Thames and Hudson.

New Zealand Immigration. n.d. Official Website. Accessed Nov. 23, 2020. https://www.immigration.govt.nz/.

New Zealand Ministry for Pacific Peoples. n.d. Front Page. Accessed May 3, 2019. https://www.mpp.govt.nz/pacific-people-in-nz.

O'Brien, Gregory. 2010. "A Portrait of the Artist as Many People." In *Hauaga: The Art of John Pule*, edited by Nicholas Thomas, 11–42. Dunedin: Otago University Press.

Pasefika Proud. 2016. *The Profile of Pacific Peoples in New Zealand*, 2016. Accessed September 1, 2020. https://www.pasefikaproud.co.nz/resources/?start=24.

Pule, John and Nicholas Thomas. 2005. *Hiapo: Past and Present in Nuiean Barkcloth*. Otago: University of Otago Press.

Stevenson, Karen. 2012. *The Festival of Pacific Arts Celebrating 40 years*. Noumea: SPC.

Stevenson, Karen. 2015. *Filipe Tohi: Journey to the Present*. Suva: The University of the South Pacific. Tautai. n.d. Tautai. Accessed Dec. 4, 2020. https://tautai.org/.

The Office of the 7th Pacific Festival of Arts. 1996. *Taeao Fou I Mea Sina: The First Pacific Festival Contemporary Arts Exhibition Catalogue*.

The University of Auckland, Fale Pasifika. n.d. Official Website. Accessed December 12, 2019. https://www.auckland.ac.nzen/on-campus/life-on-campus/pacific-life/fale-pasifika.html.

Thomas, Nicholas. 1996. "The Dream of Joseph: Practices of Identity in Pacific Art." *Contemporary Pacific* 8 (2): 291–317.

Thomas, Nicholas, ed. 2010. *Haunga, the Art of John Pule*. Dunedin: Otago University Press.

Yamamoto, Matori. 2000. "Polynesian Identity in Multi-Cultural context." *The New Pacific Review* 1 (1): 68–76.

Yamamoto, Matori. 2006. "The Eighth Festival of Pacific Arts: Representation and Identity." *Art and Identity in the Pacific: Festival of Pacific Arts*, edited by Matori Yamamoto, 5–25. Osaka: Japan Center for Area Studies.

Chapter 6

Indigenous arts in Brazil: aesthetics, cosmology and politics

Ilana Seltzer Goldstein
Federal University of Sao Paulo, Brazil

Abstract

This chapter addresses the relative invisibility of indigenous arts in Brazil, both in museums and in the art market, while at the same time signaling the emergence, in recent years, of some contemporary indigenous artists, who combine individual poetic research with political and cultural activism. At first, general information on the indigenous peoples living in Brazil today is presented. Then, an overview of their traditional artistic forms is given, pointing out the singularities and, at the same time, raising issues or practices common to several of them, such as the ephemerality of objects, the ubiquity of graphism and the agency of images and artifacts. The second half of the chapter is dedicated to the output of contemporary indigenous artists in Brazil, such as Jaider Esbell and the Mahku collective, whose works are now signed and regarded as art by the art world. Special attention is dedicated to the Amazonian artist Denilson Baniwa, whose ironical and critical work comprises painting, graphic printing, performance and video. The Brazilian state does not sufficiently protect indigenous lands against invasion by illegal prospectors and loggers, nor does it restrain the advance of agribusiness toward the Amazon rainforest. This text was written at a particularly sensitive political moment, with great setbacks in the rights of Brazil's first peoples. Presenting Amerindian artworks and cosmologies to new audiences is a way of emphasising their creativity and power but also of drawing attention to their struggles for rights.

Keywords: indigenous art, contemporary indigenous artist, museum, art market, rights

Brazil is currently experiencing a new uprise. Indigenous artists are beginning to occupy artistic spaces in the cities and in cultural institutions in general. Indigenous video makers, writers, painters, sculptors and rappers are appropriating Western technologies and languages to record traditional stories, values, knowledge and visual repertoires. They are adopting authorial artistic practices and beginning to develop unique poetics, which is inspired by and go beyond collective and traditional repertoires. The indigenous interlocutors with whom I have spoken seem to think of works of art, catalogues, exhibitions and artistic performances as interesting alternatives for communicating with the Brazilian society.

This has to be considered in a broader context. Very differently from what one may think (because some powerful images of them have been circulating worldwide), indigenous people in Brazil suffer from social invisibility and cultural marginalisation. We are now living in a particularly sensitive political moment, in which indigenous leaders and activists fear great setbacks in the rights of Brazil's first peoples.

Studying and presenting the Amerindian artistic output to new audiences is a way of emphasising their creativity and power but also of drawing attention to their struggles for rights, which are terribly threatened by a far-right president. Using the arts to promote intercultural communication can be a promising strategy that is still little explored and only recently studied in Brazil.

The chapter is organised by the idea that artefacts and images can shift between different categories: they can be understood as ethnographic testimonies, can become art, turn into merchandise, or cease being that. James Clifford developed a model that allows to situate items from traditional societies in four "zones" (Clifford 1988, 224).[1] When moving from one "zone" to another, the object changes status and value—and they raise their status as they move from being a "cultural artefact" to an "artistic object" and from "inauthentic" to "authentic".

The (re-)classifications observed by Clifford are not too far from the idea of "artification", "a dynamic process through which new objects and practices emerge and relationships and institutions are transformed" (Schapiro and Heinich 2012, 4). "Artification" encompasses practical and symbolic changes, in which recognition, legitimation and meaning attribution play an important role so that something is considered as art. One of the artification mechanisms identified by Schapiro and Heinich is the trend toward authorisation, that is, the individualisation of a product. "Objects are [then] understood to express

---

[1] In the "zone" of "authentic artefacts", there are specimens collected by researchers and housed in history and ethnographic museums (such as those mentioned in the second part of this chapter); in the "zone" of "authentic works of art", items valued by artists, curators and collectors are found (such as those covered in the third part of the chapter); in the "zone" of "inauthentic works of art", we see fake pieces; and the "zone" of "inauthentic artefacts" is the area for mass-production tourist souvenirs and goods (often found at airports and tourist places in Australia, for example) (Clifford 1988).

personal intention; they are nominal and original; and the maker's signature appears as a synthetic marker of these mechanisms" (Schapiro and Heinich 2012, 24). This is exactly what we are beginning to witness in Brazil right now.

Another central concept underlying this reflection is agency. According to Alfred Gell, the power of images and objects comes from the fact that human beings project their own intentions and agency onto the things and images they make and manipulate. They become fascinated by the "index" (material expression) of people and social relations imbued in the works. It is a process that occurs also beyond museums, collections and catalogues (Gell 1998). Works of art may play the role of mediators in the relationship between indigenous and non-indigenous worlds, serving as "traps of thought". As Alfred Gell (2006) stated, artworks are:

> "complex, demanding of attention and perhaps difficult to reconstruct fully (…). A trap or a snare that impedes passage; and what is any art gallery but a place of capture, set with what Boyer calls 'thought traps', which hold their victims for a time, in suspension?" (Gell 2006, 233–234).

From this perspective, an object, image or practice should be considered artistic only when social relations are established through and around it, when it attracts and challenges our thinking and when it is capable of triggering actions and reactions. The metaphor of art as a trap of thought helps to describe the strangeness, fascination and even the violent reactions aroused by the display of indigenous works in the Western arts system.

In August 2019, for example, an exhibition showcasing artworks by indigenous artists that was on display in Embu das Artes, near Sao Paulo, was invaded at night and completely destroyed. Canvases were torn, sculptures were broken, labels were damaged. It is as if the vandals, probably right-wing extremists, were trying to hurt the indigenous subjects and contesting their place in the world through the artworks. It can be seen as a response to indigenous artists, by means of the exhibition being present in the main cultural centre of the city, showing that they are alive and have something to say.

But just as Gell suggests artworks are never finished, the process did not end with the depredation of the exhibition. An independent and small Sao Paulo gallery called CoLabirinto organised an exhibition to display the same works with their new appearance. And at this very moment, one of our main art museums, Pinacotheca of the State of Sao Paulo, is organising its first exhibition curated exclusively by an indigenous curator, Naine Terena, to showcase again some of the vandalised pieces. As it turns out, the thought-trapping artworks carry a disruptive potential, however at the same time they may bring us closer together and establish new relationships between people. All these dimensions of agency—disruptive, relational, procedural—will emerge in an array of examples given along the next pages.

The first purpose of this chapter is to provide an introductory overview of the expressive forms of indigenous peoples living across Brazil today. Considering a readership from different countries and disciplines, the first part of the chapter offers basic historic, demographic and cosmological information about the Amerindians in Brazil. In the second part, while recognising the great diversity and heterogeneity that compose the Amerindian universe, I seek to point out common characteristics and trends in their artistic expressions. Some of the elements highlighted in the second part, such as bodies as aesthetic media, the synaesthetic experience linked to shamanism and the omnipresence of geometric patterns, appear again in new ways in the third part of the text. This is dedicated to the output of contemporary indigenous artists in Brazil. In the fourth part, I especially focus on Denilson Baniwa, an Amazonian artist.

Contextualising: Amerindians in Brazil

In the beginning of the sixteenth century, when the Portuguese settlers first arrived, there were between two and five million inhabitants in the territory that we call Brazil today, divided into approximately one thousand ethnic groups. Many of them died from European illnesses, others were killed and enslaved (Cunha 1992). The indigenous population declined steadily.

It was not until the end of the twentieth century that this demographic trend reversed. The 1991 census recorded an indigenous population of 294,000. The 2000 census revealed that this population had more than doubled. In the 2010 census 817,000 people identified as indigenous (Carvalho and Andrade 2014). One of the explanations for this big shift is that the 1988 Constitution, enacted after the end of the military dictatorship (1964–1984), assured that indigenous peoples had the right to land, cultural difference and self-determination. The prospect of a more promising future made people no longer ashamed of but wanting to claim their origins. In addition, from the second half of the twentieth century onwards, we have seen processes of ethnogenesis, that is, a resurgence of peoples who had been considered extinct (Arruti 1997; Bartolomé 2006). The ethnic groups mentioned in the chapter are circled on the map.[2]

---

[2] The author has adapted the map from two different sources. Accessed September 2, 2019. https://www.dicionariotupiguarani.com.br/mapas/ and https://pib.socioambiental.org/pt/Pagina_principal.

Indigenous arts in Brazil 107

Figure 6.1 Map of important artmaking ethnic groups in Brazil in 2019.

One way of thinking that is common to all Amerindians is perspectivism, a concept coined by Eduardo Viveiros de Castro (1996) and Tânia Stolze Lima (1996) for the attribution of human-like consciousness to supernatural beings and animals, especially those who have a status of predators and preys. This theory suggests that many species have forms of social organisation that others are unable to see. Wild boars, for example, have the same concerns as human beings it is claimed: taking care of their offspring, going hunting, working the land, drinking beer, partying, decorating their bodies, etc. While they see themselves in the same way that humans see themselves, we see them as prey to be hunted, they see us as spirits that may capture their souls. It is a question of perspective. But a perspective is not a representation: representations are linked to the mind or spirit, while the perspective depends on the body. "Since the soul is formally identical in all species, it can only see the same things everywhere— the difference is given in the specificity of bodies. (…) Bodies are the way in which alterity is apprehended as such" (Viveiros de Castro 2012, 27). The only ones who manage to go back and forth between the different perspectives and species are the shamans. In sum, the Amerindian universe is dynamic, transformational, full of non-human and extra-human intentionalities and agencies. And their arts mirror all this.

Regarding the relationship with the state, the Indian Protection Service was the first government body to deal with indigenous peoples in Brazil. It was created in 1910 but was extinguished in 1966 on charges of corruption. Its mantra was "guardianship of the incapable". In 1967, the National Foundation of the Indian (Funai) was created by the military dictatorship with an assimilationist mantra. This only changed in the 1990s with the re-democratisation when non-governmental organizations and indigenous associations were empowered. Funai is still in operation today, although its status is precarious. There are programs for indigenous health and also support for bilingual schools in the villages. Nevertheless, the state does not sufficiently protect indigenous lands against invasion by illegal prospectors and loggers, nor does it restrain the advance of agribusiness toward the Amazon rainforest and the indigenous lands.

Specificities and recurrences in indigenous arts in Brazil

Ethnographies dedicated to peoples living in the Brazilian territory today sketch a rich, although incomplete, panorama of their forms of expression. The following features—some that I have identified, and others that were identified in the literature—including elements that appear in the work of several different peoples, contrast the precepts of Amerindian arts with Western ones.

Absence of an autonomous aesthetic sphere

Amerindian forms of expression are present in daily life and in celebrations in a diffuse way. They permeate what Westerners would call political, economic, religious or medicinal domains. A body painting, a mask or a chant enables and enhances activities such as hunting, a young man's entry into adulthood, the departure of a dead soul or the healing of a sick person. Indigenous stools illustrate well the amalgam of aesthetic, ritual and utilitarian purposes. The degree of technical mastery and the plastic strength of many of them suggest that they are not just furniture to sit on. In the Huni Kuin or Caxinauá initiation ritual, for example, parents sculpt a stool out of a kapok tree.[3] The contact with

---

[3] Part of the peoples has two names, one given by the whites and a self-designation. Thus, Huni Kuin (self-designation) and Caxinauá, for example, refer to the same people. For more detailed information on the indigenous peoples in Brazil, see the website of the

Indigenous arts in Brazil 109

it is expected to bestow long life and firm roots upon their children. The stool agency is maximised by the painting made on the wood and on the skin of the boy (Lagrou 2007).

Figure 6.2 Stool shaped like a jaguar, by a Kuikuro artist. BEI private collection, exhibited at the Ibirapuera Park, 2018.

Photograph by Ilana Goldstein.

Several Amerindian peoples make solid wood chairs with no joints that can be covered or not with painting. The stool shaped like a Kuikuro jaguar in figure 6.2 probably refers to the leadership figure. In the Xingu region, chiefs are like jaguars that need calming and carry ornaments associated with the jaguar.

The central role of the body

The body of the performer plays a central role in Amerindian art as a target of scarification and ornamentation. The collective memory, in some cases, is inscribed on bodies by means of scars resulting from ritual torture. Depending on the people, the art of public speaking, important to chiefs, can be reinforced by lip adornments, just as the art of listening can be heightened by ear enlargers. The shaman usually swallows or inhales substances that allow him to have visions. Warriors receive paintings that strengthen and protect them; newborns and young people deserve body care that transforms them and conveys knowledge to them.

Social and Environmental Institute, which has an encyclopaedia in English: Accessed May 14, 2019. https://pib.socioambiental.org/en/Main_Page .

The Kayapó-Xikrin baby's body is decorated since his or her birth. At first, it is covered with red *achiote*, because the smell of this fruit keeps the child close to the living and protected from the dead. After the umbilical cord stump falls off, the child's body is painted for the first time with a black colour made out of genipap and charcoal. Cohn argues that body painting and ornamentation contribute "to promote health and the well-being of people, as well as to communicate their status. This applies to all ages throughout life and in death" (Cohn 2010, 101).

Ephemerality

Traditionally, collecting is not a practice that makes sense to Amerindians. Dance, music and oral poetry are performed live and only recently they have been recorded in audio-visual and written media by the indigenous themselves. Body painting needs to be made again and again regularly. Masks are not kept after having been worn in rituals, for they represent entities capable of bringing about transformations, illnesses and deaths. Among many peoples, the objects of an individual are destroyed when he or she dies. According to Barcelos Neto, the Wauja of Xingu consider it nefarious to retain photographs of the deceased, as this could prevent or delay the soul's journey to the celestial village. The soul and the image are not dissociated from each other (Neto 2002).

However, some groups have been trying to recover museological collections of their material culture. Tariana and Tucano representatives, for example, recently demanded the repatriation of items from the Manaus Museum of Brazilian Indians, run by missionaries (Martini 2012). Other peoples have chosen to build their own cultural spaces. The Maguta Museum, of the Ticuna people, is the oldest. Created in 1990 in the state of Amazonas, it collects and displays masks, necklaces, baskets, nets, historical photos, maps and drawings of myths. The museum upsets loggers, politicians and landowners, who threatened it on the opening day (Oliveira Filho 2012).

Presentification

If in Western art the difference between the referent and its representation is clear, for Amerindians this distance seems to be non-existent or reversible. This is why the idea of presentification works better than the idea of representation. Amerindian images or objects do not represent or replace beings which are far away—or dead. Artefacts, designs, songs and performances are meant to bring these beings and their powers to the visible world, they are an extended part of them. According to Lúcia van Velthem, the objects produced by the Wayana are equivalent to pieces of bodies of supernatural entities. If they are fully materialised in art form, they will come to life. In order to prevent a *tipiti* (a long

Indigenous arts in Brazil 111

and thin braided manioc press) from reviving in the form of a constrictor snake, its head and tail should not be made (van Velthem 1998). The fact that objects and images are imbued with agency leads to a strong association between art and shamanism.

The ubiquity of graphic body painting

Body painting and facial painting, especially in the Ge-language-speaking groups, reveals social distinctions. It indicates the individual's belonging to a certain age group, a certain clan, the state of mourning, among other possibilities that identify and situate him or her within the group. Among the Kayapó the stages experienced throughout a person's life are marked by changes in the pattern of the body painting—the couple's first child, the period of reclusion, reintegration into society, the loss of a close relative (Vidal 1992). The Xerente people, by means of designs on their bodies, indicate the exogamous moieties and the ritual halves to which the individual belongs (Silva and Farias 1992). However, in other groups, body ornamentation and graphic designs may be associated with alterity and communication with other dimensions of the cosmos.

Amerindian graphic designs seem to vibrate, or move, and figure and background merge into a possible visual translation of perspectivism (Lagrou 2009). Such an effect is present, for example, in the Kadiweu designs, nowadays mainly applied to ceramics. Formerly, the Kadiweu women daily painted their skins with the patterns shown in figure 6.3.

Figure 6.3 Ceramic vase made by Libência Rufino, from the Kadiweu people.

Photograph by Raquel Duran.

Figure 6.4 Draft of a tile made by Sofia de Souza, from the Kadiweu people.

Photograph by Raquel Duran.

One of the most frequent patterns among the Kadiweu designs is *lawile*, shown in Figures 6.2 and 6.3. It resembles a spiral or a whirlpool and may allude to the mythical lagoon around which friends consumed the fermented drink they discovered, thereby representing drunkenness; or it may refer to the hypnotic effect of a red dangerous flower that seduces children, virgins, and vulnerable people. The *lawile* pattern works as a protection against these phenomena (Duran 2017). Figure 6.2 deserves an additional comment. Architects Marcelo Ferraz and Francisco Fannucci invited six Kadiweu women to participate with them in a competition in 1998. They registered their traditional designs at the National School of Fine Arts, and then used them on tiles that today decorate the Yellow Quarter, in Berlin. Although it is not possible to delve deeper into the subject here, it is controversial that six women signed documents relating to a repertoire that is mostly collective. The concepts of authorship and individual intellectual property mirror Western conceptions. When applied to the Amerindian arts and knowledge, they can bring about real short circuits.

Synaesthesia

Often, two or more artistic languages and two or more sensory channels are triggered, thus leading to an immersive experience. The graphic art of the Wajãpi, from the state of Amapá, is a form of transmission of visual knowledge that works in conjunction with oral narratives (Gallois 2012). The Marubo's graphic repertoires show a narrative structure similar to that of their verbal arts. The Wauja heal their patients by means of a true "aesthetic therapy" composed of dances, flutes, chanting, and the shapes and colours of the giant masks. When a Wauja falls seriously ill, the patient's family sponsors a ritual in which a specialized shaman negotiates the return of the patient's soul, which has been kidnapped by the supernatural entities. The senses complement each other in the healing ritual: vision enables diagnosis; music creates the necessary atmosphere; and the beauty of dances and masks attracts and calms the *apapaatai* entities and turn them into allies (Neto 2002, 341).

Invisible and chimeric images

In Amerindian contexts, images can be relatively independent of their material existence. In the Yanomami conception, the image is an equivalent of what Westerners call a "spirit". Images populate Yanomami dreams, trances and mythic narratives, forming a repertoire of schemas, forms and colours shared collectively (Kopenawa and Albert 2013). Pedro Cesarino says that, when he asked different Marubo interlocutors to translate their oral poetry into drawings, all of them used similar solutions to transpose verbal narrative schemes onto paper, thus suggesting the existence of common mental schemes (Cesarino 2012). Even in the case of designs made on concrete surfaces, it is common for the viewer to perform a mental projection operation on the incomplete visual indices that make up that image or that object. This is what Carlo Severi has called "chimeric images". For example, a form composed of a small number of strokes, which offers the eyes a few details, impels the viewer to fill-in what is lacking in the image (Severi 2013).

Relativisation of the innovation vs. tradition dichotomy

While in the West modern and contemporary arts are often driven by the pursuit of innovation and rupture with the past, breaking with established mores and traditional forms, this dichotomy is not emphasised in Amerindian arts. However, what we call "tradition" is always changing. This is illustrated by the case of the *ritxokó* ceramic dolls made by the Karajá. Traditionally, they were children's toys gifted by aunts or grandparents, with which children learned about family members and their relationships. From the mid-twentieth century onwards, due to demands from the non-indigenous market, the Karajá potters began to fire the dolls previously made of raw clay to increase their resistance; they doubled their height from 10 to 20 cm; and added arms and legs, thus enhancing realism. But the small, old, raw-clay limbless dolls are still being produced for domestic consumption (Whan 2012). It should also be remembered that industrialised beads—preferably made of crystal and glass but also plastic—have been appreciated for decades in the manufacturing of belts, necklaces and bracelets, among other pieces, and are completely integrated with Amerindian cosmology and rituals. Similarly, the use of industrialised India ink for body painting has spread among the Xingu peoples because it is easily washable, while the genipap-based painting persists for up to two weeks. Additionally, amazingly novel body paintings have been seen in the Upper Xingu: spider man, soccer team coats and the yin-yang symbol (Aguillar 2018). New materials such as plastic straws are also used, for example for the headdress in figure 6.5, displayed in Amoa Konoya, one of the rare indigenous-object stores in Sao Paulo.

Figure 6.5 Headdress made of plastic straws, unidentified artist.

Photograph by Ilana Goldstein, 2017.

Indigenous people and the arts scene in Brazil

Contemporary indigenous artists are emerging in Brazil now, notably identified by their personal names rather than being firstly identified as part of a group. Reinventing their identities in the face of current global challenges, the work of these artists creates a dialogue between their indigenous origins and mainstream Brazilian society. These artists have a characteristic ability to incorporate exogenous technologies and signs with the application of their own endemic logics. Many aspects mentioned in the previous section of this chapter are also important in their artworks. Although few in number their emergence is an important and little-studied phenomenon.

A history of indigenous art exhibitions in Brazilian museums is yet to be written. Nonetheless, some events deserve to be highlighted. The 17th Sao Paulo Art Biennale in 1983 had a section titled *Brazilian Feather Art* with a separate catalogue. The *Rediscovery Show*, held in the Ibirapuera Park, Sao Paulo, in 2000, included a large section called *Indigenous Arts*. The third important exhibition, conceived by a professor at the Federal University of Minas Gerais, toured between 2013 and 2015. Titled *Mira!* [Look!], it brought together contemporary indigenous artworks from the whole of Latin America and included varied media: water-colour and acrylic paintings, sculptures, textiles, etc. The Museum of Art of Rio de Janeiro innovated by hosting the exhibition *Dja Guata Porã* (Our Beautiful Walk in Guarani language), in 2017, co-curated by the Guarani woman Sandra Benites with the collaboration of people from different ethnic backgrounds. It was not strictly an exhibition of visual arts, but an event that addressed the history of the indigenous peoples in the state of Rio de Janeiro, their political struggles, aspects of their mythology and it also included artefacts, videos and installations.

I will start by presenting two indigenous artists who were nominated for the 2016 Pipa Award of contemporary art: Jaider Esbell, from the Macuxi people, in Roraima, and Arissana Braz, from the Pataxó people, in Bahia. The work of Jaider Esbell is quite varied in terms of style and subject matter. One part refers to ancestry, shamanism and forest beings. The other part makes evident the problems resulting from contact with the whites, such as in the *It was Amazon* series, which portrays deforestation, river pollution and the oppression of indigenous peoples. Jaider, who has a degree in geography, is internationally known and had an article published in *Select*, a selective Brazilian art magazine, in 2018. In his opinion, the indigenous people "need to use the arts as a form of resistance" (Esbell 2018, 103).

Arissana Braz holds a degree from the School of Fine Arts at the Federal University of Bahia, but artistic activity is not her main occupation. Besides acting as an art educator among the Pataxó people, she also works with other indigenous peoples in educational courses and in the production of educational materials. In 2018 she told me that often the price offered for her canvases is low and, hence, she prefers to keep them. She also said that she produces images to "show the whites that there are natives in Brazil" (personal communication). Her paintings are predominantly figurative and of a documentary nature.

A third example is that of an indigenous-art collective which has achieved a sort of prominence in the art world: Mahku—a group of Huni Kuin artists coordinated by Ibã Sales who transpose ritual music into visual language. Mahku's work was exhibited at the Fondation Cartier, in Paris, in 2014. Two years later, the collective produced a multi-coloured figurative mural painting that spanned the corridor of the Museum of Modern Art of Sao Paulo (MAM).

Figure 6.6 Mural painting by the indigenous collective Mahku.

Photograph by Ilana Goldstein, 2016.

In the picture above, taken at the Sao Paulo Modern Art Museum, we see the centre and the edges of the wall framed by the ancestral *jiboia* (boa constrictor). This serpent, source of wisdom and creativity, is a recurrent element in Amerindian cosmologies, as we can read in the ethnological literature. Mythological snakes may be at the origin of humanity, shamanic knowledge, artefacts, drawings and songs. One of the pioneering studies on the subject was Lévi-Strauss' work *Le serpent au corps rempli des poissons* (1948).

Other Huni Kuin have developed projects with the non-indigenous well-known artist Ernesto Neto. As I have described in detail elsewhere (Goldstein and Labate 2018), in the installations he exhibited in the Guggenheim Museum Bilbao, Spain, in 2014, and for the Tomie Ohtake Institute, in Sao Paulo, Ernesto Neto designed penetrable environments of fabric shaped like the ancestral *jiboia* linked to the *ayahuasca* drink, to which he was introduced by the Huni Kuin. Shamans performed healing rituals in those spaces, with dance, songs and psychoactive tea drinking. In Vienna, the following year, the installation he conceived for the Thyssen-Bornemisza Art Contemporary incorporated *kené* graphic designs, thus expanding the Huni Kuin's participation from the spiritual plane to the formal plane. In early 2018 it was the turn of the exhibition

Una Shubu Hiwea in Sao Paulo. This time, Neto stepped out of the spotlight to act as curator. The project relied on the collaboration of Huni Kuin shaman Dua Busê, who encouraged the cultivation of medicinal plants in 35 villages. Drawings of flora and fauna occupied the centre of the exhibition, together with canvases depicting myths linked to these species. In 2019, the largest room of Ernesto Neto's retrospective at the Pinacotheca of Sao Paulo housed an installation with Huni Kuin traditional designs on the walls. In the same year they participated together in the 57th Venice Biennale, where their *Sacred Place* installation was dismissed by art critics as engaging in primitivism and colonialism (Maroja 2019, 1–2).

The Amazonian artist Denilson Baniwa

Denilson Baniwa is one of the most interesting and multi-skilled artists working in Brazil today due to the quality, quantity and activist nature of his output. He designs and prints posters for demonstrations and events of the indigenous movement, and he is one of the persons responsible for Yandé, an internet radio that has existed since 2013. On the programming of Rádio Yandé, there are shows in various indigenous languages, as well as in Portuguese, Spanish and English. Interviews, music, debates and news are broadcast. On its website, Rádio Yandé states that its purpose is to spread indigenous cultures from a traditional perspective combined with the speed and reach of new technologies.

In the domain of visual arts, Denilson works on reinterpretations and visual appropriations: he painted the Last Supper in the middle of the Amazon rainforest, for example, in addition to La Gioconda with face painting and arrows in her hands. He made sarcastic interventions in documents of Brazilian historical iconography. On a replica of a page of Hans Staden's book representing a Tupinambá anthropophagic ritual in the sixteenth century, for example, he glued an elegant waiter who asks the viewer: "Have you tasted it yet?" The footnote, written in pencil, reads: "Don't eat meat, eat heritage!" In the copy of Jean-Baptiste Debret's[4] watercolour *Wise Man Working in His Office*, he included an indigenous man sitting on a log in the gloom and watching a European man taking notes in his field notebook. At the bottom of the image, he added the provocation: "the modern anthropologist was born old."

---

[4] Jean-Baptiste Debret (1768–1848) was a French painter and draftsman who traveled to Brazil in 1817, along with other French artists, with the mission of founding a fine arts academy in Rio de Janeiro. In his book *Voyage pittoresque et historique au Brésil* (1834–1839), Debret visually documents aspects of Brazilian nature and social life in the early 19th century, including portraits of African slaves, indigenous peoples and European explorers.

In 2019 Denilson Baniwa has curated a surprising show of Brazilian contemporary indigenous artists, held at the Arts Centre of the Fluminense Federal University, in Rio de Janeiro. It was a modest event in terms of size and budget, but its pioneering spirit is undeniable in putting together indigenous artists from diverse ethnic groups and regions of Brazil. The curatorial concept of this exhibition, titled *Re-Anthropophagy*, was meant to re-cannibalise the Brazilian art by restoring to use native cultural elements and repertoires that had been appropriated by white intellectuals and artists since the colonial times.

In a solo show in 2018, *O Agro Não é Pop* [Agro Is Not Pop], Denilson discussed the industrial agribusiness issue in Brazil and the harmful consequences of the use of pesticides. One of the most impressive works was a video with old black-and-white footage of planes used in the Vietnam War spraying Agent Orange over the Vietnamese land combined and alternated with recent footage of small planes of Brazilian landowners, which sprayed pesticides containing the same poison in their chemical composition not only over their plantations, but also over nearby indigenous villages.

Denilson Baniwa's intervention in a famous historical monument consecrated to colonial adventurers was also remarkable. The so-called *bandeirantes* were explorers who crossed the land in the seventeenth century, captured Indians to enslave them and who searched for precious metals and stones. Despite their being violent and rude, they were hailed as heroes in late nineteenth century after Brazil's independence. There are many monuments in honour of the *bandeirantes* in Sao Paulo, the largest of which being the *Monumento às Bandeiras* [Monument to the Sao Paulo Expeditions], sculpted by Victor Brecheret in 1953. It lies in front of the Ibirapuera Park, one of the largest green areas in the city.

In 2013 the Guarani Yvyrupa Commission, a political organisation that coordinates initiatives of the Guarani people, held a demonstration in which a red cloth was raised. It represented their ancestors' blood spilt by the *bandeirantes*. Some non-indigenous supporters, who wanted to offer their support, painted the monument with red paint during the night. This appeared in the press as vandalism in the following days. However, as the Guarani puts it: "with this gesture, the work is no longer a monument in honour of the genocides that decimated our people and it became a monument to our resistance".[5]

---

[5] Account given by Guarani leader Marcos Tupã. Accessed September 26, 2020. http://conpoema.org/?p=373.

Seven years later, during the novel Coronavirus pandemic, Afro-brazilian curator Hélio Menezes commissioned Denilson Baniwa to video map the *Monumento às Bandeiras*. Hence, he delivered another perspective of the history of Brazil. In Denilson's five-minute video called *Brazil, Indigenous Land*, Portuguese ships are destroyed by the powers of nature, powerful plants, primordial deities and mythical animals. This was just another step in Baniwa's long term project to decolonise the Brazilian history and Western art history.

A similar situation arose with his provocative performance at the 2018 Sao Paulo Art Biennale, where there were wooden masks of an unidentified indigenous people brought from Paraguay bearing no explanation at all, as well as giant photographs of another unidentified and extinct people from Tierra del Fuego. Disgusted qualitatively and quantitatively by indigenous representation in most part of Brazilian art exhibitions, Denilson Baniw addressed himself as a shaman-jaguar (in a powerful fusion of man and beast typical of Amerindian perspectivism) and tore the book he had bought at the Biennial bookstore called *A Brief History of Art*. While he was tearing the book, he said: "The history of art written by the whites is so brief that it leaves no room for other peoples. We need to rip, rewrite this history" (Baniwa 2018). Denilson Baniwa presented a similar performance at Sao Paulo Museum of Art (MASP) in March 2019. Brook Andrew, curator of the Sydney Biennale coming later in 2019, was present at the event and invited Baniwa to attend the Biennale that year. In 2019 Baniwa was also given the Professional Art Investor Award for Contemporary Art (Pipa), one of the most important arts awards in Brazil.

The sign in Figure 6.7 was produced in a workshop coordinated by Denilson Baniwa in Sao Paulo, 2018. The participants jointly produced protest signs employing the stencil technique and showing messages related to the current indigenous situation in Brazil—land invasion, social invisibility, environmental destruction. The next day, the group distributed those signs around the city centre with messages like "Sao Paulo, indigenous land" and "Demarcating indigenous lands means protecting the forests." As this article is being written, part of the Amazon is in flames and the president-elect says that he will authorise mining and logging on indigenous lands. Finally, it is worth pointing out the reappearance of the jaguar in the Amerindian arts associated with the shaman—who is able to turn into such an animal and see the world through the jaguar's perspective. The jaguar is also linked to political power. In the Xingu region, for example, "A chief is groomed in the image of a feline: as a novice, his ears are pierced by another chief who attacks him with a sharp jaguar bone; as a young fighter, he moves and snarls like a formidable predator; as a ritual owner, he carries the necklace of claws, the belt and the hat of a jaguar" (Fausto 2017, 664).

Figure 6.7 "Forest standing, fascism on the ground." Serially-produced political sign by Denilson Baniwa, print on paper, 2019.

Photograph by Ilana Goldstein.

Unfortunately, jaguars and boa constrictors, key animals in Amerindian cosmologies, have appeared charred. As this chapter is being written, many forests and reserves are burning in Brazil, generally as a result of arson committed by agribusinessmen, miners and loggers. Apart from that, indigenous leaders, such as chief Aritana, from Xingu, died during the COVID-19 pandemic, as well as indigenous artists and educators. The federal government minimises environmental and social losses and accuses the indigenous peoples of starting the fire with the support of international NGOs.

At the same time, the Sao Paulo Art Biennale, postponed to 2021 because of the pandemic, will spotlight two indigenous artists from Brazil in its programme: Jaider Esbell and Gustavo Caboco. Such an unprecedented fact has to be celebrated. The Sao Paulo Museum of Art announced a major exhibition of indigenous art to be held in 2023, something unprecedented, too. So, the artistic realm seems to be one of the few that currently welcomes them, values their knowledge and expressive forms and raises the visibility of the indigenous cause.

Final remarks

As the reader may have noticed, these thoughts are in between anthropology and art history. Some art historians have criticised their discipline for being based on an ethnocentric and exclusionary concept that isolates Euro-American art from "contamination" by ethnic and popular arts (Belting 1995; 2008). Anthropology on the other hand, by encouraging the study of forms of expression that do not fit into the Euro-American canons and models, contributes to a questioning of this concept of "art", in preference for more elastic definitions (Morphy 2008).

In Brazil, for example, reference to indigenous "handicrafts" is very frequent. The term "handicraft", or artefact, is used to denote something produced with an economic and utilitarian purpose, that is, with extra-aesthetic motivations. But the opposite, the totally "disinterested" artwork—as in the concept of "art for the art's sake"—rarely exists. So, when someone refers to a piece of work as handicraft what is at stake is not the description of a phenomenon but, rather, the creation of a hierarchy based on hegemonic Western categories—where art is superior. In view of this the expression "indigenous handicraft or artefact" is problematic.

If the classification of objects and works of art is dynamic and reversible, as James Clifford (1988) has shown, questioning how categories are established in the art world and claiming the status of art for indigenous creations is a way of contributing to reducing the situation of marginalisation where these populations often find themselves.

There is certainly no universal shared concept that is "art", and we cannot always find words equivalent to art in non-Western societies. It is undeniable, however, that each people or culture can itself recognise its own unique forms of expression (such as dance steps, drumbeats, visual repertoires and chants) and in turn be recognised for them by others (Geertz 1993). Moreover, even without the endorsement of the legitimating authorities, many objects and practices have what Paraguayan scholar Tício Escobar calls "artisticity, which is the power to mobilize us by means of their forms, to make us feel small shocks and associate ideas" (Escobar 2008).

Alfred Gell's approach is particularly interesting here, as it depends neither on aesthetic criteria nor on institutional labels. According to the author, works of art are those in which we project our own intentions and agency (Gell 2006). This materialisation of human gestures and relations is what fascinates us about artistic objects—which may exist in any society (Gell 1998). Gell's theory helps to think about the many examples of Amerindian arts presented throughout this chapter, since all of them, including Denilson Baniwa's provocative works, have something in common: they condense and objectify relations between men or between men and things/spirits/animals.

I argue that "Indigenous arts" can be both a body painting made for a ritual in a remote Amazonian village and a painting on canvas displayed in a contemporary art museum. I believe the term is appropriate for indigenous expressive forms, with the caveat that it is used with some care: always using the plural; by keeping in mind how thorny the art category is; by being aware that nothing is produced or performed merely for contemplation. In indigenous cultures it is often impossible to separate form, meaning and the capacity for agency.

There is certainly the risk of misappropriation, asymmetry in economic negotiations, stereotyping and misunderstanding when the Western art world represents and deals with its' Others. But at the same time seduced and captivated by the sophistication and density of Amerindian arts, non-indigenous audiences, while broadening their aesthetic horizons and their imaginations, may also develop greater empathy towards and closeness with indigenous peoples, and help them cope with their current serious issues.

Macuxi Jaider Esbell wrote that "contemporary indigenous art is a specific case of empowerment in the cosmological field, a way of thinking about humanity and the environment" (Esbell 2018, 99). Guarani Cristine Takuá, in a talk delivered in Sao Paulo in April 2019, said that she sees hope in the arts for her people to continue sowing for the future.

As more indigenous creators and intellectuals have voice and space in the public sphere as well as in academic systems, and as anthropologists and art historians intensify their dialogues, we will have an increasingly open, plural and "decolonised" art history. I hope that this chapter and this book as a whole will help to strengthen the anthropological approach to the study of art, and that they will shed light on the mechanisms of physical exclusion and symbolic marginalisation that have been operating in the national and global art systems.

References

Aguillar, Gabriela. 2018. *Criatividade visual e transformações entre o povo Matipu do Alto Xingu*. Dissertation to the State University of Campinas for a Master's degree in Social Anthropology. Campinas.

Arruti, José Maurício. 1997. "A emergência dos 'remanescentes': notas para o diálogo entre indígenas e quilombolas". *Mana* 3 (2): 7–38. http://dx.doi.org/10.1590/S0104-93131997000200001.

Baniwa, Denilson. 2018. "Pajé-Onça Hackeando a 33ª Bienal de Artes de São Paulo." YouTube video, 16:09. Accessed November 7, 2018. https://www.youtube.com/watch?v=MGFU7aG8kgI.

Bartolomé, Miguel Alberto. 2006. "As etnogêneses: velhos atores e novos papéis no cenário cultural e político." *Mana* 12 (1): 39–68. http://dx.doi.org/10.1590/S0104-93132006000100002.

Belting, Hans. 1995. *Das Ende der Kunstgeschichte: Eine Revision nach zehn Jahren*. Munich: Beck.

Belting, Hans. 2008. "Contemporary Art and the Museum in the Global Age." In *Forum Permanente de Museus* [online]. http://www.forumpermanente.org/journal/articles/contemporary-art-and-the-museum-in-the-global-age-1.

Carvalho, Maria Rosário and Ugo Maia Andrade. 2014. "Índio, Índios." In *Dicionário crítico das ciências sociais dos países de fala oficial portuguesa*, edited by Lívio Sansone and Cláudio Furtado, 215–251. Brasília: Brazilian Association of Anthropology.

Cesarino, Pedro. 2012. "A escrita e os corpos desenhados: transformações do conhecimento xamanístico entre os Marubo." *Revista de Antropologia* 55 (1): 437–471. https://doi.org/10.11606/2179-0892.ra.2012.47583

Clifford, James. 1988. "Collections". In *The Predicament of Culture*, Part III. Cambridge, Mass.: Harvard University Press.

Cohn, Clarice. 2010. "A criança, a morte e os mortos: o caso mebengokré-xikrin." *Horizontes Antropológicos* 16 (34): 93–115. http://dx.doi.org/10.1590/S0104-71832010000200005.

Cunha, Manuela Carneiro da, ed. 1992. In *História dos Índios no Brasil*. Sao Paulo: Companhia das Letras/Fapesp.

Duran, Maria Raquel da Cruz. 2017. *Padrões que conectam: o Godidigo e as redes de socialidade Kadiwéu*. Doctor's degree thesis in Social Anthropology. University of Sao Paulo.

Esbell, Jaider. 2018. "Arte indígena contemporânea." *Select Magazine* 2007 (39). Sao Paulo: Editora Três.

Escobar, Tício. 2008. *El mito del arte y el mito del pueblo*. Santiago: Ediciones Metales Pesados.

Fausto, Carlos. 2017. "Chefe jaguar, chefe árvore: afinidade, ancestralidade e memória no Alto Xingu." *Mana* 23 (3): 653–676. http://dx.doi.org/10.1590/167849442017v23n3p653.

Gallois, Dominique. 2012. "Donos, detentores e usuários da arte gráfica kusiwa". *Revista de Antropologia* 55 (1): 20–49. https://doi.org/10.11606/2179-0892.ra.2012.46956.

Geertz, Clifford. 1983. "Art as a Cultural System." In *Local Knowledge: Further Essays in Interpretive Anthropology*, Clifford Geertz, 94–120. New York: Basic Books.

Gell, Alfred. 1998. *Art and Agency: An Anthropological Theory*. Third edition. Oxford, Clarendon Press.

Gell, Alfred. 2006. "Vogel's Net: Traps as Artworks and Artworks as Traps." In *The Anthropology of Art: A Reader*, edited by Howard Morphy and Morgan Perkins, 219–330. Cornwell: Blackwell Publishing.

Goldstein, Ilana, and Beatriz Labate. 2018. "From the Forest to the Museum: Notes on the Artistic and Spiritual Collaboration between Ernesto Neto and the Huni Kuin people." In *The Expanding World: Ayahuasca Diaspora*, edited by Beatriz Labate, and Clancy Cavnar, 76–94. London: Routledge.

Kopenawa, Davi, and Bruce Albert. 2013. *The Falling Sky. Words of a Yanomami Shaman*. Cambridge: Harvard University Press.

Lagrou, Els. 2007. *A fluidez da forma: arte, alteridade e agência em uma sociedade amazônica (Kaxinawa, Acre)*. Rio de Janeiro: TopBooks.

Lagrou, Els. 2009. *Arte indígena no Brasil. Agência, alteridade e relação*. Rio de Janeiro: C/Arte.

Lévi-Strauss, Claude. 1948. *Le serpent au corps rempli de poissons*. Paris: Société des américanistes/Musée de l'homme.

Lima, Tânia Stolze. 1996. "O dois e seu múltiplo: reflexões sobre o perspectivismo em uma cosmologia tupi." *Mana* 2 (2), 21–47. https://doi.org/10.1590/S0104-93131996000200002.

Maroja, Camila. 2019. "The Persistence of Primitivism: Equivocation in Ernesto Neto's A Sacred Place and Critical Practic." *Arts* 8 (2). doi:10.3390/arts8030111.

Morphy, Howard. 2008. *Becoming art: Exploring Cross Cultural Categories*. Sydney: University of South Australia Press.

Neto, Aristóteles Barcelos. 2002. *A arte dos sonhos. Uma iconografia ameríndia*. Lisbon: National Museum of Ethnology / Assírio & Alvim.

Neto, Aristóteles Barcelos. 2008. *Apapaatai: rituais de máscaras no Alto Xingu*. Sao Paulo: EDUSP / FAPESP.

Oliveira Filho, João Pacheco. 2012. "A refundação do Museu Maguta: etnografia de um protagonismo indígena." In *Coleções e colecionadores. A polissemia das práticas*, edited by Aline Montenegro, and Rafael Zamorano, 201–218. Rio de Janeiro: National Historical Museum.

Schapiro, Roberta, and Nathalie Heinich. 2012. "When is Artification?" *Contemporary Aesthetics* 4 (Special Volume Artification). Accessed September 1, 2019. http://www.contempaesthetics.org/newvolume/pages/article.php?article ID=639.

Severi, Carlo. 2013. "O espaço quimérico: percepção e projeção nos atos do olhar." In *Quimeras em Diálogo: Grafismo e Figuração nas Artes Indígenas*, edited by Carlo Severi and Els Lagrou, 25–66. Rio de Janeiro: 7 Letras.

Silva, Aracy Lopes da and Agenor Farias. 1992. "Pintura corporal e sociedade: os "partidos" Xerente." In *Grafismo indígena. Estudos de Antropologia Estética*, edited by Lux Vidal, 89–116. Sao Paulo, Studio Nobel/Edusp/Fapesp.

van Velthem, Lúca Hussak. 1998. *A Pele de Tuluperê. Uma etnografia dos trançados Wayana*. Belém: Emílio Goeldi Museum of Pará.

Vidal, Lux. 1992. "A pintura corporal e a arte gráfica entre os Xikrin do Cateté." In *Grafismo indígena. Estudos de Antropologia Estética*, edited by Lux Vidal, 143–190. Sao Paulo, Studio Nobel/ Edusp/ Fapesp.

Viveiros de Castro, Eduardo. 1996. "Os pronomes cosmológicos e o perspectivismo ameríndio." *Mana* 2 (2): 115–144. https://doi.org/10.1590/S0 104-93131996000200005.

Viveiros de Castro, Eduardo. 2012. "Nature: The world as Affect and Perspective." In: *Cosmological Perspectivism in Amazonia and Elsewhere. Four Lectures given in the Department of Social Anthropology, University of Cambridge, February–March 1998*, 105–129. London: Hau Books. https://haubooks.org/cosmological-perspectivism-in-amazonia/.

Whan, Chang. 2012. *Iny: Karajá*. Rio de Janeiro: Museum of the Brazilian Native/FUNAI.

Chapter 7
Artwork and performances in the creation of Martinican history and culture

Magdalena Sophia Toledo
Universidad Alberto Hurtado, Chile

Abstract

The focus of this chapter is the agency of artworks and performances made by two visual artists from Martinique in the process of creating Martinican history and culture. In this process of creating that specific history and culture, the search for new themes and materials reflects a specific way of becoming artists, along with simultaneously becoming Martinican and Afro-Caribbean. Therefore, historic characters or episodes, like slavery, the maroons, indigenous or African heritage, are part of a performative process of rewriting Martinican history. That process becomes stronger with a generation of artists who elaborated a project with an aesthetic on the margins of the European canons, with a marked identity and political discourse. As a result, works of art are also offerings to divinities or historical counter-narratives; performances are also rituals against the old and new masters—rituals of purification, or experiences of historical events corporally inscribed. Therefore, considering the arguments elaborated by Alfred Gell in his book *Art and Agency* (1998), these artefacts are considered as agents in the process of production of Martinican history and elaboration of a "Martinican culture".

Keywords: Martinican art, slavery, identity, aesthetic cannibalism, culture

This chapter will take as a starting point the artwork of two visual artists in Martinique, Victor Anicet and René Louise, whose works are strongly related to debates about the constituent elements of Martinican culture and identity, as well as being about the history of the island from the inhabitants' point of view. Therefore, it makes sense to view their artwork as agents, according to Gell (1998), in a performative process of creation and rewriting of Martinican history, as well as of elaboration of elements that constitute today's "Martinican culture".

I met these artists during my fieldwork in Martinique between 2011 and 2013, for my PhD research about the artistic appropriations of the Martinican writer Aimé Césaire, one of the founders of the negritude movement and its primary exponent. The island of Martinique is a French department situated in the Lesser Antilles, and debates about identity on the island were always linked to this dual position of Martinicans, both Caribbean and French, which became even more complex after the emergence of negritude approaches.

In the year 2012, during which I lived in Martinique for five months continuously, Anicet and Louise became two of my primary informants. I visited their workshops, expositions, and other events and locations that they indicated as significant on various occasions. We had long conversations, sometimes recorded, sometimes not, about their creations, artistic evolution, and memories during these visits. This dialogue was accentuated in 2013 when, in addition to the fieldwork I did in Martinique, I was able to visit an exhibition of Martinican artists held in Paris, in which René Louise was one of the exhibitors.

Although I had not observed these artists during their creation processes, their works were the catalysts for these encounters. On these occasions, they would show me artworks that they considered relevant, and from these they discussed the motivations for their creation, the materials selected for their construction, their central themes, or the contexts in which they were produced. These creations were produced based upon ideas and concepts about Martinican identity and culture, the island's recent history, and their role as artists in the face of these topics. The belief that they had a commitment to these issues as artists was central, and it was through the production of these artefacts that they connected with the issues they considered to be most relevant in Martinican society. Among these was the idea of the necessity of preserving and publicising the set of elements associated with Martinican culture. In fact, I perceived that, for these artists, their creations represented a way of constructing and communicating Martinican identities through the artefacts they produced, with the intention of provoking similar questions in the audience.

Thus, the works of art were the mediators of the relationships I established with these artists, and through them I grew to know their artistic evolution and positioning. The artefacts also revealed how these artists connected themes that will appear throughout this chapter. Thus, from the interactions with these artists, which were mediated by their works, I followed the networks (Latour 2005) that they informed me about and that, in turn, connected concepts, stories, events, and people.

In this regard, an agenda of identity debates among Martinican visual artists and the consequent production of Martinican identity through these debates has been a project for a whole generation of artists. It was initiated in the 1970s by a movement called *École Negro-Caraïbe* and expanded by the reflections of the *Fwomajé* group founded by Victor Anicet in 1984. This group was comprised of five members, which included Louise. Anicet had the objective of elaborating a Martinican aesthetic in the field of visual arts. According to Donatien-Yssa (2009), this group can be considered one of the precursors to the creation of a language in Martinique visual arts.

The debates around the creation of a Martinican aesthetic, linked to specific notions concerning the elements that constitute a Martinican cultural identity, began in the literary field with the avant-garde magazines *Légitime Défense* and *Tropiques (1941–1945)* (Ménil et al. 1979 [1932]; Césaire et al. 1994). In these magazines, Martinican intellectuals engaged in Caribbean avant-garde debates on identity through the colonial experience. They saw themselves in a dualistic position, being creators of a Martinican identity but also being French. And they can be considered as precursors in the production of an anti-colonialist discourse and identity in Martinique. In particular, the magazine *Tropiques*, created by Aimé Césaire, Suzanne Césaire, and René Ménil, presented these debates after the emergence of the ideas of the *négritude* movement (Césaire et al. 1994). These writers linked the colonial experience with the fascist repression in Martinique and the racist expression during World War II (cf. Fanon 1964). These debates influenced an entire generation of visual artists in the 1960s and 1970s and contributed to the production of Martinique cultural identities through artefacts in the new circuit.

In spite of the brief existence of *École Negro-Caraïbe* and *Fwomajé*, many artists that participated in these movements carried out the project of "Martinique identities, history, and culture" via debates about aesthetics and politics through the production of artefacts.

In the specific case of the artists that are the focus of this chapter, their artwork and performances establish a larger dialogue with the themes and literary works of Martinican writers such as Aimé Césaire and Édouard Glissant. The latter was famous for his concept of relationship as an element of articulation and production of Martinique identities. Through the use of local materials, these artists create their own aesthetic in a social and political context in which the relationship with France and its colonial history are permanently present and are re-elaborated through their artefacts. I analyse the performative creation of these artefacts, as proposed by Gell (1998), not through semiotic interpretations, conversely, I examine how "artefacts of history" (Strathern 1990), concepts, and experiences are transformed into objects of art endowed with multiple agencies.

Victor Anicet: restitution and Martinican cosmogony

The idea of restoring fragments from Martinican history that are forgotten and hidden is what moves the creation of ceramist and visual artist Victor Anicet born in 1938 in Marigot. This idea has been present since his first exposition in 1970, on the subject of memory of slavery in Martinique, and was displayed for the first time in that exposition. The exposition *Signes* consisted of panels of plywood, with signs painted in black and white, using industrial ink. It demonstrated the artist's reflections about slavery, particularly about the Maroons, understood as icons of colonial resistance and later anticolonialists. The Maroons were African and afro-descendant slaves who were the protagonists of plantation escapes, rebellions, and other episodes of resistance against slavery.

Anicet's reflections are amplified by the books *Cadastre* and *Ferrements* by Aimé Césaire and by the works of Édouard Glissant, with whom he engaged in a lifetime dialogue and whose novel, *La Lézarde,* had a profound impact on him. The artist says that his objective is "to create a visual arts' reading of Martinique history" and to return events and characters that at that time were not part of the official historical narrative "to the Martinican people". With his first series, he inaugurated a resource that would become recurrent in subsequent visual artists' works: the utilisation of literary texts as a foundation for artwork as an alternative reference to the official story and as artefacts, according to Strathern (1990), together with materials considered "not official" or "not recognized" to the production of artwork.

According to Anicet, his exposition was not understood at the time and the theme he chose was considered provocative. Firstly, slavery was considered a "taboo theme," it was simply not discussed in Martinique; additionally, plywood and industrial ink were not considered adequate materials for the creation of artwork for the local public, whose imagination about visual arts was still strongly influenced by European aesthetics, and above all else, by French "fine arts," which even ignored avant-garde experimentation in Europe.

After this premiere, the artist continued to research the theme of slavery and five years later he presented the series *Carcans*, based on the distinct types of shackles used to chain slaves in the French colonies. During his creative process, he investigated the archives of the *Musée de l'Homme* and *Musée de la Porte Dorée* in Paris, where he found different drawings that portrayed the shackles used during the slavery period. The poems in Césaire's book *Ferrements* provide the foundation for the creation of the artwork in this series.

Similar to *Signes,* the forms in *Carcans* are not representations of shackles. These are shackles elaborated by Anicet in which historical events, documents, poems, and fragments of volcanic rock are appropriated as artefacts, are put in relation to, and recreated as artwork. These artefacts are appropriated as "artefacts of history" in the sense of Strathern (1990). In proposing that the Melanesians, by the way they conceive of time, must have perceived the European advent as a performance, Strathern (1990) makes an invitation for anthropologists to rethink their notions and the manners of using "history". As the author states, "an artifact or performance grasped for itself is grasped as an image. An image definitively exists out of context; or, conversely, it contains its own prior context" (Strathern 1990, 166). Thus, being perceived as a performance, "the European advent did not have to be put into its social context. Melanesians did not have to make sense of it" (Ibid.). Hence, as the author suggests, it is possible to "switch metaphors", and "extend our concept of artefact to performance and to event" (Strathern 1990, 174). When thinking about "artefacts as the enactment of events" (Ibid.), it is possible to consider the Melanesian form of creative appropriation of history as an invitation for anthropologists to abandon the practice of "contextualisation," "translation," and "interpretation," which are occidental references. History can be thought of as an artefact, something liable to be used, performed, and re-elaborated, instead of viewing it as a series of fixed events destined only to be "translated," "interpreted," or "contextualised".

On the one hand, similar to using history, Anicet used the historical event of slavery as an artefact in his creative process, relating it with artefacts-poems, artefacts-drawings, and artefacts-documents, to form non-figurative shackles, utilising a glazed ceramic technique. On the other hand, the fragments of volcanic rock he used are emphasised as artefacts that contain events. This stems from the eruption of the Pelée volcano that occurred in Saint Pierre, the capital of Martinique in 1902, which killed all of the city's inhabitants, with the exception of one man, who was held in a prison. In condensing both nature and history, the volcanic rock, as a guide to this event, appears related to force, unpredictability, and agency, associated so many times with both natural and historical events in the Martinican imaginary.[1]

In the series *Carcans,* Anicet also started to use the colour blue as a central element in his work, as a symbol of the Atlantic crossing. This colour evokes the pain of this crossing, which can be associated with other diasporic aesthetic manifestations like the blues, a musical expression of melancholy and sadness, which we can also relate to Martinican *blès*. The word *creole* recalls a deep inner wound, which is felt, but not seen, a feeling that is born from the common experience of the African diaspora and slavery. Later, the colour blue will be

---

[1] More than once I heard in the field, "After slavery, the eruption of the Pelée volcano is the biggest tragedy in the island's history."

used in artwork by the artist as a sign of the multiple relationships that took place in the Caribbean Sea before the arrival of the first Africans.

However, despite the force and novelty of his artwork regarding the period of slavery, it would be the theme of restitution of indigenous memory that would constitute the central axis for his reflections about Martinique aesthetics. Rarely evoked as an element that constitutes the Martinican culture—taking into consideration the official discourse that claims the original inhabitants of the island were completely exterminated with the arrival of the Europeans—for the artist, the indigenous presence survived in day-to-day artefacts, such as a wicker basket and a type of boat known as *gommier*. This is a canoe-type of boat, constructed with wood from a native tree of the same name, traditionally used by fishermen, just like Anicet's father. These canoes, no longer produced today, were transformed into a key object in the artist's reflections, who started to consider them as signs of relationships before the Atlantic crossing: "the *gommiers* are boats that permitted the Amerindians to traverse the whole Caribbean Sea." This thought contrasts with the general idea of insularity associated with the Caribbean islands, an opening idea—and of a privileged locus of relations—also present in the work of Glissant (1997a). By extension, the utilisation of the colour blue as a *signe de relation* (Glissant, 1997a) acquires new meaning in his artwork, encompassing the martial interactions present in the Caribbean before the African diaspora.

But beyond the artefacts, the indigenous presence survived underneath the earth, attested to by the fragments of Amerindian ceramics. Anicet found them during his youth as an assistant to the newly arrived Father Pinchon, an autodidact archaeologist interested in the ancient vestiges of the island's indigenous people.

The discovery of the artefacts which revealed the indigenous presence on the island, that are not mentioned in the identity discourse in Martinique, become an entry point for Anicet's primary investigations about aesthetics during the whole trajectory of his career. The use of ceramics is an indicator of the impact, that latter derived in researches in the archives of the *Musée de l'Homme* in Paris about the original populations of the Antilles.

The theme of the Amerindian culture as a constituent part of Martinique identity would be present in his subsequent works, and even eventually became the main subject of his work. It is relevant to mention, that just as his first works about slavery caused an initial strangeness in the Martinican public, this theme caused the same reaction, as the Martinique public expected that an artist who graduated in France would certainly reproduce the European classical patterns. Contradicting these expectations, Anicet began to reproduce some symbols present in the ceramic fragments found in the excavations during his youth—which are today part of the collection of the *Musée*

Départemental d'Archéologie et de Préhistoire of the capital, Fort-de-France. Subsequently, he began to create ceramic pieces that take the Amerindians as an initial reference, restoring, and above all else, recreating, the indigenous presence of the island through these artefacts in the present.

In *Restitution*, a series of artworks he elaborated beginning in 1989, the artist synthesised his aesthetic research into elements he considers to be central in the construction of Martinican culture and history in an exemplary way. Anicet prefers to call this series of works "trays," referencing the trays used for ceremonial purposes, which were brought by groups of Indians who arrived in Martinique to work on the sugarcane plantations after the abolition of slavery in 1848, and which were used for religious offerings. In *Restitution*, the artist presents the trays in a vertical position, using them to support different artefacts. These artefacts, such as mirrors, pearls, African fabrics, cacao seeds, and also small zoomorphic and anthropomorphic ceramic sculptures similar to those found in excavations in which the artist participated as a child, which according to Anicet, had historically been used to establish relationships between Amerindians and Europeans, Europeans and Africans, Africans and *creoles* (cf. Bernabé et al. 1993).

For the artist, utilising these objects in the creation of the trays is a form of cannibalising[2] them by utilising and imbuing them with other meanings, "creating his own cosmogony".[3] In fact, the Martinican writer and philosopher Édouard Glissant defined Anicet's work in *Restitution* as "aesthetic cannibalism" (Hachad and Loichot 2012). For Anicet, this act of creative cannibalisation could also be considered to be a continuation of the acts of appropriation and creative incorporation made throughout the Martinican history of the same elements present in the work. In this manner, making the trays is also a way to recreate Martinique's history, marked by silences, omissions, and voids.

---

[2] The way the artist uses the idea of cannibalism resonates with the concept of "cultural anthropophagy" articulated by the Brazilian Oswald de Andrade. Although Anicet, at the time of his reflections, was not familiar with Andrade's *Anthropophagic Manifest*, it is a similar use of "swallowing of the other" (whether it is the "other external," European, or the "other internal," indigenous or African) for thinking about how to constitute Brazilian identity. Swallowing is an active movement, linked to the idea of incorporation, which excludes the possibility of thinking about contact with foreigners as a passive acculturation. It is interesting to note that, at the same time as the *Anthropophagic Manifest*, the Martinican writer Suzanne Roussi Césaire thought similarly about the emergence of the Martinican poetry: "La poésie martiniquaise sera cannibale ou ne sera pas" ("Misère d'une poésie, John-Antoine Nau". *Tropiques* 4, janvier, 1942).
[3] As the artist remarked in an interview (Martinique, May 17, 2012).

The idea of creating one's own cosmogony is particularly significant in Martinique (as well as in the Caribbean in general), if we keep in mind its heterogenous formation. That formation was marked by, among other events, "the swift genocide of the aboriginal populations, the early integration of the region into the international circuit of capital, the forced migrations of enslaved African", as Trouillot (1992, 20) expressed it.

In the same way, authors such as Hall (1990), Mintz (1996), and Clifford (1998)—the latter, using this constitutive heterogeneity as an image that is "good for thinking" of his project as postmodern anthropology—consider the ruptures and discontinuities as constituting the Caribbean's own brand. The theme of "origins" becomes a discursive field that is, by definition, permanently disputed and constructed.

Thus, the theme of origins was part of the reflections from innumerable intellectuals and artists, stemming from the negritude movement started in Paris in the 1930s—the Martinican poet Aimé Césaire was one of its main exponents—to the debates promoted by the authors of the *créolité* from the 1980s in Martinique's literary field (Césaire 2004; 2006; 2009).

In this area, one of the most interesting topics refers to how to establish a debate about "identity" in a society constituted by "non-autochthonous" peoples who, moreover, by the very situation of violence and depersonalisation in which they arrived on the island, have countless reasons to enact Glissant's idea of the "clamour for the right to opacity" (Glissant 1997b, 194). In response to this dilemma, the same author (Glissant 1990, 1997b) suggests that, instead of a search for the African origins of the Martinique people based on a notion of fixed identity—as suggested by the negritude movement—consideration should be given to the relationship itself as the element establishing and instituting the Martinican people. A relationship that was initially born on the slave ships, from the pain of the Atlantic crossing and the progressive and necessary forgetfulness: in the displacement produced by this historical event, it is the ocean itself that preserves the memory of this relationship. Hence the artist's choice of the colour blue.

Blues, which can be associated with Martinican *blès*, as previously mentioned, a Martinique *creole* word, is a term that denominates a type of deep wound that one feels but cannot see, and can be linked with the common diasporic experience. Anicet understood the elaboration of the tone of blue in one of his paintings, a search that concluded with what he called, "the blue of *blès*," a repository of history as well, as are the images evoked by the poem of Derek Walcott *The Sea of History*. Thus, poems and concepts can also be thought of as artefacts and agents of relationships, in the process of elaboration of the artist's artwork.

Additionally, the idea of the ocean as an immense blue of *blès* is also understood as a locus of relations in the context of the African diaspora. Thus, it is possible to establish a link between the concept of Relation of Glissant (1990, 1997b), utilised by Anicet, and the idea of *The Black Atlantic* (Gilroy, 1993). In his famous book, Gilroy considers the crossing of the Atlantic as an event that produced a painful but common experience among black people in the Americas and the Caribbean, and he also sees this as an installer of new forms of creativity which will later form a "counterculture for modernity" (Gilroy 2001, 33). Like Glissant, Gilroy considers the boat to be a locus from which the first diasporic experiences were formed.

Thus, we see that the slave ships are very powerful artefacts for thinking about the diasporic experience, both for its evocation of the pain of this experience and for being the place where the first exchanges, alliances, and interactions between Africans and the Caribbean took place. Stemming from this concept, authors such as Mintz and Price (1973) locate this artefact as the initiation place for African-American society's product of these first trades.

In the case of Martinique, the boat is constituted as the first locus of creation of new alliances and identities, which were strengthened and diversified in the plantations. Moreover, it witnessed, according to Glissant (1990, 1997a), the rhizomatic character of the relationship. The author evokes the concept of the "rhizome as antigenealogy" in this sense, initially elaborated by Deleuze and Guattari (1995). He reflects thus on the Antillean issue: like a rhizome, the first instances of contact that are established are, at the same time, installers of new relationships.

Moreover, for Glissant (1990, 1997a) the populations that are constituted by this experience of the African diaspora and slavery carry with them the "sign of Relation": "There is a difference between the displacement (by exile or dispersion) of people that continue to exist in another part [of the world] and the transportation (or trafficking) of a population from one place to another that *transform themselves into another thing*, a new data in the world" (Glissant 1997a, 40).[4] For the author, the Antilles are *multi-relational*—"the sea of the Antilles is the estuary of the Americas"—and he proposes a new conception of the common situation of insularity. Instead of isolation, this new idea offers openness, and, above all else, the notion that new relationships are constantly formed, instead of solely imprinting a fixed image from the first contact. The idea of insularity as imprisonment is associated with the concept of a fixed, tree-like identity (Deleuze and Guattari 1995) and with a lack of perception of the creative potential of the relationship. For these philosophers, the tree-like

---

[4] English translation from the French original.

matrix has dominated occidental thought, which bases itself in hierarchies that predate the individual and limit or suppress the expressions of multiplicity, rupture, and continuity.

Following the concept of *relation* created by Glissant to define the fundamental base of Martinican identity, the Tray is selected by Anicet as a *signe de relation* (Glissant 1997a, 41) par excellence in his cosmogony of Martinican society. Trays initially performed a religious function. Through their use as ceremonial trays by the Indian plantation workers, they were progressively redefined. The plantation's inhabitants used them for the most basic daily tasks. They transformed them into containers for transporting sugar cane and other objects, into cribs for babies who accompanied their mothers that worked on the plantation, and later, in the emerging cities of the late nineteenth century, they were used for displaying fruits and vegetables at street markets. In their various uses throughout Martinican history, the tray condenses the experience of the African, Indian, and creole workers of the plantations and first Martinican cities, as an agent of diverse social relationships.

Additionally, by putting the tray in an upright position—removing the horizontal position that permits its everyday use—Anicet intended to restore its original sacred function, considering that it was distorted by the different appropriations it was subjected to throughout Martinique's history. Similarly, by putting reproductions of Amerindian amulets in his works, Anicet restores the ritual functions of these artefacts, which were underestimated by the Europeans in their attitudes of contempt and ignorance about their uses and meanings. Thus, by "making his own cosmogony," the artist also seeks a way to restore the potency of these artefacts, through art.

Furthermore, Anicet selects the tray as a key object from which he begins his reflections on the material conditions in which the first Indians arrived in 1848, after the abolition of slavery in Martinique, as compared to the first Africans who arrived at the island's ports. For Anicet, a fundamental difference, in relation to the Africans who arrived in conditions of slavery, was the Indians' possibility to carry artefacts from their culture with them on their journey. Expanding upon this idea, it can be said that the Indians could bring their "entire" culture with them as an artefact, which strongly contrasts with the fragmented experience of the first Africans.

Thus, the artist proposes that Indian culture is not only "represented" by the tray artefact, but Indian culture is, in itself, an artefact that the Indians could carry with them. And because they brought with them a "whole" artefact-culture (also via artefacts of their culture such as the trays), upon their arrival they could immediately establish relationships. The multiple uses of the trays, rapidly incorporated into the daily life of the plantations, are the best example of these relationships, which were given above all through the exchanges and appropriations mediated by this agent. This image of an artefact-culture that could be brought "whole" can be extended and contrasted with the fragmented artefact-culture of the first enslaved Africans who arrived on the island (they themselves were also fragmented, morally and psychologically), as well as with the fragments of Amerindian culture that diminished after French domination. Hence the artist's choice of this artefact, in particular to structure his cosmogony of Martinican society.

Thus, from the proposal in *Restitution*, the tray can be seen as an agent that contains and structures other ephemeral elements of the relationship, via the allegory of Martinique's creation from the artist's viewpoint. As a type of object-synthesis of multiple appropriations, the tray can be considered to be an agent of multiple relationships throughout the history of Martinique, and it holds this expanded meaning in the work of Anicet. In the *Restitution* series, the artist not only used this artefact that is, in itself, an agent of social relations, as a support for other artefacts. Within the piece, he also connects other artefacts that can equally be considered agents of relationships, such as Amerindian amulets, native seeds and leaves, pearls, mirrors, and tissues, all objects that were exchanged in the first instances of contact between the original inhabitants of the islands and the first colonisers. Hence, he establishes the creation of a Martinican universe by way of a demiurge, re-created in the new relationships among the artefacts that have been reimagined in the trays he created. From this perspective, the work of art itself establishes new relationships.

Once more the artist chooses a group of people that, in the discourse of Martinican identity constitution, has been considered to be of lesser importance as the centre of his reflections. The choice of an artefact which was used by the Indians in their religious ceremonies as an object that will support other artefacts in his allegory of Martinican creation is a subversive act by the artist, especially if we take into account that African culture is commonly considered to be the basis of Martinican culture. Thus, the Indian artefacts can be considered as even more foreign elements in the common discourse of Martinican identity. Furthermore, we should not overlook that the Indians who arrived in Martinique along with the end of slavery held jobs with extremely precarious salaries, suffering distinct forms of discrimination that were perpetuated for decades.

Anicet's tray can also be considered as a "vehicle of complex intentionalities," as Gell explains in his article "Vogel's Net" (1996). Reinforced by the use of historical artefacts as a medium for his artwork, the viewer's gaze is directed to the complex intentionalities incorporated in the artefacts themselves. Thus, by transforming them into works of contemporary art, the artist allows for a reflection upon the network of meanings incorporated in them, revealing the complexity of non-western creativity present in the process of constituting the Martinican culture.

René Louise: artefacts of power and the power of the work of art

Art and ritual go hand-in-hand in the creative process of René Louise, and in the production of his paintings, installations, and performances. Martinican history is re-elaborated from the connection with divinities, especially with those from Haitian voodoo. In his work, the artist relates these divinities to specific episodes of Martinican history, also presenting them as interpretive models of important historical characters present in the Martinican imaginary, such as the Maroons.

René Louise chooses the figure of the Maroon as an image-synthesis of colonial resistance. He appropriates this character and re-creates it in many of his pieces. In Martinique, the meaning attributed to the *nègre marron* on various occasions is associated with the demarcation of political positions, indicated in the post-departmentalisation period, particularly with an anti-assimilationist and anti-colonialist position linked with the creation of an identity discourse (Jolivet 1987). Thus, the *nègre marron* became an icon in the process of "identity reconstruction" (Jolivet 1987, 290), to the detriment of characters like the French abolitionist Victor Schoelcher, associated with the assimilationist position in this new context. In the same way, the three biggest literary movements in Martinique (*négritude*, *antillanité*, *créolité*) played a fundamental role in the constitution of that historical protagonist. This became a target of distinct disputations of meaning, relating to different political stances (Jolivet 1987; Price and Price 1997).

For Louise, the image of the *nègre marron* as a resistance icon offers countless possibilities, not only as a critique of the colonial period but also as a way of thinking about modern Martinique. Hence, the Maroon is appropriated as a powerful icon in creating a narrative of resistance to the colonial regime, apart from its use as an icon of resistance to the complex forms of oppression present in contemporary Martinique.

Furthermore, the phenomenon of marronage is taken as a starting point from which the artist formulates his artistic manifesto. In Louise's *Manifeste du Marronisme Moderne* (1998 [1979]), he elaborates an aesthetic theory related to the identity discourse that discusses the elements that form a Martinican identity, beginning with their relationship with the Caribbean, Africa, and Latin America. Thus, marronage is used as a subversive image that should be applied to artistic performances. In this context, Louise creates the term "conceptual marronage," a reflection very close to the concept of "cultural marronary" by René Depestre. He considers it to be a response to the "conceptual violence" which weighs upon the Caribbean and Latin American artists, as they suffer from the "imposition of models of expression," the exoticisation or exclusion of their artistic manifestations in big international events (Louise 1998 [1979],16).

In the semi-colonial context lived by Martinicans, the artist composes his theory, beginning with his condition as a Martinican artist, whose possibilities of entering the international circuit are mediated—and strongly delimited—by legitimation criteria defined by the French capital, especially during the period when the book was written. Since Martinique is a French region, these artists can eventually access more resources, in comparison to other Caribbean artists. Paradoxically, for the same reason, the circulation of their artwork is limited by the category of "ultramarine artists," with all the colonial exoticism inherent in that expression. In this sense, the possibility of interlocution and insertion in certain international circuits, including dialogue with other Caribbean artists, is limited. This is one of the many paradoxes of departmentalisation so well-analysed by Glissant (1990, 1997a). In his creation of an aesthetic theory, Louise not only shows Martinican specificities but also shows the situation of partial and peripheral integration into French society by the Martinicans (and consequently, their artists). He seeks an approximation with other Caribbean and Latin American societies, understanding them as models of society that are equally dominated. This explains the presence in his manifesto of certain generalizations of the current forms of domination, taking the Martinican model as a point of reference.

Thus, starting from conceptual marronage as a form of resistance, Louise conceives the artistic creation as a way of recovering the "visionary role" of the artist, and defines himself as a "shaman artist." He compares his process of creation to a ritual, referring to the learning process as well as referring to the effects generated by the produced artefacts in the artist and also in the audience.

The ritual aspect of art is evidenced above all else by his performances. These occur outdoors, in places such as on the beach, in a forest, or on the banks of a river, according to the spiritual forces he wishes to evoke. As the artist revealed to me: "I come to the place, and I ask a spirit to inhabit me. And then I proceed".[5] This mixture between spirituality and artistic creation manifests via a bricolage of elements of diverse, non-occidental religions. Thus, in his installations and performances, he uses symbols of voodoo *loas*, African masks, shamanic symbols of different traditions or precious stones, all considered to be sources of power and transcendence. In accordance with what he explains

---

[5] Conversation during fieldwork. Martinique, 2012.

in his performance *Hommage aux ancêtres,* what he is seeking is to create a synthesis, in which he evokes the Amerindians, Africans, and Indians that constitute the Martinique people, by appropriating their rituals and symbols. In this process, he permits himself to be affected by the artefacts incorporated in his artwork, deliberately mixing the boundaries between the spiritual and the artistic in practice and aesthetic discourse.

In his artistic production, it is also possible to find elements that reflect this conceptualisation of the combination of art with a sort of spiritual experience. One example is the story about the production of the work *Le Masque Sacré,* inspired by the experience of the Martinican poet Aimé Césaire in Casamance, Senegal. Césaire found a mask that displayed red horns and small mirrors used in an initiation ritual and he was impressed with its similarity to the Red Devil mask used in a Martinican carnival. When reflecting upon this episode, the poet was convinced that this was, ultimately, the same mask that survived slavery and the diaspora. He remarked: "And so, what has happened? In this colonial society, the God of the defeated was transformed into the devil of the victor".[6] Thus, Césaire referred to the disqualification of the African' gods from the Christian tradition, and above all else, to the process of re-elaboration of meanings and uses of artefacts of African power in a colonial society as a form of survival. Moreover, he pointed to the admirable capacity for resistance (simultaneously "cultural" and "spiritual") demonstrated by the African populations enslaved in the Caribbean and the Americas. It is important to remember that various "creole stories" portray the devil as an omnipresent character, who permanently torments the supposed victors who are not capable of anticipating nor containing their agency. In the artwork, Césaire's story about the Senegalese mask and its connection with the Martinican mask was more than a source of inspiration. It served as a foundation and a structure for the artwork, indicating the connections that the artist would make.

Le Masque Sacré is part of the *Cercles Solaires* series created by the artist: non-figurative metal paintings in circular formats, 80 to 90 centimetres in diameter on average, with applications of materials such as precious stones and other objects. On the metal structure painted in gold and red, three horns, as well as blue and red stones, stand out. In the centre of the work, which makes reference simultaneously to the red devil mask from the Martinican carnival and to the

---

[6] Excerpt from an interview in which Césaire reflects on the episode: "Or, ce masque, je le connaissais fort bien; mais chez nous on ne le porte que durant le carnaval et il représente le diable. *Alors, qu'est-ce qui est arrivé? Dans cette société coloniale, le dieu du vaincu est devenu le diable du vainqueur*". Accessed October 12, 2014. http://www.potomitan.info/cesaire/politique.php.

traditional Senegalese mask *Ejumba,* he presents a deformed face. Louise refers to this work as a "loaded" work, with "weight," and reports that, as he progressed in its production, he had a difficult time looking at it straight on. As Louise pointed out to me while commenting on the process of creating this work, "I worked looking to the side; it seemed that a spirit had come to inhabit the work."[7]

This account condenses the way the artist understands many of the artefacts he produces, suggesting the intervention of multiple agencies in his creation process. In the case of *Le Masque Sacré,* it is a hidden force, which one does not know how to classify. This is reminiscent of Gell (1999) when he analyses the frequency in which works of art are seen to be transcending the technical schemes of their creators (Gell 1999, 181). In his analysis of technical production, Gell argues that the magical effects generated by works of art, magic, and technical efficiency are interconnected: "magic haunts technical activity like a shadow; or rather, magic is the negative contour of work" (Gell, 1999, 181). That confers upon the artist an ambiguous position, "half-technician and half-mystagogue" (Gell 1999, 182). For Louise, it is this "ambiguity" that gives meaning to his creative process, and he allows himself to be "captured" by the magical effects of the work of art—letting himself be guided, as well, by different agencies in his creative process. This is part of, and is something to be expected during the process. Because he was trained as an artist-shaman, Louise allows himself to be affected in the same manner by the effects of his technical efficiency (which, in turn, is a double efficiency, artistic and mystic). Moreover, the artist himself aims for this undefined aspect, and the last indecipherable analysis, between the magical and the technical, are both presented in his works and in his creative process.

Another example is *Voyage Triangulaire,* which references slave ships and the Atlantic crossing, presented in conjunction with the work *Hommage a Ogun et a les ancêtres africains* in the *Agora Mundo* exhibition, in 2013 in Paris. In the centre of *Voyage Triangulaire,* part of the *Cercles Solaires* of Louise, is a painting that summons an image of a ship, and small dolls lying down and overlapping each other, barely contained by the ship's borders, give a sensation of being piled up. These bodies in relief reinforce the visual sensation. Contrary to other *Cercles Solaires,* in this work, Louise intentionally uses more figurative language.

Elaborated particularly for this exhibition, *Hommage a Ogun et a les ancêtres africains* draws attention for its similarity to that of the *candomblé* in Brazil, known as an *ebó,* an offering made for an *orixa* (divinised African ancestors) with

---

[7] Conversation during fieldwork. Martinique, 2012.

the aim of producing a certain effect on a person or a situation. The work is supported by a tray with a black background, upon which stylized *vèvès*, drawings used to evoke divinities from Haitian voodoo, are painted in red. These are of Ogun Ferraille, the leader of the phalanx of the Oguns soldiers. He is a warrior spirit who is also evoked as a protagonist in the historical narrative of the Haitian Revolution (Dayan 1995). In this, Ogun is not only a "representation" of the "spirit of the bellicose resistance that, in the Haitian nationalist mythos, dominated the history of the country of the rebellious slaves and bands of maroons of the eighteenth century" (Burton 1997, 250). It is also important to emphasise his role as an agent of this revolution, standing at the side of the men and women with their legions of "horses," and of the phalanxes of the Ogun soldiers.

Along these lines, Louise evokes this powerful agent in his installation—*ebó* and, in the centre of the tray, he places a caiman, painted red, which has a copy of the *Code Noir* tied to its mouth. Toads or lizards with their mouths tied, in turn, are buried in Martinique in the rituals of *quimbois* with the intention of producing a certain effect, a practice that had previously been used on plantations by former slaves against their masters. In turn, the *Code Noir*, a legal instrument created in colonial France in 1635 that regulated the lives of and relations between slaves and free people in the French colonies, appears to be manipulated like a spell in the work. Thus, this work suggests proposing the production of a spell against the French colonial empire, similar to the spells produced by the slaves against their masters in the colonial era. Hence, it would almost be on the border between a work of art and a religious offering, intriguing precisely because of this ambiguity. More than this, his work constitutes a vehicle for questioning the new relationship of coloniality in contemporary Martinique and, perhaps, for producing new spells.

Regarding this productive ambiguity, Louise uses the intervention of multiple agencies in the process of developing his works clearly at various moments. Once they are produced via a creative process in which divinities and trances are often evoked, once the works are finished, he intentionally refrains from defining the nature of the artefact produced. Moreover, without knowing whether it is a work of art or an artefact inhabited by entities that are sometimes unknown, he allows himself to be affected by its effects and by the agency of the various indexes that compose them. The works themselves, furthermore, can be seen as indexes (Gell 1998) of these multiple agencies which operate through the artist-shaman. Following the analysis of Dayan (1995) in relation to voodoo as "historical rituals" capable of responding to the dispossession generated by the institution of slavery with a model of possession, "by making a man not a thing, but a spirit" (Dayan 1995, 42–43), the transformation of these artworks into artefacts of power can also be interpreted as a response to a situation of domination that, similar to the religion, carries the marks of slavery and colonialism.

Final considerations

Through the multiple appropriations made by these artists, "artefacts of history" (Strathern 1990), concepts, and experiences are transformed into artwork endowed with multiple agencies in a process through which history, culture, and Martinican identity are elaborated through artefacts.

These works also function as indexes of conceptualisations of certain historical events or aspects of the Martinican culture. More than "representations" of previously existing events, they are agents themselves, creating identities and indexes of elements that, together, these artists defined as "Martinican culture." These works are also measures of political, aesthetic, or spiritual experiences, at a personal level or in relation to the public, that establish connections which would not have been possible without them.

Victor Anicet, in creating his cosmogony of the history of Martinique via art, produces not only an allegory about the way the Caribbean formed itself but also "makes" Martinican culture via artefacts, from the new relationships established within his works. René Louise considers his artistic creation as a mode of marronage and a spiritual practice and evokes what he considers the deep roots of Martinican identity. He experiences, through his produced artefacts, a specific form of creation and a narrative of Martinique's history mediated by these objects.

Thus, the artists perform the actual constitution of the Caribbean society in their creative work (Mintz and Price 1973; Mintz 1996; Clifford 1988; Trouillot 1996). In that work the relationship is presented as a constituent mode (Glissant, 1997a), creating culture, history, and Martinican identities via these artefacts. Hall emphasises that it is through "acts of imaginary rediscovering," as well as through the recognition and updating of the "ruptures and discontinuities," that Caribbean singularity is constituted (Hall 1990, 224, 225). Through creative appropriations of artefacts of distinct order, they cannibalise elements of domination as well as modes of liberation, bringing the margins into tension and proposing other relations, in this way expanding the "circumstances of meeting and relationship" that are at the genesis of these societies (Mintz 1996, 296). Moreover, the artwork and performances produced by these artists are constituted as agents of the creation of history and Martinican culture, becoming artefacts that incessantly build new forms of resistance to current forms of colonialist domination.

References

Bernabé, Jean, Patrick Chamoiseau and Raphaël Confiant. 1993. *Éloge de la créolité*. Paris: Gallimard.

Burton, Richard D. E. 1997. *Afro-Creole: Power, Opposition and Play in the Caribbean*. Ithaca and London: Cornell University Press.

Césaire, Aimé. 2004. *Discours sur le colonialisme*. Paris, Dakar: Présence Africaine.

Césaire, Aimé. 2006. *La Poésie*. Org. Daniel Maximin and Gilles Carpentier. Paris: Éditions du Seuil.

Césaire, Aimé. 2009. *Cahier d'un retour au pays natal*. Paris: Présence Africaine.

Césaire, Aimé, Suzanne Césaire and René Ménil. 1994. *Tropiques (1941–1945)*. Collection Complète. Paris: Jean-Michel Place.

Clifford, James. 1988. *The Predicament of Culture: Twentieth-Century Ethnography, Literature and Art*. Cambridge, Massachusetts, and London: Harvard University Press.

Dayan, Joan. 1995. *Haiti, History, and the Gods*. Berkeley, Los Angeles, London: University of California Press.

Deleuze, Gilles and Félix Guattari, Félix. 1995. *Mil Platôs: capitalismo e esquizofrenia*. São Paulo. Ed. 34.

Donatien-Yssa, Patricia. 2009. "Fwomajé and Totem: The Beginnings and Consolidation of an Artistic Language in Martinique." *Small Axe: A Caribbean Journal of Criticism* 30: 115–127.

Fanon, Frantz. 1971. *Peau noire, masques blancs*. Paris: Seuil.

Gell, Alfred. 1996. "Vogel's net: Traps as Artworks and Artworks as Traps." *Journal of Material Culture* 1: 15–38.

Gell, Alfred. 1998. *Art and Agency: An Anthropological Theory*. Oxford, New York: Oxford University Press.

Gell, Alfred. 1999 [1992]. "The Technology of Enchantment and the Enchantment of Technology." In *The Art of Anthropology: Essays and Diagrams*, edited by Eric Hirsch, 159–186. London: Brunswick, NJ: Athlone.

Gilroy, Paul. 2001. *O Atlântico Negro: Modernidade e dupla consciência*. Rio de Janeiro: Editora 34.

Glissant, Édouard. 1990. *Poétique de la Relation: Poétique III*. Paris: Gallimard.

Glissant, Édouard. 1997a. *Le discours antillais*. Paris: Gallimard.

Glissant, Édouard. 1997b. *Poetics of Relation*. Michigan: The Univesity of Michigan Press.

Hachad, Naïma and Loichot, Valérie. 2012. "Victor Anicet: Le Pays-Martinique ou le Bleu de la Restitution." *Small Axe* 39, volume 16, no. 3: 39–57.

Hall, Stuart. 1990. "Cultural Identity and Diaspora." In *Identity: Community, Culture and* Difference, edited by Jonathan Rutherford, 222–37. London: Lawrence and Wishart.

Jolivet, Marie-José. 1987. "La construction d'une mémoire historique à la Martinique: du schœlchérisme au marronnisme." *Cahiers d'études africaines* 27 (107–108): 287–309.

Latour, Bruno. 2005. *Reassembling the Social: An Introduction to Actor-Network-Theory.* Oxford: Oxford University Press.

Louise, René. 1998 [1979]. *Manifeste du Marronisme Moderne.* Case-Pilote: Lafontaine.

Ménil, René, Thélus Léro, Etienne Léro, Jules-Marcel Monnerot, August Thésée, Michel Pilotin, Maurice-Sabas Quitman, Pierre Yoyotte et Simone Yoyotte. 1979 [1932]. *Légitime défense.* Paris: Jean-Michel Place.

Mintz, Sidney. 1996. "Enduring Substances, Trying Theories: The Caribbean Region as Oikoumene." *The Journal of the Royal Anthropological Institute* 2 (2): 289–311.

Mintz, Sidney and Richard Price. 1973. *The Birth of African-American Culture.* Boston: Beacon Press.

Price, Richard and Sally Price. 1997. "Shadowboxing in the Mangrove." *Cultural Anthropology* 12 (1): 3–36.

Strathern, Marilyn. 1990. "Artifacts of history: Events and the interpretation of images." In: *Culture and history in the Pacific,* (ed.) Jukka Siikala, Finnish Anthropological Society, 25–44.

Trouillot, Michel-Rolph. 1992. "The Caribbean Region: An Open Frontier in Anthropological Theory." In: *Annual Review of Anthropology* 21: 19–42.

Part III.
New Forms of Art and Ethnography in Museums and Development

Chapter 8

Material culture and art practice in Ladakh: notes from a collaborative art project

Abeer Gupta
Achi Association India

Abstract

Ladakh is a trans-Himalayan frontier of the Indian subcontinent, but until recently it was part of a vibrant network of Central Asian and Himalayan trade which gradually disappeared since the mid 20th century with the reconfigurations and militarisation of the borders. Over the past few decades, the material culture of the region has become inexorably linked to India and has reconnected with global circulation through tourism. The author relocates Ladakh as a contact zone of various streams of cultural production and commoditisation through transformations in groups of objects. These artefacts narrate a historical assimilation of various regional traditions and local productions and the shifts in present times as they are outsourced to production centres in India. Further, the author shows how they negotiate and influence industrial products as they are traded next to contemporary substitutes and alternatives, alongside recycled, second-hand goods and international brands. Together with Chemat Dorjey and Gulzar Hussain, contemporary artists from Ladakh who displayed two site-specific installations in conjunction with a set of objects, Abeer Gupta explores these ideas for an exhibition at the National Ethnographic Museum in Bhopal (IGRMS). The chapter documents the journey of this collaboration and in the process raises questions around artist-artisanal agency and representation at the peripheries.

Keywords: trade, artefact, contemporary art, museum exhibition, collaboration

Located in Ladakh, this chapter attempts a study of contemporary material culture, through a collaboration with artistic voices from the region, unpacking the idea of a traditional or ethnographic artefact and the manner in which it exists today and enacts ideas of agency of artefacts (Gell 1998) which this volume explores.

A trans-Himalayan region of India bordering both Pakistan and China, Ladakh often appears in the popular imagination of mainland India within either the framework of nationalism and conflict, or monastic spiritualism. In recent years, while the geographic alienation may have reduced, mainstream Indian representation displays limited interest or understanding of the socio-cultural aspects of the region—comparable to the regions in the North East of India—where individuals are often stereotyped for their "Mongoloid" features and regarded as foreign. The landscapes, however, are used as backdrops for advertisements or musical sequences in Bollywood and appropriated within the geographic diversity of India. Ladakh's marginalisation in representation continues within contemporary international perception as a periphery of Tibet's religious-cultural sphere. Baltistan was referred to as Little Tibet (Bernier 1989 [1914], 395), a term popular in various accounts since the 19th century, however the term is often used for Ladakh while being sold as an international tourist destination. While ideas of tradition have been profoundly influenced by Tibetan Buddhism (Harris 2005, 83–93), and Ladakh and Tibet do share aspects of material culture, they differ significantly within contemporary socio-political formations. Its cultural articulation is appropriated by a primarily Buddhist identity although the region has a diverse socio-religious population (van Beek 2004).

Ladakh has transformed from a vibrant centre of the network of Central Asian and Himalayan trade to a periphery of the Indian subcontinent. The Main Bazaar in Leh, one of the two principal urban spaces in Ladakh, becomes a significant site for this chapter, to map this transformation not only through the production and circulation of a group of objects, but also evolving social relations and transactions—from a unique and local cultural system to an aspirant in a new global-capitalist economy.

Clare Harris, for the past few decades, has provided insights into the development of a contemporary art movement (Harris 1997, 160–177) by a group of Tibetan artists. They have responded to a classical-religious domain of art, rearticulated a cultural identity and developed an artistic voice in the global art world. This process has involved reconnecting with ideas from material culture studies, challenging existing paradigms of representation in order to re-examine ideas of authorship and realigning with issues of migration, globalisation and commoditisation. A similar process is currently underway in Ladakh.

A significant number of museums have come up in the region in recent decades, narrating ideas of tradition and various cultural identities, usually encircled by ideas of spiritualism. These tropes of representation extend themselves not only in the manner in which Ladakh is sold in tourism brochures, but often displayed in art galleries. The emerging contemporary art movement in Ladakh, while similar in its quest for articulation, like the Tibetan artists, finds itself in the space of an illustrative tradition celebrating ethnographic subjects and religious art, in a journey from an act of veneration towards a critical, reflective articulation. This project, a collaboration between the curator and ethnographer and two emerging artists from Ladakh, exemplifies issues around representation—how the display of artefacts provokes the spectator to consider various cultural nuances through curatorial interventions and how art practice might evolve as a site of critical reflection in the region. Together with the Main Bazaar, the recent development of museums in Ladakh provides a backdrop for the project.

Ladakh and the evolution of the Main Bazaar in Leh

Ladakh was largely shaped in the 11th century by the Western Tibetan kingdom of *Ngari*, which created a new region by joining Gilgit and Baltistan in the west to more Tibetan-influenced central and eastern territories. By the 16th century, the Namgyal dynasty made it the centre of a kingdom that extended from Guge in the east (Western Tibet) to Baltistan in the west (Petech 1939, 167). Ladakh's domination in the region started to collapse in the late 17th century in the aftermath of a Tibetan invasion that caused Kashmir and Delhi to intervene in the favour of the Namgyal kings (Francke 1907, 90–135). As a result, the whole of Western Tibet was lost to Lhasa, amputating the country of over two-thirds of its area and giving it almost its current eastern border.[1] With the Treaty of Amritsar,[2] Kashmir came under Dogra rule (Rizvi 2012, 90–99) and between 1834 and 1947 the regions of Baltistan, Gilgit and Ladakh came under unified governance from Jammu, with growing British intervention in the area. Along with sustained interaction with European missionaries (Bray 2011, 20–21) and a growing number of colonial agents (Hopkirk 2006, 92–93), this period saw the introduction of industrial objects in the region.

Historically, Ladakh was largely a trading post, although not much that was manufactured in Ladakh was meant for trade apart from food products. Local traders from western Ladakh bartered basic supplies in Changthang in eastern Ladakh for *pashmina* and raw wool. The people of Rupshu in Changthang (Rizvi 1999, 69–107) brought salt to Zanskar and took barley in exchange. Balti traders from Skardu brought dried apricots, vegetables and butter, and traded them in Leh for rice, tea and sugar. Leh, situated centrally between northern Indian and

---

[1] "Treaty of Tingmosgang." Accessed February 10, 2020. https://tibet.net/wp-content/uploads/2014/10/political-treaties-of-tibet...pdf.
[2] "Treaty of Amritsar." Accessed February 10, 2020. http://jklaw.nic.in/treaty_of_amritsar.pdf.

Central Asian trade routes, was bustling with socio-economic activity between Tibet, Central Asia, Chinese Turkistan, Baltistan, Kashmir, Delhi and Punjab. Built in the 16th century at the peak of the Namgyal Dynasty, the Main Bazaar (Gompertz 1928, 159–172) in Leh (Joldan 2018, 30–68) was the epicentre of this interaction. Traders from different regions were allocated space and it was known for its plural cosmopolitan nature (Pallis 1949, 251–256).

The presence of the two main mosques—for the Sunni and Shia communities—the Moravian Mission Church, a small Hindu temple just south of the Polo Ground, and the imposing Gompa Soma Buddhist temple at Leh Palace corroborate the relation between economic and religious practices at the core of its socio-cultural life. Both the administration as well as the clergy participated in this trading activity. Famous summer trade fairs once took place in Leh, Shey, Rampur and Palampur. Ladakh did export wool, sulphur, borax, dry fruits and quantities of opium came from Yarkand, but it was the trade of *pashmina*, and tea from Tibet and China, that had the most significant influence on its political economy (Rizvi 1999, 56–67). Trade agreements and missions such as the *Lopchak* caravan to Lhasa were in effect well into the 20th century (Radhu 2017, 61–63).

Since 1947, with the Instrument of Accession signed between the Maharaja of Jammu and Kashmir and India,[3] Ladakh came under the administration of India, via Srinagar and Jammu—the summer and winter capitals of the state of Jammu and Kashmir. The historic trade routes were closed (Albinia 2008: 252) except the road to Srinagar via Kargil. In the period that followed, Ladakh witnessed armed uprisings in both Tibet and Kashmir, and a steady rise in militarisation and multiple reconfigurations of its borders through several covert and overt operations between India's wars with Pakistan (1947–48, 1971 and 1999) and with China (1962). The introduction of military paraphernalia, specially catered for the extreme weather conditions, found quick popularity: jerry cans, direct-moulded and waterproof boots soon became household goods alongside army surplus canned dried eggs and condensed milk. After a couple of decades of confinement, government establishments such as the Border Roads Organisation and the Public Works Department made the first inroads into Ladakh in the 1970s and 1980s, bringing with them a modern imagination of space and materials for construction. Institutional buildings were fashioned with a sub-continental aesthetic, with a few regional embellishments. Constructions in reinforced cement-concrete with iron

---

[3] "Instrument of Accession." Accessed February 10, 2020. http://jklaw.nic.in/instrument_of_accession_of_jammu_and_kashmir_state.pdf.

beams, aluminium, tin, asbestos and glass set the standards of development, gradually replacing vernacular materials such as stone, mud and wood.

Since the 1970s, alongside the development around a robust military infrastructure, the region was reopened to foreigners, which ushered the advent of scholars and tourists. With the formation (van Beek 1999, 435–459) of the Ladakh Autonomous Hill Development Council (LAHDC), in Leh in 1995 and in Kargil in 2003, the region entered a certain degree of democratic-political process within the state of Jammu and Kashmir. More recently, in August 2019, the Indian government abrogated Article 370 and Section 35a[4] bifurcating the state into two Union Territories, one consisting of the regions of Jammu and Kashmir, and the other Ladakh, comprising the districts of Leh and Kargil. The new Union Territory is triangulated by three nuclear powers of the world, namely China, Pakistan and India and is now administered directly from New Delhi through the office of a Lieutenant Governor.

Today, Leh is a rapidly growing urban space, and the goods traded here cater to the needs of a different population including large groups of migrant labour (Dewan 2011, 132–136) from India and Nepal. Apart from those who have lived in Leh for several generations, Ladakhis from rural areas are settling in Leh for purposes of business, employment or education. Leh is no longer a stopover, but a Mecca for traders from across India, drawn to cater to either the tourism sector or the armed forces. In the last few decades, though an increasing number of Ladakhi Buddhists are entering trade, much of the fare is still in the hands of the Muslim descendants of Arghons (Fewkes 2009, 63–75) and families of Hindu and Sikh traders from Punjab, who have settled in Leh for several generations.

A number of Tibetan Refugee Markets, a recognised trade network across India, are located south of the main Bazaar, two permanent ones at the top of Old Road, and several smaller clusters are popular either for trinkets or for a range of duplicate mountaineering gear, clothes and accessories, available across the Himalayan circuit. Initially dealing in products of the grey market, populated by covert cross border trade till the 1990s, they are increasingly shifting to the sale of mass produced, inexpensive goods from India and China. Merchants from Kashmir, like their Tibetan counterparts, deal in a range of textiles, antiques, and junk jewellery for tourists, apart from dealing in second-hand clothes and covertly selling contraband items such as narcotics and *shahtoosh* (fleece from Tibetan antelope).

---

[4] "Article 370 and Section 35a". Accessed February 10, 2020. http://www.jklaw.nic.in/constitution_jk.pdf.

Leh's Main Market today is enabled with 4G Internet, national and international travel agencies, local boutiques, cafes with Italian coffee machines, and is ever-present on social media. While basic utility goods and domestic wares continue to arrive by road via Srinagar, a variety of seasonal or luxury goods find their way up to Leh either by road from Manali in Himachal Pradesh or simply by air.

Harris, along with Monisha Ahmed, has discussed new approaches to art and material culture in Ladakh (Ahmed and Harris 2005, 11–20) recontextualising artistic production, bringing into focus everyday objects of regional significance and a role and history of a diverse set of agents in their making. The material culture of Ladakh developed over centuries, close to its natural resources due to its geographic remoteness, accentuated by objects of luxury arriving through trade. The cultural marginalisation and economic deprivation of Ladakh, which has been described at its worst under the Dogra Rulers of Jammu, outlived the period of feudalism well into the threshold of economic liberalisation of markets in India in the 1990s. Limited agency within the state legislature of Jammu and Kashmir, coupled with poor connectivity of roads and (still) being cut off from the mainland of India for several months of winter, produced a deep impact on a largely self-sustaining society. Up-cycling, recycling and reuse was deeply embedded in local cultural practices; and a great amount of economy was practiced and continues to be done in remote areas.

Museums, identities and representation

While the Main Bazaar in Leh becomes a significant site to map the circulation of commodities, it continues to be the space for both political and artistic expression, offering not only a historical context but a somewhat secular backdrop. The museums on the other hand present a space of articulating or appropriating traditional and religious identities of the region. Over the past two decades the major monasteries and certain affluent families have attempted displays of their collections. The objects displayed provide the occasion to question how the ethnographic objects dwell in the space between local traditions and religion. While a large number of such artefacts have been sold off to foreign buyers, there is now a growing appreciation for saving and showcasing what remains for posterity.

Another reason for the proliferation of monastic museums could be to offer basic interpretation to the growing number of Indian tourists, with the added incentive of monetising entry, which was otherwise left to voluntary donations. This provides an opportunity to reflect upon the representation of Ladakh for the outsider's (touristic) imagination. During the 19th century Ladakh entered the visual imagination of Europeans through colonial agents, and its art was represented as an extension of a broader Tibetan artistic production in terms of architecture and painting. But Ladakh encompassed a much wider and diverse populace which developed due to its vicinity to Persian and Central Asian cultures and therefore developed a multicultural syncretism. However, Ladakh is largely marketed, even today, as a Buddhist Shangri La (Korom 1997; Lopez 2018 [1998]), with ideas of tradition continue to be defined by Tibetan-Buddhist religious art.

Ladakh, although it is similar to Tibet in many ways, developed a very distinct culture, with a significant influence of Tibet especially in religious domains. Geographically akin, in the 1960s Ladakh was one of the regions in India which accommodated a large section of the Tibetan diaspora, especially in Choglamsar, a neighbourhood a few kilometres south of Leh town. Several institutions, significantly, the Central Institute of Buddhist Studies, were built here and some of them built their own museums, such as the School of Buddhist Dialectics in Choglamsar and the Men-Tsee-Khang, the Tibetan medical and astrological centre in Leh. This museum includes iconographic, botanical and geological collections relating to Tibetan medicine and astrology.

The monastic museums are a local assertion and celebration of Buddhist identities and culture. Grand monasteries, belonging to the various sects of Tibetan Buddhism, such as Hemis, Chemrey (belonging to the Drukpa order), Likir, Thikse (belonging to the Gelugpa order) were the pioneers of this movement along with the Stok Palace Museum—the rest of the palace is a hotel and the current home of the erstwhile royal family of Ladakh. While the tendency was to convert certain old chambers into museums, Hemis and Thikse monastery were some of perhaps the first to construct modern galleries and display cabinets, within the premises. These institutions had elaborate collections of ritual objects, iconography and often eclectic personal collections belonging to a high priest or royal. While the physical space of the museum was seemingly distinct, collections often moved freely between the ritual spaces of worship and the premises of the museum. In the last few years a number of monasteries such as Hemis and Chemrey have reinvested into extension projects while several other monasteries such as Matho (Sakyapa) have initiated new museum projects.

The Central Asian heritage of Ladakh has often been linked to the Islamic populations of Ladakh, with the Buddhist populations looking eastwards to Tibet to define their aesthetics. The rich history of Central Asian trade along with objects from the colonial period of trade are represented in the Munshi Aziz Bhat Museum of Silk Route[5] in Kargil, and more recently in the Central

---

[5] "Munshi Aziz Bhat Museum of Silk Route, Kargil." Accessed February 10, 2020. http://kargilmuseum.org/.

Asian Museum[6] in Leh. The latter is the first museum whose premises were conceived from scratch as a museum.[7] Designed in the form of a Central Asian watchtower, it hosts a large collection of artefacts attributed to the Islamic heritage of the region. Ghulam Mustafa, trained at the Institute of Music and Fine Arts, Srinagar, is a senior artist and accomplished painter. He brought in much-needed curation and consistency to the display at the Central Asian Museum. The objects in the museum are largely historical artefacts from the Jama Masjid (Sunni) or have been donated by affluent members of the community. Such private family collections have also been presented in luxury hotels such as the Grand Dragon, owned and largely visualised by Ghulam Mustafa and his family. Such artefacts have often been used as decorative elements in the more affluent hotels and resorts, towards providing a glimpse of the cultural history of the region for tourists. Several private guest houses such as the Gyap-thago House in Stok, boast elaborate museum-like showcases within their premises.

A number of smaller private collections belonging to prominent families of traders along the highway from Srinagar to Leh, such as Tsaskan House in Nurla or Moljoks House in Saspol have been considering formal spaces for museums within their stately homes. The Balti Heritage Museum in Turtuk and the Himalayan Museum of Labdak Culture and Heritage in Garkone focus on important subcultures of the region (Albinia 2008, 275). They are thus finding a voice. Belonging to families of prosperous traders, these collections represent a secular, vernacular and more domestic history of material culture. Apart from ritual objects, the collections include colonial and trade artefacts and local production of pottery, woodcarving, textiles, jewellery and objects of popular culture. These collections allude to various accounts of production, circulation, trade and aesthetics before the region's accession to the state of India in 1947, when the northern and eastern borders were mostly sealed off and historic trade suspended.

The other predominant narrative, most relevant to the domestic tourist in Ladakh, is about its borders with China and Pakistan, with a number of wars, continuing border skirmishes and a large resident military population. The Hall of Fame in Leh and the War Memorial in Drass showcase India's military and nationalist narrative. It is noteworthy to mention that these museums record

---

[6] "Central Asian Museum, Leh." Accessed February 10, 2020. http://www.tibetheritagefund.org/media/mediablog/image/caml_flyer.pdf.

[7] Andre Alexander, the chief architect for the Tibet Heritage Fund/ Ladakh Old Town Initiative. Accessed February 10, 2020. http://www.tibetheritagefund.org/pages/projects/ladakh/leh-old-town.php.

the largest footfall and most engaged audiences of all local museums, as they appropriate a culture within overreaching narratives of patriotism.

The Textile Museum of Ladakh[8] near the Polo Ground in Leh, conceived and executed by a designer Jigmat Norbu (who started the boutique Jigmat Couture), is perhaps the first thematically curated museum in the region. The space has been designed to highlight aspects of regional architecture and is executed in local materials; the artefacts have been curated and displayed through an insightful and inclusive narrative. The museum project complements the proprietor's design practice as well as furthers his efforts for education and outreach among local school children.

While a significant amount of anthropological and ethnographic research (Fewkes 2009, 1–34) has been conducted in Ladakh and discussions[9] have taken place over the years towards building a new museum for Ladakh, a distinct void still remains in reframing a narrative of the region along contemporary ideas of visual and material culture. The geopolitical flux in the region and the evolving articulation of local political identities paves the way for religious or nationalist contexts within which artefacts continue to be presented with insignificant space for interpretation. A few institutions, such as the Munshi Aziz Bhat Museum of Silk Route,[10] the Textile Museum of Ladakh, and the Central Asian Museum in Leh have displayed artefacts along histories of trade or material culture. Projects in craft documentation have also created opportunities for discussions on materials and processes (Jaitly 1990, 2012, Ranjan and Ranjan 2005, 35–45). This led to reflections on the historic evolution of and access to technology. Such moments are also opportunities to reflect upon intersections of local and western knowledge systems, and to distinguish these ideas from predominant development narratives.

Developing curatorial ideas

With the gradual acceptance of alternative histories, interdisciplinary approaches have evolved in locating ethnographic objects within the materiality of cultural production (Bourdieu 1993). These objects have juggled several identities and notions of authenticity (Svašek 2007, 140): from being a

---

[8] "The Textile Museum of Ladakh." Accessed February 10, 2020. http://jigmatcouture.com/projects.php.
[9] "International Seminar on Museums and the Changing Cultural Landscape, Ladakh: Conference and Project Report." Accessed February 10, 2020. https://www.berghahn journals.com/view/journals/museum-worlds/1/1/air-mw010113.xml.
[10] "Latika Gupta, Archival and Museum Fellowships at Munshi Aziz Bhat Museum of Silk Route, Kargil 2014–2015." Accessed February 10, 2020. http://indiaifa.org/grants-projects/latika-gupta.html.

colonial artefact in museums, a tourism souvenir, an antique, researchers have established their connections with the intangible aspects of culture and discovered scientific knowledge coded into them by indigenous communities. But essentially, for the communities themselves, these objects have often remained a bridge between time and space—they codify memory when seen within the context of migration, urbanisation and the making of a global economy. Simultaneously, the space-location of some of the more recent museums and access to their collections have transformed considerably from distant, elite archives for academic research or display of popular curiosity, to interactive spaces for the community itself to participate in, and build the museums' narrative (Svašek 2007, 146).

In 2017, a fellowship to work with a Himalayan collection at the Indira Gandhi Rashtriya Manav Sangrahalay (IGRMS), National Ethnographic Museum in Bhopal, offered opportunities to explore ethnographic artefacts in the contemporary world along with their display and interpretation within the space of the museum.[11] The fellowship also provided the opportunity to collaborate with two artists from Ladakh, to create intersections with ideas from contemporary art practice.

The project was an opportunity to explore how the ethnographic museum might become a site for rebuilding cultural connections. For this, it would be important to acknowledge the existence of the new along with the old and create a space for dialogue incorporating the diversifications and improvisations that came along the way, to facilitate an interaction (agency) between a given ethnographic collection and the community they belong to and finally inform display. The project would be materialised by reimagining the display of the *chansa*—a Ladakhi kitchen. The IGRMS had recreated a *chansa* as a permanent installation as part of the Himalayan Village, one of its open-air exhibitions.[12] The edifice of this *chansa*, though recast in concrete, has the visual elements of a traditional Ladakhi building. Inside, a large central traditional oven (*thab*) (Clarke 2005, 52–54), a set of shelves where utensils are stored (*langs*) and floor seating with the traditional low tables was created. This became the site for the curatorial intervention: to recreate the experience inside with a set of objects and art installations.

The process started with the identification of a small group of objects from Ladakh, interconnected with the collection at the IGRMS. Some of these

---

[11] Abeer Gupta, Archival and Museum Fellowships at Indira Gandhi Rashtriya Manav Sangrahalay, Bhopal 2016–2017. Accessed February 10, 2020. http://theifaarchive.org/user/single_grant/379.

[12] "Indira Gandhi Rashtriya Manav Sangrahalay: Open Air Exhibitions, Himalayan Village." Accessed February 10, 2020. http://igrms.gov.in/en/exhibitions/exhibitions.

objects were obtained from the Main Bazaar in Leh, where they were being sold either as antiques or in commercial forms. But most importantly, these objects, drawn from daily life, are found commonly in homes across all regions of Ladakh, both rural and urban spaces and across social and religious groups. Research was initiated to build a fresh set of narratives around these objects, to relocate Ladakh as a contact zone of various streams of cultural production and commoditisation. The research mapped these objects, in the process of their making, manner of use and patterns of circulation today. These would open up conversations on the transformation of trade routes, the evolution of those objects made locally to those industrially produced and about existing local skills and practices.

This process was in collaboration with two contemporary artists from Ladakh, Chemat Dorjey and Gulzar Hussain. I met Chemat, a sculptor and mixed media artist from Sakti, a village 50 km south of Leh, and Gulzar, photographer and a resident of Leh's old town, during a workshop and exhibition[13] at the Ladakh Arts and Media Organisation (LAMO) in 2010. Chemat had worked with local potters and stone carvers and was familiar with the historical change in materials and processes, and Gulzar had photographed craft and textiles across Ladakh and Kashmir extensively. The aim of the collaboration was to create two mixed media, site-specific installations based on the research generated during this project, displayed in conjunction with a set of objects from the museum and personal collections alongside Gulzar's photographs mapping the transformation in these objects.

Gulzar has co-authored *Journey Through Paradise: Kashmir, Ladakh and Jammu* (2015), which used his photographs, and co-founded CHANRI,[14] in Puga, Changthang. He is a self-trained photographer, and his practice has evolved from creating images for advertising and tourism to capturing cultural nuances. In 2017 Gulzar was featured in the anniversary issue of *Condé Nast Traveller* as one of the "50 people to know in the Himalayas". His archive of images formed the initial research for the textiles part of the exhibition. Then, following discussions with Chemat and Gulzar, the photographic documentation of specific objects was initiated. This exercise was an attempt to create an archive of images, documenting a shift in the cultures of the region.

---

[13] "Wash Exhibition, Water, Sanitation and Hygiene in Old Town, Leh 17 June–17 July, 2011." Accessed February 10, 2020. http://www.lamo.org.in/wash_exhibition.html.
[14] The Changthang High Altitude Nomadic Research Institute (CHANRI) is a Trust whose headquarters are located in Puga Valley, Changthang. It was set up in August 2019 by a group of people committed to supporting the rich ecosystem of the Changthang and the self-determination of the Changpa as they continue to pursue the nomadic way of life.

In the course of the documentation, key facets were identified which would then be interpreted and represented through the art-installations. The *bog*, a Tibeto-Himalayan cape, was one of the identified objects. It has developed a unique range of sub-regional visual identities within Ladakh. It was and continues to be a product of trade textiles, and points to the convergence and assimilation of various textile traditions into the region. The other selections were *pabu* and *lapul*, inexpensive yet extremely functional warm local footwear, which are products of a cultural recycling of a range of leftover textiles. The *tibril* and *melang* were also chosen. These are two parts of a utensil made for serving tea, and exemplify the continuity of local craft production, defined by the need to store and serve hot drinks, such as sweet tea and butter tea, into widely used industrially manufactured thermos flasks imported across the border from Tibet, China. While the industrial products now take care of the functional aspects, the *tibril* and *melang* occupy important ceremonial and ritual spaces.

The *bog* presents a rich history of the diversity of textiles that have passed through Ladakh, connecting it to distant places. In Korzok, Changthang weaves akin to neighbouring Kinnaur in Himachal Pradesh are used to make the *bog*, while in Turtuk, simple woollen shawls are worn like the *bog*. Today a variety of *gyaser* (Ahmed 2014a) brocades from Varanasi, and Chinese brocades via Shanghai and Delhi continue to reach Ladakh and are on the visible surface of the *bog*. Plain and printed cotton, used as backing, continues to arrive from the Indian mainland. A range of wool and fur for the insulation and lining of the garment used to be sourced locally from the region, but synthetic substitutes are prevalent today to meet the increase in demand.

The surface of this garment-accessory embodies the rich exchange of textiles, both within the various regions of Tibetan cultural influence in the Himalayas as well as local adaptations within those regions. In Ladakh a diverse range of *bogs* can be found both as daily wear as well as in ceremonial use and continue to be handed down along with the *perak*, the turquoise head dress worn by women of a household (Aggarwal 2005, 56–64). In the high, cold nomadic regions of Changthang, for instance, the *bogs* are much larger in size and are lined with heavy animal fur; used as a windbreaker by women who have hard working days tending their flocks. As we move westwards from upper Ladakh, along the lower Indus basins, the *bogs* reduce in size and gain more decorative elements, seen more often during monastic or seasonal festivals and marriages. While elderly ladies can be seen wearing it in the Main Bazaar, for the younger generations it has become ceremonial.

A number of embellishment techniques are also visible on its surface such as appliqué, from Tibet, and *aari*, chain stitch and embroidery from Kashmir. Recycled brocade borders, often from Banarasi saris, were commonly used to strengthen and highlight the edges. Alien till recently to the visual language of the region, embellishments broadly termed as *kinari* work have been adapted to the surface of the *bog*. This may be seen as an influence of Delhi, which is a primary influence for latest fashion. The surface of this artefact has been a receptacle of textiles, techniques and patterns and is a document of rich exchanges in material culture.

As Chemat had been a part of the field work, his responses and plan for the installations developed simultaneously. In the past years, Chemat had been engaging with a range of local craftsmen, with stone carvers in Turtuk in the Nubra valley and with the potters in Likir. The form of the spindle was becoming a *leitmotiv* in his work, including in his first solo show at the Lalit Kala Academy, New Delhi in February 2017. Chemat interpreted the research and photographic material on the *bogs* as a centripetal movement—with Ladakh at its centre. The *bogs* also presented a rich spectrum of colours, due to the diverse embellishments. Both these aspects were incorporated in the final installation. However, the installation germinated from the idea of the spindle, which for Chemat embodies the core of weaving—the transformation of raw fibre into thread. Spinning and weaving are imagined as a source of life in Ladakh and were, historically, common household skills. Chemat wished to develop the *Reclining Spindle* (made in papier-mâché and exhibited earlier at the Lalit Kala Academy) further into an installation.[15] The form of the *Reclining Spindle* was inspired by a young lady, pregnant with her first child, who was learning to spin. At first, Chemat observed, her spinning was not uniform, but she continued to make an effort, and hide her embarrassment, till she mastered it. He wished to associate this facet into the new installation, in some ways trying to evoke the nurturing spirit of a mother through elements from the textile traditions of Ladakh (Ahmed 2014b, 27–36). Chemat wanted to respond to the next set of objects—the *pabu* and *lapul*, and the *tibril* and *melang*—together through one artwork. These objects were constructed of multiple materials and their transformation evoked a more centrifugal motion, with the objects originating in Ladakh but moving outwards.

The *pabu* and *lapul* form part of a range of textile-based footwear, for domestic use as well for outdoor travel, made from locally produced woollen

---

[15] Catalogue of Chemat's first solo exhibition, artworks inspired by the form of the spindle, including Reclining Spindle. Accessed February 10, 2020. https://docs.google.com/a/krishna kriti.in/viewer?a=v&pid=sites&srcid=ZGVmYXVsdGRvbWFpbnxjaGVtYXRsZWh8Z3g6NWU2 ZDAxZjdiZTg3MDk5YQ.

and felted textiles and worn widely in the past by both men and women. While the *lapul* is used extensively at home, especially during the colder months, the *pabu* is still common in the rural areas among the older generations and in more urban spaces in ceremonial use during both religious and cultural occasions. Ornate versions lined with animal hide soles are frequently seen during the *chams*, the monastic ritual dances. A number of local producers around Leh, in Zanskar and Nubra Valley, continue to make shoes. The materials used for making the *pabu* and *lapul* are leftover locally woven woollen cloth (*nambu*) either dyed in maroon, green or black, or embellished by a resist dying process (*thigma*)[16] and often include a further process of felting still prevalent in Zanskar, called *spuruk*. A range of synthetic materials, mass-produced woollen yardage and waste bits from tailoring shops, also go into their making. The soles of the *lapul* are often lined with rubber, but a lone Muslim cobbler from Kargil in Phating Bazaar in Leh continues the craft of attaching leather soles both for elaborate monastic boots as well as the *pabu*.

The footwear embodies a transition from local products to introduction of items by the military to international contemporary brands of trekking gear. Changing lifestyles and professional requirements have introduced over the decades a new set of functions. The army introduced a range of outdoor shoes, low or high ankle canvas shoes, direct moulds, and waterproof gumboots, which are useful both in farming as well as to navigate in snow. With the advent of adventure tourism, hiking and climbing shoes have become popular daily fashion, connecting international designs and technologies both in original as well as cheaper reproductions. A range of warm shoes for both men and women with inner lining of insulation, which imitate Ugg boots, have also been in circulation, providing a stiff completion to the *pabu* and *lapul*.

A two-part utensil used for serving tea is made up of the *tibril*, the teapot, and *melang*, the base pot where hot embers keep the tea warm. Historically, this set of utensils was produced either in metal using copper and brass, or in clay. Once an essential in the *chansa* (the Ladakhi kitchen), in present times it has acquired more ceremonial or decorative use after the arrival of the thermos flask. These are now seen widely in both homes and restaurants, serving both butter and sweet tea. The kettles too represent the journey of domestic object into a space of ritualistic and ceremonial use. They continue to be produced by the *sergar*, the goldsmiths of Chilling (Clarke 2005, 45–50), master craftsmen who work with brass and copper as well. Their rich repertoire includes ritual objects such as statues and *chortens* (stupas), and domestic objects such as

---

[16] Ahmed, "The Fabric of Life: Nomadic Textiles from the Ladakh Himalayas," 2018. Accessed February 10, 2020. https://www.sahapedia.org/the-fabric-of-life-nomadic-textiles-the-ladakh-himalayas.

chabkyan (beer pots), *thumbu* (ladles), *druklungma* (elaborate dragon-headed teapots) and *thagu* (simpler tea pots). They work with metal sheets and are experts in gilding with metal and with insets of semiprecious stones such as corals and turquoise. The master craftsmen of Chilling are said to have migrated from Nepal in the late 16th century and introduced the making of elaborate metal ware in Ladakh. The *tibril* and *melang* in a range of sizes are one of their significant contributions. A range of motifs such as the dragon, the eight auspicious Buddhist symbols, an interlocking pattern known as the *rgya-nag-lcags-ri* and *yumdumlagyut* are found adorning the surface.

Nepal continues to produce a great volume of metal ware seen widely in both antique shops and Tibetan Refugee Markets selling trinkets in tourist destinations across the Himalayas. Among the many groups of migrant labourers, which inhabit Ladakh seasonally, a group of young Nepali coppersmiths run a repair shop for a range of domestic and ritual metalware in Leh near the Polo Ground. Production centres like Moradabad and Aligarh in India are accepting commissions, and they are entering the market of Tibetan or Himalayan artefacts. Designs from Chilling are sent for reproduction to the semi-industrial workshops, with larger capacities of production in brass and copper, making the objects more affordable for the local markets in Leh. Silver and gold-plated versions are available at Moti Market in Leh, either as decorative artefacts, part of a young lady's trousseau or ceremonial purposes within monastic or domestic spaces. Further, the form of the *tibril* has been simplified and industrially cast in aluminium to make it even more affordable.

Likir, a village in western Ladakh continues to have several families of potters. Apart from the *chodme*, clay butter lamps, and a range of simple clay pots, they produce the *tibril* and *melang*. The *tibril and melang* are products of free hand pottery and their surface carries embellishments, perhaps inspired by the ornamentation done on the ones made of copper and brass in Chilling. Historically, it is rare to find pottery in the extended Himalayan and central Asian region with examples of such relief work. The clay *tibril* and *melang* were extremely popular cheaper substitutes in the region, when industrial kettles were still not available. This could be one of those rare contributions to pottery from Ladakh, where pottery has adopted an embellishment technique from regional metalware.

The journey of this set of objects alters significantly with the entry of the thermos flask into the region, which almost replaced the need of the kettle and base pot, providing an industrial alternative for the same purpose today. A range of Chinese made thermos flasks, in varying sizes, with plastic and aluminium exteriors are imported across the Tibetan border in Demjok in Changthang. These flasks have adapted to local needs in their designs, including a handle for pouring, a simple stopper and often a tapering snout for better flow. The printed surface of these thermos flasks is produced in China, for use mostly in the Tibetan region. They bear mostly colourful renderings of Tibetan and Chinese motifs, sometimes a photograph of the Potala Palace in Lhasa, and flowers such as the chrysanthemum. Subsequently, more secular motifs, in the form of flowers such as roses and daisies influenced by European Romanticism or photographs and geometric patterns are seen. Further, while on one hand, painted images of European hamlets, or even the Kremlin have appeared, so has the *Durgah of Nizamuddin Auliya* for specific clientele.

Chemat had created, while studying for his Bachelor degree in sculpture, at the Institute of Music and Fine Arts in Jammu, a wood-cut print and fibre glass sculpture of a shoe and a kettle and hat in Ladakhi styles morphing into an abstract form. It was titled *Welcome to Ladakh*. The form was derived from three objects, the *tibi* hat, the *chabkyan* beer pot, and the *pabu* shoe. These are essential items of clothing worn or carried during a formal reception by women of Ladakh and have developed into the most commonly represented traditional attire.

This artwork had been discussed for our project due to its direct connection with the shoe, however Chemat was inspired by the idea of transformation, from the research on the kettles and shoes. The process of transformation is often complex and not an easy one, and he wished to add this element while developing it further. A similar form would be created in clay and cast into a pair of sculptures in fibreglass. But this time the form is physically divided in half and cut into two from the middle. Each of the internal surfaces carries a digital screen that displays a photomontage. Each of the screens would be used to represent the stories of transformation in the kettle and the shoes. The external surface would be adorned by the motifs, patterns, textures from both cultural objects as well as foreign brands that pass through Ladakh.

The research on the objects also resulted in a final selection to be displayed alongside. For this, a selection of *bogs* was made from different regions, the surfaces of which were adorned by a range of silks brocades, wool and embroidery. The textile-based artefacts narrate a historical assimilation of various regional traditions, local productions and an evolution of materials and processes. At the same time, the kettles speak of the shifts in present times as production is outsourced to manufacturing-centres in India. A selection of old and new traditional kettles, made by local artisans as well as those made outside Ladakh, were displayed next to a range of thermos flasks. For the footwear, which speaks of a culture of recycling, a range of local shoes were displayed to highlight the sustainability of a diverse local production.

The objects on display were intended to create an opportunity to provoke conversation around how locally made products negotiate and influence industrial products as they are traded next to contemporary substitutes and alternatives and raise questions on the authenticity of cultural artefacts and the

Material culture and art practice in Ladakh

essential hybridity of cultural processes (Phillips and Steiner 1999). The artefacts showcased also illustrate Ladakh's historical connections with cultures at the heart of Asia, and how over the past decades, the material culture of the region has not only become inexorably linked to India but has reconnected with global circulation through tourism.

The *chansa* (the Ladakhi kitchen) is the epicentre of Ladakhi culture, the site of conversations, storytelling and interaction especially during the long winters. The *chansa* at the IGRMS included the *langs,* (a traditional wooden shelf) which is seen commonly in kitchens across Ladakh and is a storage facility and a display of the family's possessions—a range of utensils across generations and places. It was used to display the selected range of *bogs* and local footwear along with the kettles and the thermoses. It seemed to extend itself quite naturally to the display and it was repopulated with a range of ethnographic objects to form the backdrop for the artistic installations.

The display included two central art installations. The photographs by Gulzar of the kettles and shoes were presented in the first installation that the visitor encountered as they entered the *chansa*. It was titled Welcome to Ladakh II. A set of screens placed inside the fibre glass cast sculptures played a set of photomontages on the making, use and circulation of the *pabu* and *lapul,* and the *tibril* and *melang,* in a loop. The external surface was adorned by traditional motifs and contemporary brands related to these objects. The intention was to create an engagement with the objects and ideas of making through the provocation of the form.

Figure 8.1 Mother Spindle, Installation by Chemat Dorjey at IGRMS.

Photograph by Abeer Gupta.

The *langs* at the back of the *chansa* was used to display a set of textiles, accompanied by photographs of those textiles as they were being used. The second installation, *Mother Spindle*, in wood, wool and papier-mâché, was placed in front of the *langs*. The installation is created using different stages of production of cloth. From the raw wool, the *yokto* and the *zhutphang* (men's and women's spindles), which create the yarn, to the *nambu*, which is the final product. The installation also alluded to the process of dyeing, as the yarns were dyed into the seven colours of the rainbow strung on a hundred *phangs* (bobbins). The rainbow symbolised, for Chemat, the diverse traditions and materials that are assimilated in the region, to point to the essential hybridity of culture. The threads converge onto the previously made papier-mâché sculpture, *Recycling Spindle*. The intention was to create an engagement with the material and the process, and further to reflect upon the idea space and location. Text panels exemplifying the contexts of making and circulation were also installed.

Figure 8.2 Welcome to Ladakh, Installation by Chemat Dorjey at IGRMS.

Photograph by Abeer Gupta.

The aim was to create a visual experience where the artefacts and art installations were provocations for the viewer to consider the materials, processes and circulation of these artefacts, beyond their aesthetics, form and function. The scheme of the display proposed to create the interaction between the art objects as central provocations to reflect upon the ethnographic material alongside the photo documentation.

Concluding remarks

Ladakh has a rich history of artistic production, from the ancient petroglyphs, murals and *thangkas*[17] to various craft practices. While advanced skills always found patronage with religious or imperial subjects and were often imported, the craft practices of the region were robust and functional. Ladakh was very sparsely populated and only a small proportion of that population had social and economic mobility and the exposure or access to advanced education. All of that is changing. A group of young men and women, equipped with the latest technologies and engaged with the socio-political dynamics are getting involved in art. The Progressive Artists of Ladakh,[18] trained in institutions of national repute, are working either within Ladakh or are based in other parts of India. While Ladakh gets stereotyped and commodified for a globalised tourism economy, these artists are exploring parallel, nuanced representation as they enter the imagination of a digital world. While perceptions of contemporary art are nascent and largely obsessed with the figurative within Ladakh, artists from Ladakh have been in recent years accommodated within exhibitions of contemporary Buddhist art in New Delhi.[19] Their practice—which is a precarious balance between this stereotype and catering to the market of tourism souvenirs—is one of the few spaces (for the future) to reclaim a range of socio-cultural issues in a critical-empirical manner, within a society still heavily moderated by religion and politics determined by communalism.

The participatory manner in which this project engaged with research allowed for developing a common ground for conversations. Ladakh has been in the past, seen as a traditional subject for external experts. However, gaps in technology and communication are decreasing rapidly and the challenge is to engage with an, albeit dissimilar, but alternative experience of modernity. Ladakh is currently passing through a phase of rapid, unplanned urbanisation and introduction of products from a global market of commodities, which are bound to impact both the local environment and local production. A certain shift of focus is therefore required for revitalising the links between ethnographic objects and renewing a

---

[17] A Tibetan Buddhist painting on cotton, silk appliqué, usually depicting a Buddhist deity, scene, or mandala.

[18] *The Progressive Artists of Ladakh*, a group of 30 odd youngsters who are engaging in contemporary art, their Facebook group. Accessed February 10, 2020. https://www.facebook.com/ProgressingArtistOfLadakh/.

[19] Chemat has been part of several group exhibitions in New Delhi, namely, *The Inner Path* – festival of Buddhist film, art and philosophy, National Gallery of Modern Art, 10–13 October 2019, *Benevolent Gaze, Buddhist Imprints in Art* group show, Ojas Art, 15 December 2017 to 14 January 2018, *The Inner Path* – festival of Buddhist film, art and philosophy, Alliance Francaise, New Delhi, April 7–11, 2017.

sustainable engagement with local materials and skills. The collaboration this chapter reflects upon exemplifies a small instance of that.

Traditionally, museums have focused largely on classical art and iconography, which have been the domain of art historians and religious scholars, often requiring a highly trained eye. Ethnographic artefacts shift the attention towards vernacular materials and skills and open up conversations around local aspects of culture, thus enabling a larger community to be drawn into conversation. The interactions around the installations had a much deeper sense of belonging rather than veneration. While the familiarity of the objects and materials made the exhibit more inclusive, the juxtaposition of these ideas in the installation made it provocative, interactive and non-hierarchic. The setting, while it emulates a domestic feel, was located in the premises of a national institution and furthered the importance of displaying these artefacts and installations inspired from them, within larger circumferences of access. Chemat, along with other members of the Progressive Artists of Ladakh, have engaged successfully in numerous public art projects in Leh as well as the Main Bazaar. These artists have continued to work with materials relevant to their environment, such as ice, recycled motor parts, and recycled pieces of textiles to create installations in public spaces. *Mother Spindle* was installed permanently in a special chamber in a café[20] run by Chemat and members of the group in the Main Bazaar in 2018.

References

Aggarwal, Ravina. 2005. "The Turquoise Headdress of Ladakh." In *Ladakh: Culture at the Crossroads*, edited by Monisha Ahmed and Clare Harris, 56–64. Mumbai, India: Marg Publications.

Ahmed, Monisha. 2014a. "From Benaras to Leh: The Trade and Use of Silk-Brocade." In *Art and Architecture in Ladakh: Cross-Cultural Transmissions in the Himalayas and Karakoram*, edited by Erberto Lo Bue and John Bray, 329–347. Brill's Tibetan Studies Library, Volume: 35. Leiden: Brill.

Ahmed, Monisha. 2014b. "Duguma's Legacy: Sacred Textiles in Ladakh." In *Sacred Textiles of India*, edited by Jasleen Dhamija, 35–36. Bombay: Marg.

Ahmed, Monisha and Clare Harris. 2005. "Introduction." In *Ladakh: Culture at the Crossroads*, edited by Monisha Ahmed and Clare Harris, 11–19. Mumbai, India: Marg Publications.

Albinia, Alice. 2008. *Empires of the Indus: The Story of a River*. London: John Murray.

Bernier, François.1989 [1914]. Travels *in the Mogul Empire, AD 1656–1668*. Translated by Archibald Constable. London: Oxford University Press, New Delhi: Atlantic Publishers.

---

[20] Accessed February 10, 2020. https://www.instagram.com/spindle_art/. Accessed February 10, 2020. https://www.instagram.com/spindle_artstudio_cafe/.

Bourdieu, Pierre. 1993. *The Field of Cultural Production: Essays on Art and Literature*. New York, Columbia University Press.

Bray, John, ed. 2011. *Ladakhi Histories: Local and Regional Perspectives*. Dharamsala: Library of Tibetan Works and Archives.

Clarke, John. 2005. "Metalworking in Ladakh." In *Ladakh: Culture at the Crossroads*, edited by Monisha Ahmed and Clare Harris, 45–50. Mumbai, India: Marg Publications.

Dewan, Parwez. 2011. *A History of Ladakh, Gilgit, Baltistan*, New Delhi: Manas Publications.

Fewkes, Jacqueline H. 2009. *Trade and Contemporary Society along the Silk Road: An Ethno-History of Ladakh*. London: Routledge.

Francke, A.H. 1907. *A History of Western Tibet*. London: S.W. Partridge.

Gell, Alfred. 1998. *Art and Agency: An Anthropological Theory*. Oxford: Clarendon Press.

Gompertz, M. L. A. 1928. *Magic Ladakh: An Intimate Picture of a Land of Topsy-Turvy Customs and Great Natural Beauty*. London: Sealy, Service & Co. Limited.

Harris, Clare. 1997. "Struggling with Shangri La: A Tibetan Artist in Exile." In *Constructing Tibetan Culture: Contemporary Perspectives*, edited by Frank J. Korom, 160–177. Quebec: World Heritage Press.

Harris, Clare. 2005. "Reshaping Tradition: The Life and Work of Nawang Tsering." In *Ladakh: Culture at the Crossroads*, edited by Monisha Ahmed and Clare Harris, 82–93. Mumbai. India: Marg Publications.

Hopkirk, Peter. 2006. *The Great Game, On Secret Service in High Asia*. London: John Murray.

Jaitly, Jaya. 1990. *Crafts of Kashmir, Jammu & Ladakh*, Ahmedabad: Mapin.

Joldan, Eliezer. 2018. *Central Asian Trade and Other Essays on Ladakh*. Srinagar: Gulshan Books Kashmir.

Korom, Frank J., ed. 1997. *Constructing Tibetan Culture: Contemporary Perspectives*. Quebec: World Heritage Press.

Lopez, Donald S. Jr. 2018 [1998]. *Prisoners of Shangri-La, Tibetan Buddhism and the West*. Chicago: University of Chicago Press.

Pallis, Marco. 1949. *Peaks and Lamas*. New York: Alfred A. Knoff.

Petech, Luciano. 1939. *A Study on the Chronicles of Ladakh (Indian Tibet)*. Calcutta: Calcutta Oriental Press.

Phillips, Ruth B. and Christopher B. Steiner. 1999. "Art Authenticity and the Baggage of Cultural Encounter." In *Unpacking Culture: Art and Commodity in Colonial and Postcolonial Worlds*, edited by Ruth B. Phillips and Christopher B. Steiner, 3–20. Berkeley: University of California Press.

Radhu, Abdul Wahid. 2017. *Tibetan Caravans: Journeys from Leh to Lhasa*. New Delhi: Speaking Tiger.

Ranjan, Aditi, and M. P. Ranjan, eds. 2005. *Handmade in India*. Ahmedabad: Mapin.

Rizvi, Janet. 1999. *Trans-Himalayan Caravans: Merchant Princes and Peasant Traders in Ladakh*. New Delhi: Oxford University Press.

Rizvi, Janet. 2012. *Ladakh: Crossroads of High Asia*. New Delhi: Oxford University Press.

Svašek, Maruška. 2007. *Anthropology, Art and Cultural Production.* London: Pluto Press.

van Beek, Martijn. 1999. "Hill Councils, Development, and Democracy: Assumptions and Experiences from Ladakh." *Alternatives: Global, Local, Political* 24 (4): 435–459.

van Beek, Martijn. 2004. "Dangerous Liaisons: Hindu Nationalism and Buddhist Radicalism in Ladakh." In *Religious Radicalism and Security in South Asia,* edited by Satu P. Limaye, Robert G. Wirsing and Mohan Malik, 193–218. Honolulu: Asia-Pacific Center for Security Studies.

Chapter 9

Poets from the refugee camps in Rwanda talk to the world

Andrea Grieder

University of Technologies and Arts of Byumba, Rwanda

Abstract

This chapter explores "poetic efficacy" based on a poetry project with young people in three refugee camps in Rwanda. The term poetic efficacy is inspired by Alfred Gell (1998) and an ethnopoetic perspective on the power of words. Gell has argued that an anthropological study of arts needs to focus on arts in terms of social interactions. Efficacy brings to light the intentionality and impact of an art object. With the poetic voices from the Refugee Camps, we learn how poetry creates an agency by expressing self-conceptions beyond stereotypes and by narrating stories of exile, violence and war through poetry. A life in an unstable world can find a home in words, constructing meaning and strengthening resilience. Through the ethnopoetic lens of Jerome Rothenberg, we understand the empathic capacity of poets to be *we* and *them*. Poetry does not only give wings in a metaphoric way but gives access to a world beyond the borders of a refugee camp. The authors of the discussed poems are young, artists, part of a youth community inhabiting the virtual space of YouTube, WhatsApp and Facebook, and they are refugees. With Spivak, we may ask: Can the Refugee Speak? The answer is: Yes, they can, and poetry gives them a language to talk to the world.

Keywords: ethnopoetics, war, refugee camps, resilience, social media

> "On how that journey began
> To a destination we didn't know
> Of all the things we left behind
> Our land
> Our belongings
> Even our dreams."
> (Transpoesis 2019)

I am a refugee but… is the title of a poetry music performance that was on stage at the international *Ubumuntu Arts Festival* in Kigali, Rwanda in 2019 (Transpoesis 2019). The refugee camp poets, originally from Burundi and the Democratic Republic of Congo, told their stories in poetic language. As a collaboration between poets from Kigali and others from different refugee camps in Rwanda, the performance speaks about stereotypes about refugees within society as well as sharing self-conceptualisations by the young talented poets themselves as human beings, as artists, as strong and beautiful beings.

The performance was the culminating artwork of a one-year project with the title *Voices from the Refugee Camps*, run by the Rwanda-based poetry organisation *Transpoesis*. On the basis of this project, I explore how poetry contributes to the empowerment of refugees, people from the margins in general, and how poetry has the potential to provoke a transformation of both the individual and the community. In this essay the following questions are addressed: What is the meaning of poetry in an unstable and transitory world? How do arts connect youth with their past and relate them to a war-affected history? I discuss these questions with reference to the main thematic topics of this collective publication: marginality, art and anthropology, tradition and modernity. Within anthropology, the notion "ethnopoetics" has contributed significantly to the re-thinking of poetry. Rothenberg (2017 [1968]) initiated a valorisation not only of poetry but of arts in general from non-western societies. More broadly, ethnopoetics creates innovative forms of expressing and speaking about the surreal, the emotional, the un-representable and the mystical dimensions—the sounds and rhythms—of our existence. This perspective allows us to analyse the emotions and instability of life in refugee camps. The poems created within this universe contribute tremendously to our understanding of the experience of being a refugee. As a shared inspiration of this collective publication, Alfred Gell's anthropological theory of the arts orients my analysis towards the efficacy of poetry (Gell 1998). With *Voices from the Refugee Camps*, we learn about the power of poetry, or in my words, its "poetic efficacy". We also learn what it means to be human in a transitory place of home, the capacity of resilience and of creating a world of meaning, using poetry as a language to speak from the margins to the wider world.

Poetry in anthropology

Poetry is a "muse" of anthropology. The relationship between poetry and anthropology goes from an understanding of the beauty of the (oral) poetry of the other (Prattis 1985; Tedlock 1993), to an expression of anthropological knowledge in poetic form (Kusserow 2013; Jones 2006; Smith 2002).

In the 1960s, the American author and poet, Jerome Rothenberg, introduced the term ethnopoetics and generated a rich field of work which aimed at the rethinking of poetry within anthropology. He initiated a valuing of poetry within the academic world. This discourse on ethnopoetics was nourished by *Alcheringa*, a journal founded in 1970 by Rothenberg and Tedlock, and different conferences on Ethnopoetics since 1975. In *Symposium of the Whole* Rothenberg and Rothenberg (1983) bring together a group of artists, anthropologists and poets, among them Tristan Tzara, Claude Lévi-Strauss, Léopold Sédar Senghor, Victor Turner, and Mircea Eliade. They all share an interest in poetry and the "poetics of performances" (Schechner 1983) of non-western cultures.

As much as the poems from the refugee camps are rooted in tradition, a poetic culture—its rhythms and sounds—and metaphoric thinking, these poems are at the same time an expression of modernity. The youth of Africa today, not only from the camps but also from the urban spaces, aspire to express themselves in English rather than in their mother tongues—be it Kinyarwanda in Rwanda, Kirundi in Burundi or Swahili or Lingala in the Democratic Republic of Congo. English is seen as a door to the world. The poems are first written, then performed with the way to the final performance stage in itself a moment of empowerment: of acquiring confidence, of conquering a new world. In terms of form and content, as well as the diffusion of the poems as art works (on social media), the distinction between non-Western and Western references becomes fluid.

With "as poets, *we* are *them*", Rothenberg expresses the reflexive moment of poets as anthropologists, which means "to say, articulate, our sense of being in the world, however changeful, dangerous, and slippery" (Rothenberg 1975, 61). Ethnopoetics is about the voices of people who "struggle to make, create, an instrument of language, discourse, to map the changes, to facilitate them, live in the hope of transformation, of a deepened, heightened, sense of who we are and where" (Ibid, 61). Rothenberg calls for a philosophical understanding of what we are as human beings, but also as an understanding of ourselves through "the other".

Interestingly, the poets use their poetic sensibility to be *us* and *them* at the same time. During a joint workshop with poets from Kigali and those from the refugee camp, groups of three to four poets began writing and performing about stereotypes within the society. For the group presentations, I expected the poets from Kigali to represent the voices of the society, to speak out against the stereotypes. Surprisingly, all poets spoke in the first place as refugees, expressing an empathetic act. We can thereby understand the creative potential of a poetic imagination to be "I" and "you".

We also find the fluidity of understanding of the self and the other in the reflections of Walt Nopalito Smith (2002) who created a poem to describe his bi-cultural experiences. He argues that a large part of his writing stems from his frustration with "scientific thinking" and the realisation that "the reality in which I am participant—observing is *not* objective but is emotion-full rather than emotion-*less*, and that reality is *not* separable from my own being" (Smith 2002, 461). For Smith, the process of ethnopoetry is also about his "own identity metamorphosis," which links his "creative power" to move away from "the perceptual shackles of monocultural identity," (Ibid, 461) and, in particular, the lens of the scientific method.

With ethnopoetics, the anthropologist is the poet. In *Refuge* Adrie Kusserow (2013) uses her poetic sensibility to speak about the experiences of Sudanese refugees based in Uganda, Sudan and the United States. Barbara Jones (2006) writes a fourteen-stanza poem in the first person based on a survey carried out with 131 social workers, to express a myriad of emotions around the death of children. In *The Ethnopoetics of Space and Transformation: Young People's Engagement, Activism and Aesthetics*, Stuart Aitken (2014) finds in poetry a language to capture the change and instability in the world of cerebral palsy, and the US Health System, or school yard violence. Integrating poetic stanzas and images of young people struggling against statelessness in Slovenia or child work in immigrant communities in the United States, he expresses the unrepresentable of conversations and the emotions which precede the written text. With his ethnopoetic approach, Aitken underlines "the importance of *affect* as a political push in the world" (Aitken 2014, 9)—a push which comes from capturing poetically a world of transformation and change as well as the emotions embedded in space. With reference to Tarek al-Tayeb Mohamed Bouaziz, the young Tunisian who set himself on fire to protest against harassment and humiliation, thereby sparking a Tunisian uprising which started the Arab Spring, Aitken argues: "There is an aesthetic to this push that comprises who we are, what we say, how we say it, what we do, when, where with whom." (Ibid, 8). Aitken sensitises us to the embeddedness of the self within space and the forms of expression showing how people and emotions and spaces are connected.

For a deeper understanding of the refugee camp and its poetics of space, I outline some aspects of the reality in the refugee camps. By the fact of their existence, a refugee "camp" is a spatial experience.

Life in refugee camps in Rwanda

Rwanda currently accommodates around 150,000 refugees in six different refugee camps around the country: Gihembe (Northern Province), Kiziba (Karongi District, Western Province), Nyabiheke (Gatsibo District, Eastern Province), Kigeme (Nyamagabe District, Southern Province), Mugombwa Camps (Gisagara District, Southern Province) housing people from the Democratic Republic of Congo (DRC), with Mahama Refugee Camp accommodating Burundian refugees. As a result of the volatility and conflicts within the Great

Lakes Region, the camps were constructed at different periods in the region's history. The Great Lakes Region knows much about the flows of people in the rhythm of conflicts. We remember the Genocide against the Tutsi in Rwanda which took place in 1994, and which resulted in a tremendous loss of human lives, the destruction of infrastructure and the negative impact on the country's mental health. But it is also to be remembered for the important movements of people between Rwanda and the Democratic Republic of Congo, with the *genocidaires* fearing revenge and persecution, and crossing the borders in great numbers. At the same time, citizens from the DRC fled as a response to different political turmoils in their own country to find a home in one of the refugee camps in Rwanda. The oldest camp, Kiziba, was opened back in December 1996. The most recently constructed camp is the Mahama Refugee Camp, built in 2015, and home to about 50,000 people from the conflict-affected neighbouring country of Burundi.

The movements of people in the rhythm of those conflicts are captured in individual refugee stories. One of these stories is by Eric Kamanzi. Originally from the Democratic Republic of Congo, Eric came to Rwanda in 1996 when he was 10 years old. He lived in several camps. He recalls, "Before being brought to Gihembe Camp, we lived in the Mubano Transit Centre. I was a child, and we were without a father; my mother was pregnant and unable to do any work. We lived in a community hall, with more than two hundred others. We slept on the cement floor, and getting enough food was very hard. To get water, we used the water from Lake Kivu to cook and drink" (interview with Eric Kamanzi, May 23, 2019). He remembers being "exhausted and discouraged by the miserable life in the camp", so the family tried to be repatriated in both 2003 and 2005. But the insecurity in the Congo brought them back to a life in the refugee camp in Rwanda.

Having not only spent almost all his early years in refugee camps, but having also kept a strong network of contacts with people from other camps, Eric is an appropriate and valid observer of "refugee camp reality". He speaks of some older men who have never accepted the situation and reality of their new lives in the camp. "There are many cases of depression; some people commit suicide," Eric reports: "I have witnessed different cases during my time in Gihembe Camp, with people hanging themselves on a tree".

The American Refugee Committee Rwanda (ARC) provides a range of support services: primary health care, HIV/AIDS prevention, treatment and training in gender-based violence prevention. In addition, they ensure the provision of potable water, nutrition, shelter and infrastructure construction, and the maintenance of sanitation and hygiene. However, as time has passed, the food provided to refugees has been decreased. Today, the World Food Programme

(WFP) provides money instead of food.[1] Shelters are provided for the refugees, but the population density in the camps is high. Eric narrates the reality thus: "A family of seven people live in a house measuring four-by-three square meters; the tent shelters are separated from each other by just one metre". These living conditions are creating both health and social problems: the transmission of infectious diseases and AIDS, while other diseases result from poor diets leading to malnutrition. Young people also suffer due to a lack of employment opportunities, which creates more juvenile delinquency, prostitution, gender-based violence, rape and conflicts within families. Parents are unable to carry out their duties as parents, such as buying the basic things needed for their families. With no life goals or no or little vision, many refugees have lost hope.

Over time, various support services in the camps have decreased. The Jesuit Refugee Service (JRS) used to provide Primary to Secondary School level education for refugee children, and also introduced a series of Vocational Training programmes (in subjects such as car mechanics, sewing, arts and handicrafts), but these activities were stopped in 2009. The United Nations High Commissioner for Refugees (UNHCR) then took responsibility for providing the Government of Rwanda's standard 9-Year Basic Education programme. However, the young people in the camps felt frustrated that they had no opportunities to complete their senior school education to then try to go on to university.

Out of a growing feeling of disappointment, the youth from Gihembe Refugee Camp initiated the Forum for Congolese Refugee Students in 2008. The aim of the Forum was to support young refugees in their aspirations to attend higher education. The Forum established not only the Hope School for Senior 4 to Senior 6 students, but also prepared them for the Rwandan national exams. With the support of UNHCR and the Adventist Development and Relief Agency (ADRA), the Forum campaigned successfully with the Rwanda Government to have a 12-Year programme set up for refugee students. They were then integrated into local secondary schools. Within the last few years, World Vision has also funded refugees so that they can attend Rwandan schools. Others have received scholarships from the Albert Einstein German Academic Refugee Initiative (DAFI), a German Government scholarship programme. To some extent, the decrease in camp services has pushed the youth there to advocate for their own rights, and this has brought about changes, including a more integrative approach to the refugee situation.

---

[1] 6,500 Rwandan Francs (RWF) per month per person, which is approximately 7 US dollars.

Poetry for the youth in the refugee camps

Aware of the vulnerability of people living in these refugee camps, Transpoesis initiated a one-year poetry programme in 2018 in three Rwandan refugee camps: Gihembe, Nyabiheke and Mahama camps. The programme comprised workshops, competitions and performances, and aimed to encourage the young people in the camps to use poetry to express themselves. Founded in 2015, Transpoesis' vision is to identify poetic talents and create a platform for those talents, not only in the camps but also in society at large. The organisation's vision has two conceptual pillars: one is a strong poetry tradition in Rwandan culture (as well as the neighbouring countries); the other considers poetry as a therapy that can contribute to the development of the society (Obiora et al. 2018). While I am the founder and director of Transpoesis, this essay is written from my primary position as an anthropologist.

All non-refugees need to obtain a special permit from the Ministry of Emergency Management (MIDIMAR) to enter any refugee camp, especially if it is for a cultural or artistic project. Once Transpoesis had received the necessary authorisation to enter the camps, the poetic journey in the camps could start. The description of the journey to one of the camps provides an idea of the atmosphere in such a camp, although the level of organisation and the mind-set of the camp's population may differ, depending on when it was set up. The Mahama refugee camp is one hour's drive from the main road, and when we visited it, our driver drove slowly and carefully because the road was not tarmacked and had a lot of potholes. The UNHCR vehicles and the drivers of other non-governmental organisations (NGO), such as Save the Children, and the American Refugee Committee, drove fast over the same road as they were used to its condition. The NGO staff has to travel every day from Kirehe, where the humanitarian staff is accommodated during the working week. The Transpoesis team of three poetry trainers and myself, as a coordinator of the project, stayed in Kirehe during the two-day programme. On the Friday afternoon representatives of UNHCR and Save the Children returned to Kigali, which is located a four-hour drive away, returning to see their families, and to relax away from refugee camp life.

The Mahama Camp has been built over an immense field close to the border with Tanzania and comprises some 5,000 brick-built houses set out in straight lines. From the air, the camp looks as if it has been drawn with a ruler, but the closer you get, the more visible the misery of camp life becomes. These small houses are packed with entire families, where privacy and intimacy are difficult to maintain, and everyday activities such as cooking or washing, occupy a lot of people's time due to the scarcity of water, and the long days full of empty hours.

All camps are organized like a village with "heads" for different units, and a camp committee director for overall camp coordination. To ensure the success of our programme, it was important to understand the organisational structure in each camp to gauge the best channels of communication when in search of poetic talent, and to encourage the poets to attend the workshops and the competition.

In each camp, we trained a group of 30 to 40 young people aged between 17 and 27. The Transpoesis poetry training focused on the notions of "home", of the love of one's neighbours and of hope. The most talented poets from each training were selected to participate in a camp intern competition.

Arts as a humanitarian intervention

The *Voices from the Refugee Camps* project is in line with a changed perspective in humanitarian intervention in refugee camps. The value of offering arts for refugee communities has gained international importance and recognition in the recent past. The numerous artistic programmes now on offer meet a range of objectives. Some activities focus purely on "entertainment", others may contribute to an "international awareness-raising" or use arts as a way of healing, or empowerment or capacity building. Along with an increased awareness of the therapeutic aspects of the creative arts, many projects have a direct link to human rights issues, promote a holistic understanding of humanitarian interventions and policy-making around refugee crises and foster participatory solutions to problems faced by refugees.

A number of artistic programmes are managed under the UNHCR's broad umbrella. The UN Agency for Refugees has, for example, established non-profit art initiatives implemented by Film Aid in the Kakuma and Daadab Refugee Camps in Kenya. "The project aims to give the refugees a voice and an opportunity to express themselves, using art as a source of livelihood, and also as a form of therapy. The project also seeks to keep refugees occupied to avoid the potential risks of getting involved in criminality" (Rodriguez 2017). Artistic activities are known and recognised as being a powerful way of contributing to the healing of individual experiences after war and violence. Working with Syrian and Sudanese refugees in Egypt, the NGO Care International-Egypt uses art therapy to allow refugees to express their painful journeys and to learn how to manage their emotional pain more effectively. The groups *Clowns without Borders (CWB)*, *Cirus2Iraq* and *Mimi the Clown* use clown performances to make kids in refugee camps laugh (Peacock 2016). Laughter is a therapeutic form used in different conflict or post-conflict contexts. In Rwanda laughter is an approach used in theatre (McFarren 2011) or in combination with yoga.[2]

Other artistic programmes aim to provide knowledge and mentoring in artistic self-expression. Such arts projects create opportunities for storytelling, cultural expression and personal reflection. These activities may bring some vibrant colours to the monotony and everyday routines found in the camps, and the formalistic interactions with humanitarian organisation staff. Another well-known organisation, Theatre for Refugees, operates in many countries, such as Kenya, France, Germany and Palestine to name a few. In his inspiring essay *Health Theatre in a Hmong Refugee Camp*, Dwight Conquergood (1988) shares his experience of theatre in the refugee camp Ban Vinai, in Thailand. The camp was home to Hmong refugees who had fled the Communist rule in neighboring Laos. While running a health education programme for the International Rescue Committee (IRC) in 1985, Conquergood realised that performances like storytelling, folk singing, drumming, lamentations for the dead, and shamanic practices were taking place in the camp and were helping the refugee camp inhabitants as a way of coping with the "camp reality". According to Conquergood, these performances served to preserve the Hmong culture, constituted a sense of "community" and added stability to the uncertainty of the people's daily lives.

Building on his observations, Conquergood started using performances as a method for developing "critical awareness" amongst the refugees. Here, arts become an initiator to foster new ways of thinking about the surroundings and to stimulate the transformation of behaviours. In such a creative process, an old way of life would be integrated in the new. Arts help to creatively deal with challenges of the lived reality found and experienced by those in the camps.

Poetic efficacy

Alfred Gell argues for the impossibility "of using 'aesthetics' as a universal parameter of cultural description and comparison" (Gell 1998, 3). An anthropology of arts cannot be the study of the aesthetic principles of a culture, but of the mobilisation of aesthetic principles in the course of social interaction. Gell clearly states: "Aesthetic judgments are only interior mental acts" (Gell 1998, 3). Gell's interest focuses on the relation of the art object to the external world, in the production and circulation of art objects in the social world (Gell 1992, 3). Therefore, Gell's anthropological theory of the arts is explored in terms of relationships. With his interest in intentionality, Gell makes a strong reference to the notion of agency. According to Gell, art is seen as a kind of technology that

---

[2] Accessed April 7, 2020. www.rrgo.org/category/laughter_yoga/.

captivates and ensnares others in the intentionality of its producers. Art objects are considered devices "for securing the acquiescence of individuals in the network of intentionality in which they are enmeshed" (Gell 1992, 43). With the notion of the "efficacy of the art object", Gell focuses on intentionality and its impact on social relationships.

How can we understand the efficacy of poetry? In which way can we identify poetic agency? In *Art's Visual Efficacy*, Jakub Stejskal provides insights into understanding the visual efficacy of art objects by asking: What has their being offered to a gaze achieved? (Stejskal 2017, 81). For poetry, we can therefore ask: What has their being offered to an ear or to a performance achieved? This project, *Voices from the Refugee Camps,* provides us with some answers and knowledge to these questions. I can identify poetic efficacy on two levels: on the level of the poet, on an individual dimension, and on the level of the community, as the impact within a network of social relationships.

Poetic agency—transcending stereotypes

Liisa Malkki (1995) has comprehensively analysed and criticised the reality of refugee camps, as well as the discourses on "refugee-ness" as an institutionalised dependency through the creation of permanent transitional homes. Poems have the potential to emotionally reflect and question these narratives, to contribute to a re-writing and (re-)shaping of other narratives. In a similar vein, with the aim of breaking through a monolithic, one-dimensional representation of refugees, Jehan Bseiso and Becky Thompson conducted poetry workshops in refugee camps around the Aegean Sea. Their project, conducted in 2019, was called *Making Mirrors: Writing/Righting by and for Refugees.* Jehan Bseiso, a Palestinian poet, and US-based Becky Thompson collected examples of the artistic voices they heard in the camps in order to refute the negative stereotypes of refugees, and to create different narratives around being a refugee. The poetic voices attempted to re-write the image of refugees as being essentially passive and needy individuals, with nothing to contribute to society or to the world at large. Art has the power to challenge this perspective by engaging with refugees as active agents and by enriching the cultural life of the society.

Voices from the Refugee Camps used a similar approach. The title of the poetry performance *I am a refugee, but…* expresses the two moments of construction of meaning. *I am a refugee* is about one's identity as a refugee, which is written on official documents and which concerns the refugees' experiences of having fled their home country due to war, terror and persecution, or famine and fear of death. It is also about stereotypes found within the society. *But…* expresses that space where the "I" speaks out in its own right, where self-perception beyond the norms is aspired to, and spoken out loud. *But…* and *I am a refugee* are performed in different intervals and in the form of a dialogue.

Bahati Innocent,[3] a poet based in Kigali, speaks about stereotypes in his poem:

"You [society] think: someone lazy is given a day off, UNHCR has given them shelter.

The heart which thinks about work has become shrunken.

It didn't exist at all.

You think that you cook a meal and when food is ready, you bring it to me.

I just eat.

This is my life, you think.

We didn't have one courageous farmer and now, my people came to escape hunger, you say about me. When hunger attacked us, we left our country for a foreign country that hosted us, gave us food without work.

All this is not true."

With the aim of reshaping the narratives of dependency and laziness, Kenny Ndayiragije's poem also speaks out against stereotypes and gives value to the strengths within the refugee experience.

"And I say: Think again

We don't beg, we apply

We don't trick, we ask

We are not the results of our circumstances, but of our choices

Though we appear vulnerable, we have beautiful destinations

And in the end,

We survive a tough history

With our uniqueness

We are refugees. We are humans."

Poetic writings beyond victimhood and stereotypes contribute to the reshaping of collective narrations. "We have beautiful destinations. We are humans"—this is the voice of empowerment and self-affirmation. The concepts on refugee-ness may change not only through the content of the poems written in the camp, but also by the presence of talents in the camp on different stages. The Swiss Consulate in Kigali, one of the partners for this project, *Voices from the Refugee Camp*, invited Transpoesis to perform an extract of *I am a refugee, but ...* at their Swiss National Day celebrations on August 1, 2019. With an audience of diplomats, Swiss nationals, representatives of the Rwandan government and of cultural and artistic institutions, many ears (and mouths) were busy with small talk, but the content reached out to some important listeners. A Rwandan Minister expressed how deeply he was touched by the poetry performance that

---

[3] The poet has disappeared since February 7, 2021. https://pen-international.org/news/rwanda-investigate-and-publicly-account-for-the-whereabouts-of-poet-innocent-bahati

evening, asking his Swiss diplomatic colleague: "Are these performers really from the refugee camps?" The performance was a stimulation, asking the audience to think differently: "refugees" may indeed be in need of support and a safe "home", but they also need recognition and appreciation of their talents.

In his ethnopoetical work, Aitken explores the capacity of poetry to express its affects in the spaces of marginality. Considering the potential of young people, he hopes "that—through words and silences—their lyrical subject expands and pushes the politics" (Aitken 2014, 28). It is a beautiful argument, which focuses on what I call a "poetic push": the poem's capacity to shake the world and re-create words of meaning. The presence of these poets from the refugee camps in Rwanda at an international festival stage, or at a diplomatic event, can create a small but meaningful poetic push, poetic voices reaching out from the margins of the camps to the ears, hearts and minds of a government representative, of a national and international audience.

Home and poetic nostalgia

"Home" is a recurring theme in the poems written from the camps. With "My Home, why don't you care for me?"[4] Janvier Nsabimana was not only the winner of the Nyrirarumaga Trophy at the poetry competition, *Kigali Vibrates with Poetry*, Edition 9 in October 2017, he was also a pioneer of contributing a voice from the refugee camps to the artistic and poetic landscape of Kigali. Simone Weil emphasised the basic human need of being rooted, most often associated with a specific place, thus: "to be rooted is perhaps the most important and least recognized need of a human soul" (Weil 1987 [1952], 41). For refugees, the rootedness to a place—one's home or country—has been painfully disrupted by war, distance and trauma. Liisa Malkki has pointed to the problematic naturalised link between places and people. Especially in the discourses on refugees, this results in a pathologisation of uprootedness in the national order of things. She does not intend to deny that displacement can be a traumatising experience, but the "sedentarist assumptions about attachment to place lead us to define 'displacement' not as a fact about socio-political content, but rather an inner, pathological condition of the displaced" (Malkki 1992, 33) which can take a political, medical or moral form. In consequence, the blame for this condition is put on the refugees. But what we need here is a socio-political understanding and analysis of the refugee context.

Depending on individual refugee experiences, "home" has very different meanings for the young people in the camps. In an unstable world—and a refugee camp is an unstable world by its very nature—people experience home very strongly in their memories, "memories of, and claims on, places that they

---

[4] Accessed February 21, 2020. https://youtu.be/kbL0LKRTR14.

can or will not corporeally inhabit" (Ibid, 24). For example, for people living in the Gihembe refugee camp, the notion of home has a quite different meaning than for the inhabitants of the Mahama camp. The Gihembe refugee youth, originally from the DRC, more usually born in Rwanda, and more specifically in the camp where they now still live. They have no personal experience of their homeland to hold on to. They know of "home" mainly through the media, or from stories told to them by community and family members. Others arrived in Rwanda at a very early age. In contrast, Burundian refugees left their homes about three years ago, and express their nostalgia for home through sharing their vivid experiences, describing "home" as a place of abundance and joy, glorifying their friends as taking care of them, treating them "like royalty". Their experience in the camp is seen in reference to the beauty of these memories of home, and this creates deeply painful experiences of a life without future perspectives. Iribuka Jedidja writes in her poem "From Town to Exile":

> "Tell my lover, that I don't wear jewellery anymore
> That I eat beans, mixed with pebbles."

And she continues with an observation of the camp as the space of NGOs:

> "I only see cars during working hours."

The poet expresses the everyday camp reality, which is organised and structured around the activities of the NGOs, within the framed presence of the vehicles belonging to UNHCR and other NGOs within the camp, which create a hierarchic division of space.

During the workshop in the camp, the Transpoesis team also realised how strongly the concept and reality of time is regulated. At 5 p.m. all those who were not refugees had to leave the camp confines. We often had to leave in a rush, with a feeling of deserting people as we made our way back into a safe world, with no more time to exchange ideas, and talk any longer, or to listen to the voices eager to connect—voices eager to know that someone cares for their talents, for their lives and futures.

In some of the poems from the workshop we find "home" as a place of memory, a place to be kept alive as a form of coping with the conditions in the camp.

> "How can I say here is home.
> While my heart is hungry for my homeland?
> My heart is full of sadness
> Because my siblings stayed in my homeland.
> Here is not home!
> Home is not where I am now
> Home is where I departed from
> Here is not my home."

The deep sense of nostalgia found in the poem "Here Is Not My Home", written by Emery Tuyisenge, is what can be defined as a coping mechanism. In *Imagined Homelands: British Poetry in the Colonies* by Jason R. Rudy (2017) he writes about the poetry of British immigrants in Australia. Rudy considers poems as a tool for mitigating nostalgic pain, as a coping mechanism with loss and trauma: "The emigrant poet inhabits a nostalgic structure so as to understand his own experience of difference and absence" (Rudy 2017, 38). The poems express "what it means to be displaced, and yet still attached" (Ibid.). Unlike the emigrant, the refugee is forcefully deprived of his or her country of origin, which adds to the feeling of loss through distance and absence, the pain of deep un-rootedness and the feeling of rejection and abandonment.

Beyond the feeling of nostalgia, we find other ways of re-creating and re-defining the notion of home. During the Transpoesis workshop, the trainer, King Kivumbi, shared his own experiences thus: "As a kid, the feeling of 'home' was when I came back "home" and my sisters or mum gave me a shower." Interestingly, this experience of "home" is not rooted in space itself but is relational. King had grown up in Rwanda, Burundi and Uganda, living his life on the move, not as a refugee, but with the experience that home can be found in relationships, rather than in land or territory. During a conversation with refugees from the DRC living in Uganda, at the Byumba Arts Festival, Jean, an artist living in the refugee camp, brought to light another meaning of "home" when he said: "The day I leave the refugee camp, I will also miss it." In this way, he underlines that "home" is not only places and experiences, or of relations, but home is also the story of the lives we are writing through our poems. The poem thereby becomes a place of home. Janvier Nsabimana, who lives in the Nyabiheke refugee camp, writes: "My second home is everywhere I find a true smile", where "home" becomes detached from a place, but is rooted in an emotion, in its relatedness to others. "I don't have a home. I have the world" expresses Janvier with his emotional voice. The door to this world is poetry. In 2018, Janvier's journey to becoming a poet began: winning the Nyirarumaga poetry award empowered him with confidence to develop his poetic talents. In 2019, he organised his own poetry event, called *A Pen*, to celebrate how poetry has changed his life.

From despair to symbols of strength—strengthening resilience

We find in some of the poems a feeling of despair and frustration, of unlived potential. In "The Voice of Destiny", regarded as the best poem in the *Mahama Camp Competition*,[5] Kenny Ndayiragije speaks out about how the camp is

---

[5] Accessed February 22, 2020. https://youtu.be/Zxrzb9FjZUY.

Poets from the refugee camps 183

indeed a safe and secure place, but for that, the price is of lost freedom: "In vain you realise that what has been before an unconditional freedom, and joy of living, has been transformed into a jail where you're condemned to stay because it provides security."

Recognising the camp as a secure place, the poet evokes the social and cultural misery found among the inhabitants:

> "I found myself in the middle of nowhere.
> Ahhh, and I still do not understand how life has become so tricky and unfair.
> Destiny guides me by using the long rope of life.
> So as to give my soul hunger and thirst for security and the joy of freedom
> I used to triumph in.
> Ultimately, I am here in this 'pretend' exile of peace,
> Which appears as a secure place to travellers...
> But a jail I'm condemned to stay in."

With Ghislaine Nishimwe, we found another talented young woman on the poetry stage. Her poem, written in Kirundi, and called "Agahinda kabaho kagashira", she speaks about a sorrowful life, but also speaks out for an end of those sorrows. She came second in the competition. With a microphone in her hand, Ghislaine captured the audience with her emotionally intensive and interactive stage presence. From an ethnopoetical perspective, with a focus on the sounds and rhythms, it was clear that the audience's participation in the performance created an emotional connection, lasting beyond the poet's actual time on the stage. The competition took place on a basketball court inside the refugee camp, with the audience forming circles around the poet in the centre. Children of all ages, from small kids to school pupils made up the first row, with adults standing behind them, all curious but, at the same time, hesitant to come closer. Dressed in a long flowing pink dress, Ghislaine gave her emotional poetic performance making long Ehhh! sounds, repeating this between the lines of the poem's content, thus creating an echo in the audience. This refrain became a chorus: the poet's voice and the interactions with the audience—becoming the collective.

> Ghislaine: Ehhh!
> Audience: Ehhh!

It is a joyful and interactive sound, similar to the culturally used sound to comment a story. The dividing line between "performer" and "audience" no longer exists—they are in fusion. The audience is part of the performance and connects beyond the time of the performance. This Ehhh! Still echoes now in my ears—a poetic echo, a vibration of content and sound—continuing long after the performance and competition.

During the Transpoesis workshop, we tried to strengthen that feeling of hope and strength. Poetry can have a healing power through guided work on our emotions, and through the use of symbolisation, the creation of images and metaphors (Grieder 2018). Writing in symbols is a poetic way of exploring an intuitive truth. At the same time, such writing can allow us to mobilise our resources of resilience. During the workshop in the camp, we asked participants to choose a symbol that they felt represented their qualities, their personality. Alice expressed herself with the symbol of a stone, a stone that can also be a pillar of a house. Jacques spoke of a stone in its capacity to construct a road, a house: "I am a stone, I am strong and cannot be destroyed by any means," he says. The stone has the capacity to be useful, as well as for its resilience to external forces, such as the violence that exists in one's home country, or poverty and unemployment in the camps, a challenging environment where the dependency on external international organisations undermines young people's desires to be agents in charge of their own destinies.

Steve Kwizera chose the elephant as his symbol. "I am bigger than other animals" he writes. Steve contextualised his chosen symbol in the different places where he had been living—in his home country, Burundi, in the refugee camp and in an imagined future place, of hope.

> "I am in struggle
> Though awkward
> Challenging life 'cause of them
> I was living in a forest, where many animals tried to kill each other
> In search of security
> I left my forest to find another one
> I am intelligent, but because of losing the security in my heart,
> I have no occasion to use it.
> I am overburdened because of these small animals we lived with,
> Who are still wanting to eat my body.
> I am so big that I can be shared with them
> Another thing, I may say, I'm still looking for another forest far away,
> Where I ran to before and where my animal neighors cannot reach me."

With the symbol of the elephant, Steve brings to light that although he lives in an apparently safe place, fear of the past and of violence is captivating the heart of people. And peace of the heart is difficult to find in a refugee camp, which can never be a home. Steve expresses resilience and an anchor in faith:

"But actually, I'm satisfied with who I am, I like my origin because I was created by Almighty God. It puzzled my best friend how I am satisfied even though I've not had much food."

With animals of strength as symbols, we find an association between strength and resilience. Jean Paul chose the lion heart as his symbol, with the notion of the lion's strength, and the capacity of generosity of heart, and thus a person who is powerful, but who uses this power to help others.

The language of the world

Speaking of people living in the margins, not only from the arts but in more general ways, Spivak has pointed correctly to the language that people possess—in this case, the subaltern—to speak out and reach the world with their voices (Spivak 1983). In *Can the Subaltern Speak?* Spivak asks us to consider why the subaltern is not heard, because they do not know the language they need to use to reach out to their audience, the public. The subaltern does not know the language to use to speak from the margins to the centre.

As with Spivak, we can also ask: Can Refugees Speak? If yes, in which language do they speak? Bringing poetry to the young people in the refugee camps was not only an important moment of creating a space for their stories and talents, but also of providing them with a language to speak out loud about their life experiences. It may be a story of suffering and trauma, but also one of hope. The poetic voices from the camp oscillate between pain and victimhood on the one hand, and hope, resilience and empowerment on the other. Poetry is the language that refugees can use to speak out. In the poetry performance *I am a refugee, but…* we hear the voice of Dinah Nzirakaneza, a young woman living in the Nyabiheke refugee camp, and originally form the Democratic Republic of Congo. She says:

"Don't call me trouble-maker. I just live in troubles.
Don't call me tragedy, tragedy make me homeless.
Don't call me something. I call myself a human being.
And if you call me a refugee, start with human being first.
I know that I am a refugee. I have a refugee card.
If I am thin, I am a small refugee.
If I am fat, I am a big refugee.
If I am too fat, I am the biggest refugee.
It all has the same end as refugee.
But if you call me a refugee, start with a human being
Just say a human being and add that she is a girl
And end with refugee. You will be saying me the right way I am."

Dinah challenges the way people are named and labelled. It is her way of saying: "I am a human. I am a talent." Her poem points to words that name and categorise, words used to marginalise. Poetry is the language to re-name and to re-create words, and therefore meaning. This young woman speaks out to ask others to validate and recognise her talents instead of opposing people and their language—to stop them putting her in a box, of being a refugee.

> "I am a human being with an everlasting time
> In class, you can come after me
> In knowledge, I can be your role model
> In art, I can make you confused
> In poetry, I can make you back at home as you came."

Poetry gives people a language to say who they are. Beyond the creative space in the camp or on the stage of a festival, poetry brings those marginalised voices into the virtual space of the Web (and of YouTube and other social media channels) and to a real space, of a dream to travel and of leaving the camps behind. With Gell, we understand that the efficacy is created through social relationships, and the power of poetic words is the cement that creates connections.

David Ndagijimana, a young poet from the Mahama Camp, using his artist's name of 'No-Stress', is living testimony to this connection to the world. Originally from Burundi, David arrived in the Mahama Refugee Camp on May 5, 2015, and came all alone. When writing about his life, he says: "I am 23 years old. When I was 14 years old, I lived with my parents. But I left them many years ago." The silence of "how and why" creates a space for stories to be imagined or to be told later. David was part of the Transpoesis poetry training and performance. Despite his name, No-Stress, David challenged everyone by developing a strong voice and stage presence, and he conquered his fears and feelings of stress so that in the end he was without stress and became the symbol he had chosen to represent him: a lion.

Some weeks after the performance in Kigali at the International Arts Festival, David wrote to me using WhatsApp to say:

> "Maybe it is true
> People help when it is too late.
> But when poet Andrea and Transpoesis
> Came to our camp
> I became another one
> Because of poetry.
> You saved my life."

No-Stress speaks not only about change in his own life, but also of a transformation among young people in the camp. He told me: "We won that competition, and we really must acknowledge that Transpoesis changed our minds here in Mahama camp." This change can be seen in reference to a world of hope in the camp, and maybe also of a recognition by others of being a poet, being a star, or of the connection David and the other young people were able to make with other poets in Kigali, in the society outside and beyond the camp.

Putting things more clearly, David shared how poetry has changed his life: "We love you, our mother. I sometimes think about your work (…). I really appreciate your help because before coming there (Kigali and the Ubumuntu Arts Festival), I didn't have a smartphone. But now, I have an expensive one. I thank you so much."

With a smile, I realised that poetry impacts others by giving them a smartphone! This point is simple and deep at the same time. A phone is a status symbol, but also provides access to wider communication. Using an integrative approach, where the workshop and the performance in Kigali brought poets from the refugee camps together with poets from Kigali, the capital city, enabled those from the camps to learn and be inspired, to feel part of a wider community, not just of refugees but of artists. In a world where the Smartphone is used for "likes" and "friends," where self-promotion and views are part of an artistic career, a Smartphone offers access to the immense global world of the Web. It gives access to the imagination, to dreams and the magic of broader encounters and support, which a poet in the refugee camp would never have without such a phone.

In another conversation I had with No-Stress, he told me that he now goes regularly to the studio to record his poems "because people in the camp love them so much." Within the digital world, another dimension of connecting and of the YouTube poetic presence takes place.

Conclusion

With the poetry music performance *I am a refugee, but...* I have explored poetic voices from the margins of the refugee camps in Rwanda (Transpoesis 2019). The poems are rooted in the poetic tradition of metaphor, of sounds and rhythms. At the same time, the poets aspire to speak out, in English, the language of the real world and of the virtual world, or the world-wide web.

Using the notion of the efficacy of art from the anthropological theory of art by Alfred Gell, I discussed the notion of poetic efficacy: the capacity to create a sense of agency by speaking out against stereotypes on refugee-ness using the power of poetry to name things and people differently, to use words to recreate a different world of meaning. From the individual, we can see the potential to reshape collective narratives on refugee-ness which focus on dependency and the source of instability and problems. Poems allow the young people from the camps to speak out about their problems instead of being seen themselves as the problem. Beyond the content, an ethnopoetic approach highlights the sounds and rhythms of poetic performances with their capacity to create an echo in the audience, with the capacity to touch the hearts of the audience. This poetic efficacy may thereby resonate with the need to be considered first as human—a young woman, a girl, an artist, a talent—before being considered as a refugee. Once the poem is spoken out, it can enter the public space in its content and form and can thus create a poetic push: to transform the perceptions and discourse on refugee-ness within society, and within the political space.

Knowledge of poetry provides the young people in the refugee camps with a language that gives them access to a potentially huge network within the camps, in the society outside and also beyond—in the world of social media. Poetry allows refugees to have and use a language that can speak from the margins to the wider world.

References

Aitken, Stuart C. 2014. *The Ethnopoetics of Space and Transformation: Young People's Engagement, Activism and Aesthetics*. Ashgate: Routledge.

Bseiso, Jehan and Becky Thompson. 2019. *Making Mirrors: Writing/Righting by and for Refugees*. Massachusetts: Olive Branch Press.

Conquergood, Dwight. 1988. "Health Theatre in a Hmong Refugee Camp: Performance, Community and Culture." *The Drama Review* 32 (3): 174–208.

Gell, Alfred. 1992. "The Technology of Enchantment and the Enchantment of Technology." In *Anthropology, Art and Aesthetics*, edited by J. Coote and A. Shelton, 49–67. Oxford: Clarendon Press.

Gell, Alfred. 1998. *Art and Agency. An Anthropological Theory*. Oxford: Clarendon Press.

Grieder, Andrea. 2018. "Poesie in Rwanda: Kühe und Schmerz." In *Wenn Sprache heilt. Handbuch für Poesie—und Bibliotherapie, Biographiearbeit und Kreatives Schreiben. Festschrift für Ilse Orth*, edited by Hilarion G. Petzold, Brigitte Leeser und Elisabeth Klempenauer, 425–443. Bielefeld: Aisthesis Verlag.

Jones, Barbara. 2006. "Tucked in My Heart: The Use of Ethnopoetry to Represent Meaning-Making of Social Workers in Pediatric Palliative Care." *Journal of Palliative Medicine* 9 (3): 789–90.

Kusserow, Adrie. S. 2013. *Refuge: Poems*. Serie: American Poets Continuum. No. 137. Rochester. NY: BOA Editions.

Malkki, Liisa. 1992. "National Geographic: The Rooting of Peoples and the Territorialization of National Identity among Scholars and Refugees." *Cultural Anthropology* 7(1): 24–44.

Malkki, Liisa. 1995. "Refugees and Exile: From 'Refugee Studies' to the National Order of Things." *Annual Review of* Anthropology 24: 49–523.

McFarren, Cheryl Kennedy. 2011. "Laughter Diplomacy: Transcultural Understanding at Play in Rwanda." *Theater Topics* 21(2): 163–173.

Obiora Ike, Andrea Grieder and Ignace Haaz. 2018. *Poetry and Ethics. Inventing Possibilities in Which We Are Moved to Action and How We Live Together.* Geneva: Globethics.net Global No.16.

Peacock, Louise. 2016. "Sending a laughter around the world." *Humor* 29(2): 223–241.

Prattis, J. Iain. 1985. *Reflections: The Anthropological Muse.* American Anthropological Association.

Rodriguez, Melissa. 2017. *Art Becomes Therapeutic.*

Rothenberg, Jerome. 1975. "Pre-face to a Symposium of Ethnopoetics." In *Alcheringa (Selections): Ethnopoetics,* edited by Jerome Rothenberg und Dennis Tedlock, 60–66. Accessed August 5, 2019. www.durationpress.com/archives/ethnopoetics/alcheringa/alcheringa.pdf.

Rothenberg, Jerome. 2017 [1968]. *Technicians of the Sacred: A Range of Poetries from Africa, America, Asia, Europa and Oceania, Revised and Expanded.* Berkeley: University of California Press.

Rothenberg, Jerome and Diane Rothenberg, eds. 1983. *Symposium of the Whole: A Range of Discourse Toward an Ethnopoetics.* Berkeley, Los Angeles, and London: University of California Press.

Rudy, Jason R. 2017. *Imagined Homelands: British Poetry in the Colonies.* Baltimore: Johns Hopkins University Press.

Schechner, Richard. 1983. "From Ritual to Theatre and Back: The Structure/Process of Efficacy-Entertainment Dyad." In *Symposium of the Whole. A Range of Discourse Toward an Ethnopoetics,* edited by Rothenberg Jerome, and Rothenberg Diane, 311–327. Berkeley, Los Angeles, and London: University of California Press.

Smith, Walt Nopalito. 2002. "Ethno-Poetry Notes." *International Journal of Qualitative Studies in Education* 15 (4): 461–467.

Spivak, Gayatri C. 1983. "Can the Subaltern Speak?" In *Marxism and the Interpretation of Culture,* edited by Cary Nelson and Lawrence Grossberg, 24–28. London: Mcmillan.

Stejskal, Jakub. 2017. "Art's Visual Efficacy: The Case of Anthony Forge's Abelam Corpus." *RES Anthropology and Aesthetics* 67/68: 78–93.

Tedlock, Dennis. 1993. *Breath on the Mirror: Mythic Voices and Visions of the Living Maya.* Albuquerque, NM: University of New Mexico Press. Accessed June 3, 2019. www.warscapes.com/art/art-becomes-therapeutic-refugees.

Transpoesis. 2019. *I am a refugee, but…* Video, 20 Min. Accessed September 4, 2019. https://youtu.be/aAZo_s3EpPs.

Weil, Simon. 1987 [1952]. *The Need for Roots: Prelude to a Declaration of Duties Towards Mankind.* New York: Ark.

Epilogue
Art in/from the margins: some comparative and theoretical reflections

John Clammer

O.P. Jindal Global University, India

Abstract

In the epilogue John Clammer reflects on the issue of art in or from the margins comparatively and theoretically. He attempts to give a shape to the edited volume as a whole by tying the individual case studies into a theoretical and politically aware whole. In doing so, he critically scrutinises the term "margin" and its use in different contexts, particularly with regard to art history. Moreover, with his special focus on ethnography, museums and the development of the arts in non-Western regions he uncovers the often invisible richness of the historical and contemporary regional arts worldwide in their visual and performative forms as well as their great potential for the near future.

Keywords: polycentric aesthetics, museum, development, postcolonialism, aesthetic justice

The notion of art from the margins raises many practical and theoretical issues, and indeed, political ones too. The basic argument of this essay is that there are no "margins", but those artistic spaces and processes considered as such are considered in this way because of the politics of the art world, a failure to develop and accept a polycentric aesthetics, the biases of art history and the negative aspects of the professionalisation of art and art education. In other words, the category of "margins" is a social construct, and as such can be contested on many grounds, historical, sociological, geographical and ideological.

As we know from art history, a number of categories of artistic production have been at some time considered "marginal", and yet many of these, when "recognised" by the formal art world in Howard Becker's (1982) sense of the term, have been drawn into that world and become the subject of exhibitions, publications and even films. Examples might include so-called "outsider art" or "Art Brut", the productions, often of high aesthetic standards, known collectively as crafts (including weaving, pottery, jewellery, and carving), "folk" or tribal arts, and the art of the handicapped. Where, in the case of visual arts, such productions are displayed when and if they enter a gallery or museum situation, is important—in an "art" gallery or in an ethnographic museum for instance—the former being "real" art, the latter of primarily anthropological interest as "objects", of cultural interest certainly, but somehow not "real" art. This is a position now vigorously opposed by the growing field of the anthropology of art (e. g. Coote and Shelton 1994; Gell 1998; Morphy and Perkins 2006; Schneider and Wright 2010; Westermann 2005). The thesis advanced here is that the notion of margins does not refer to an actual spatial, temporal or sociological location: it is a constructed category reflecting thinking among curators, critics and art historians and is not a reflection of the aesthetic qualities of the actual productions. This is a problem with material forms of art; with intangible ones such as dance, theatre and other modes of performance, these problems are, if anything, intensified.

Evidentially the notion of marginal arts has been contested from a number of directions other than that of anthropology. These include the creation of dedicated museums showing particular categories of such art, for example the museum of Art Brut in Lausanne, Switzerland, founded by the artist Jean Dubuffet, devoted specifically to "Outsider Art", the Indira Gandhi Rashtriya Manav Sangrahalaya in Bhopal, India, which is devoted to Indian tribal arts (Wolf and Wolf 2015), the Bharat Bhavan in the same city which showcases side by side Indian modern and contemporary art and tribal art, and the increasing practice of "mainstream" art galleries to stage exhibitions devoted to forms of art or artists that would previously have been considered outliers. Examples in my own fairly recent experience in Japan alone include a major show of masks from Africa, Oceania and elsewhere at the Tokyo Metropolitan Teien Art Museum, a show at the Mori Art Museum on contemporary art of the Arab world, and two shows at the prestigious New National Art Center, one on *Forms*, many of them from the arts and crafts of the non-Western world, and an entire exhibit devoted to the Australian Aboriginal artist Emily Kame Kngwarreye. Such museum-based initiatives have been increasingly reinforced by more theoretical work in the field of visual anthropology and its application to history as well as to contemporary societies (e. g. Motrescu-Mayes and Banks 2018), interest in comparative aesthetics, the rapid expansion of the fields of visual culture and performance studies, and magazines, networks and exhibitions devoted to the "craft arts" (often in fields such as ceramics or textiles.)

These initiatives have in turn been reinforced by art educational projects designed to overcome the artificial distinction between arts and crafts, such as revived interest in the movement pioneered in England by William Morris, or the philosophy of the original Bauhaus, designed to encourage its students to work towards the "total work of art" (*Gesamtkunstwerk*)—and indeed the original Weimar Bauhaus had workshops in weaving and textile arts, pottery, bookbinding, furniture design, mural painting, and stained glass, as well as for painting and sculpture. In a sense its "successor", the Black Mountain College in the US, not only continued this tradition, but also emphasised literature and poetry (Harris 2002). In some cases, as in the Bhopal examples cited above, attempts have been made to bring together tribal artists (of which a substantial community exists in India) and contemporary professional artists, often resulting in significant cross-fertilisation. A significant recent book entitled *Indian Contemporary Art* for example, is actually a major survey of tribal arts, and in particular painting, in the sub-continent (Perdriolle 2012), and interestingly does not include examples of what might more conventionally (at least in "art world" terms) be considered as contemporary art at all. As this essay was in preparation, an exhibition was in progress at the National Gallery of Art in Washington, DC, on the theme of "Outliers and American Vanguard Art", where the term "outlier" has been substituted for "outsider" and "vanguard" for folk art. The term "Outsider Art" now seems to have become itself formalised as an accepted term as referring to work by non-professional artists, often suffering from some form of mental or emotional handicap, and in many cases institutionalised in hospitals or care facilities and whose work often exhibits an obsessive quality and concern with repetition and minute detail (Peiry 2001).

Mainstreams and margins

All these categorisations of art forms raise their own interesting conceptual and aesthetic questions. Attaching labels indeed creates such categories, say "Art Brut", into which certain forms of artistic production are slotted, and so, while certainly recognising such forms as genuine expressions of art, also reinforces their marginalisation as somehow separate from "mainstream" forms. As suggested above, the theoretical basis of this paper is that there are no "margins", only zones categorised as such by critics and curators in the "art world" who have the power to label. What requires interrogating is thus not the status or aesthetic quality of the works produced in such zones outside of the conventional mainstream, but rather the ideology and politics of that very "mainstream" that works to exclude whole areas of artistic production and expression from its purview and fails to grant legitimacy to works of beauty, utility and qualities of design that often surpass those of much "contemporary art". This is indeed a question of politics, since it bears not only upon the exclusion or incorporation of certain categories of artistic production in a formal sense (craft/art, outsider/insider, work of art/utilitarian object, work of art/religious object), but also of a larger politics of exclusion.

Whereas in principle globalisation should have made available to many of us access and exposure to many forms of art, both historically and cross-culturally, and of the different aesthetic systems underlying or expressed by these objects, in practice what it has often done is simply expand the hegemony of certain styles, techniques, and forms of display and representation. This is a problem faced not only by "outsider" artists (in the sense defined above), but also by post-colonial artists in particular, and certainly by the producers of craftworks, vernacular architects and, in the case of the performance arts, dancers or musicians who produce movements and sounds deeply indigenous to their own cultures. If they paint like their Western counterparts they are accused of copying and producing derivative art; if they do not, then they run the risk of not being "understood" and denied access to the larger global circuits of display, publicity, recognition, sales, and even fame.

Writers on post-colonial literature have examined this issue at considerable length, but the whole field of 'post-colonial studies' is heavily dominated by literary studies; much less has been said or written about the visual or performative arts. Without undertaking (the, in any case impossible) attempt to list examples of visual art or performance that have fallen outside of the "mainstream", and either remain there unacknowledged, or are, through processes of "discovery" by the gate-keepers (critics, art historians, art journalists, or even, in some cases media-savvy anthropologists and designers) recognised, publicised, made the subject of exhibitions, and becomes "collectable" by individuals and museums which have the financial means to do so. The point however, one effectively illustrated by the essays in this volume, is that the notion of "margins" is a shifting and fluid one. The ability to define such a category resides only with those who possess the power to define—a circular situation in that "power" is itself conferred by the very art world institutions and social scientists that have created a notion of centre and periphery. Those inhabiting a "margin" are unlikely to even know that: for them their productions are naturally authentic and indigenous. It is only through non-recognition or active stigmatisation that the sensation of being marginal to something else arises. It is, after all, an entirely relative term.

This is not to say that the process or experience of marginalisation does not have profound consequences. In many ways artistic marginalisation shares essential features with any other form of identity politics: the need for recognition and the possibility of having voice. It can have economic consequences if nobody buys or displays or views that particular art form). It can have profound psychological consequences: the suicide of the Indian tribal painter Jangarh Singh Shyam who had suddenly become famous, rich and much displayed and very much "discovered" by the international art world, is usually attributed to the huge pressures of publicity, fame and sudden dramatic increase in income placed on an individual who had no cultural resources to cope with these forces. He literally had no language to understand what was being said to or about him without an interpreter, and yet was subject to rapid and unmediated exposure to a world and to travel for which he was completely unprepared (Luis 2019). The dangers of cultural appropriation are also all too evident, and unfortunately abundant examples exist of indigenous artists being exploited and even abandoned by their (foreign) promoters. The 19th-century practice of world fairs and expositions dramatically underlined this, with "native" artisans, dancers and musicians often being displayed in virtually a zoo-like situation (Mathur 2000), although the positive influence was also possible, such as the influence of Javanese and Balinese dance seen at such fairs on European ballet and emerging forms of modern dance. There have also been cases where this situation of display, as if in a zoo, has been turned into a critical art form itself, forcing viewers to radically interrogate their own perceptions and cultural assumptions. A wonderful example of this has been the work of the performance artists Coco Fusco and Guillermo Gomez-Pena, who have displayed themselves in many different places in a cage, pretending to be wild natives from the jungles of Latin America, and have had their assistants record the reactions of audiences.

While artistic "quotation" or borrowing has always existed, the point at which this becomes appropriation is a complex one, but examples abound in which a "marginal" art form or performance style has been adapted and incorporated into mainstream productions without due recognition being given to the actual sources of that inspiration. There is even politics to this. The leading creator of what is now considered to be modern dance in India, Uday Shankar, whose productions were widely acclaimed in the West for their exoticism, was severely criticised within India for not cleaving sufficiently to the canons of Indian classical dance, and, in his blending of Western and Indian forms of being both inauthentic and not sufficiently nationalist enough in the context of the years immediately before and after Indian independence in 1947. His cosmopolitanism was "exotic" outside of India (itself potentially a form of marginalisation), and marginal within, it only being later that his innovations were seen as highly creative and as actually rescuing Indian dance from the potentially stultifying effects of strict adherence only to classical forms. Creating the "modern" was itself a position of marginality in the Indian dance world of the 1940s (Purkayastha 2014).

In her presentation at the conference from which this volume arose, Andrea Grieder made two important statements, notably that "The voices from the margins need to find poetic empowerment in the affirmation of a positive original capacity for social creativity in themselves", and through this means to create the capacity to challenge 'normalcy' and through this power of using poetic imagination to connect people in the process of sharing expressions. This essay takes up a similar theme, but not specifically in relation to poetry, but to other forms of performance such as dance and theatre, and to the visual arts, and in particular painting. A number of case studies can be drawn from a large range of marginalised groups including handicapped persons in Japan,

India and the UK, refugees and internally displaced people in India including Rohingya from Myanmar, Sri Lankan Tamils who fled the only recently concluded civil war in their country, and Bangladeshi illegal migrants to West Bengal and Assam. Looming large in this picture in South Asia are the survivors and descendants of the 1947 Partition of India and Pakistan and the many traumas that accompanied that event and the huge displacement of populations that it entailed.

This catalogue is tragically large, given that many of the artistically marginalised are also displaced, whether geographically, politically, conceptually or socially. Such cases might also include tribal artists in India and on work with children in remote areas of the Indian states of Odisha and West Bengal, on Dalit ("Untouchable") artists and on displaced people in Kashmir, an area disputed between India and Pakistan, all of which have been documented. This essay will also refer to comparative work from other similar situations in the Middle East and elsewhere on which literature exists. In particular, it raises the question of the nature of "performance from the margins" and what it might tell us about the nature of contemporary "world encounters". While there is no space to discuss these case studies in detail, broad continuities between them will be noted and the significance of these for the larger discussion of "marginal art" indicated and some theoretical conclusions will be drawn.

Performing/contesting marginality

Many other examples abound, including ones from the highly "developed" world reveal, as examined by Eriko Aoki in the context of contemporary Japan in this volume (Chapter 4). Others which have drawn attention to the artistically and usually also socially marginalised in other such societies include the literature on the work of the British drama group *Extant*, which is widely regarded as the UK's leading blind and visually impaired theatre group, the London based Entelechy troupe which works with individuals of many kinds of learning and physical disabilities, and the US-based Amaryllis Theatre which produces plays with deaf actors. In rather different situations Community Performance (or theatre) has proved to be highly effective not only in empowerment, but also in, as the name suggests, community building in such contexts as inner city, ethnically divided housing estates (Crehan 2011). Likewise, work has been done with the physically disabled, in hospitals, prisons, the streets, residential homes for the elderly, and in "developing" world situations where it often appears as an instance of "applied" theatre directed towards educating audiences in such areas as gender relations, AIDS/HIV and caste (Kuppers 2007). The whole subject of the so-called "theatre of the oppressed", traced to its charismatic founder Augusto Boal, has attracted a great deal of attention and will not be gone into in any detail here (Boal 2008;

Wong and Clammer 2017; Clammer 2015a, 63–82), although case studies of its application with truly marginalised groups such as long-term prisoners and street children in India show its transformative potential (Chakraborty and Munsi 2018). Refugees and those in situations of, hopefully, temporary displacement as a result of natural disasters, also demonstrate the power of art in reflecting the voices of those regarded as being on the "margins" of mainstream society (Duggan and Peschel 2016).

It is important to note the significant role that "applied theatre" has played in refugee situations and ones of internal displacement of peoples, where the ability to not only create entertainment (a far from insignificant value in the boredom and seeming futurelessness of the refugee camp), but to express in corporeal form emotions, hopes, critique, rights, desires and possibilities—in other words to express social imagination—has proved to be a powerful act of creativity. This is especially the case when the subject and form of drama or dance is evolved from within the displaced community itself and not introduced from the outside (Balfour 2013; Wickstom 2012). These examples all touch upon deep existential issues of loss, injustice, hope. Continuing as well as historical examples of conflict and civil war (Kashmir, Syria, Congo, Palestine, Somalia, South Sudan) generate profound poetry and narratives of suffering, loss and displacement. War has stimulated not only poetry and painting, but increasingly those most contemporary of art forms—photography and film. In his beautiful book on Kashmir, Suvir Kaul, himself a member of the largely displaced and marginalised Kashmiri Pandit (Hindu) community, has combined poetry by local poets, his own essays, and photographs by Javed Dar to give a brilliant sense of the everyday trauma of living in a zone of virtually permanent conflict, curfew, death and disablement, as well as political betrayal by the central Indian government which has failed to keep its promises to the region and responded to the disorder that it itself has largely engineered through increasing militarisation and oppression (Kaul 2018).

These examples all illustrate the significance of "performing identity". Identity is a complex subject and a highly contested one, both conceptually and politically. It is now accepted that notions such as gender and ethnicity are performative (Clammer 2015b) and that the notion of the "self" is largely a socially and culturally constructed one. It is perhaps significant that the very period in which there was an anthropological upsurge in literature on alternative aesthetic systems, there was also a parallel and intersecting upsurge of interest in the question of self-identity, the two being linked by notions of an aesthetic of "proper" behavior. This is exemplified for example in Bradd Shore's *Sala'ilua: A Samoan Mystery* (Shore 1982) in which a detailed ethnographic case is presented showing the relationships between ideas of deportment and propriety and an extended view of aesthetics that extends far beyond the production or appreciation of art objects. But then, as we know from Margaret Mead's classic, if contested, accounts of Samoan society, that culture has always been highly performative in its modes of self-presentation, with dance being an important part of that process. Underlying these discussions is the idea that the sense of self is constructed in many cases through creative activity, whether performative in the sense of theatre or dance, or in some form of material expression such as painting, pottery or weaving. While this is true in all cases, from the perspective of disability and displacement it takes on additional power and points to the extent that, despite the absence of such factors from conventional development discourse, these elements are in fact vital to social as well as individual transformation and empowerment, the latter in fact often taking cultural forms and leading to the expansion of the total repertoire of cultural expressions and possibilities.

Aesthetics from the "South"

Aesthetics as a formal discipline, one usually practiced within the space of philosophy rather than of art practice, is still dominated by Western approaches, assumptions and examples. Major surveys of art history give little space to non-Western examples, the Western ones still being the norm. Herbert Read's major text on the subject mentions only six Asian artists—all Japanese or Korean, has only four illustrations of their work out of over 300 depicted, and no Indians or Africans and only a tiny handful of Latin Americans (Read 1997). In fact, however, the existence of radically different art forms, the struggles of post-colonial artists to find a distinctive and authentic voice, the existence of art forms still very much tied to religion and ritual, and the many expressions of "outsider" art, all point to the necessity of what has been termed a "polycentric aesthetics" (Shohat and Stam 2002).

Interestingly in the anthropology of the arts, the 1970s and 1980s saw a burst of activity on what might be called alternative or polycentric aesthetics, expressed in works such as John Chernoff's *African Rhythm and African Sensibility* (1979), Edward Schieffelin's *The Sorrow of the Lonely and the Burning of the Dancers* (1976), and perhaps pre-eminently in Steven Feld's *Sound and Sentiment: Birds, Weeping, Poetics and Song in Kaluli Expression* (1982) in which he examines a culture in which the world is interpreted through sound rather than vision. Surveys of non-Western aesthetics tend almost always to discussions of "classical" aesthetic systems with little or no reference to contemporary thinking and practice (Sasaki 2010). In fact, it is in contemporary practices, which may or may not be theorised in formal terms, that aesthetics is quite literally embodied, and it is from these embodied actions that aesthetics needs to be derived. This is as true of any expression of "marginal" art as it is of the "mainstream". The performance practices of the handicapped make this very clear and represent exemplary cases of emergent aesthetics, but of course a similar case can be made for "crafts", Art Brut, tribal art, and for ritual.

This point can be extended even further to suggest that it is often from the margins that creativity comes. This is now recognised in Western art history where it is the *fauves*, the Expressionists, and the multitude of rebels against academic art, who are seen as the sources of renewal in the visual arts, and with figures like Stravinsky in music, Isadora Duncan in dance, and Bertolt Brecht and Samuel Beckett in theatre. The extension of this to modes of artistic creativity outside of the canon greatly expands the fertility and application of aesthetics, and links it to the *uses* of art as well as its formal qualities. It is interesting that under the impact of the environmental crisis, the notion of environmental aesthetics has quite powerfully emerged and has spread, if not again much into the visual or performing arts, certainly into literature under the rubric of eco-criticism (e. g. Huggan and Tiffin 2010). The idea of "world music" is now a familiar one and the typical music store, at least in the affluent world, will have a section devoted to the music of many parts of that world—in Japan for example Arabic music including modernised forms ("Arabic Groove"), Javanese classical music, Tibetan chanting, Greek Orthodox plainsong, Turkish pop music, Balinese music, music from the Andes (often to be heard live in the streets of Tokyo), Hindustani classical *ragas* and many other forms. The anthropological significance of this still awaits further exploration, as does its impact on aesthetics.

In 2014 the Portuguese social theorist and critical commentator on colonialism and, as some would argue, its successor, "development", Boaventura de Sousa Santos, published his book *Epistemologies of the South: Justice Against Epistemicide* (de Sousa Santos 2014) in which he powerfully argued that among the most damaging of the consequences of colonialism has been what, a generation before, the distinguished Kenyan novelist Ngugi wa Thiong'o had dubbed (thinking of its antithesis) "decolonizing the mind" (Thiong'o 1986). That is, the inculcation of patterns of thought and language, and hence of the categories through which one understands the world, alien to the indigenous sensibility and philosophy of the spaces colonised.

To succeed in genuine and thorough decolonisation it is not enough to simply get rid of the colonisers, to break the negative economic links that they had established between the colony and the metropolis and to "nativise" and localise institutions (courts, universities, the bureaucracy and the army), but also, and perhaps even more importantly, to identify and overcome the categories of thought that had been often subtly imposed through education, language use, access to positions and other cultural means. These, when carried to their extreme, result in what de Sousa Santos calls "epistemicide", meaning the death of indigenous categories of thought, or at the very least, their reduction to a second-class status in relation to the colonial modes of thought. It is significant that Thiong'o, after publishing the just cited book (in English and published in London), announced that thereafter he would only write in his native languages, even though this would obviously greatly restrict his potential audience to readers of Kikuyu or Swahili. The act of translation (which has indeed happened with some of his subsequent books) is thus fraught with philosophical as well as technical problems: is it in fact the rendering back into the colonial categories of thought the indigenous epistemology embodied in the original? And if not, would an "authentic" translation have to somehow match the aesthetics and style, or even physical layout, of the original, however initially alien that might be to foreign ears or eyes? Given that much "traditional" literature (including the scriptures of many religions as well as poetry) is or was oral in nature and is meant to be sung or recited, not read, the very process of reception is greatly influenced by not only the literary form, but also by the mode of transmission.

Thiong'o is of course a novelist and his primary medium is therefore the story. Santos' argument, powerful as it is, is a cognitive one: it has to do with patterns of thought, logic and rationality. But Thiong'o's position raises another set of possibilities—that of the existence of different forms of aesthetics such that patterns of beauty, form and representation, the structure of narratives and myths, the modes of performing (rather than just reading) a literary work, vary substantially from one culture to another. If there can be "epistemologies of the south" can there also be "aesthetics of the south"? A basic argument of this essay is that, of course, the answer is very much "yes" there can, and that such systems do indeed exist in abundance, although rarely captured by comparative philosophy, even forms emanating from such contexts as contemporary Africa (Eze 1997; Chimakonam 2017). This is significant for several important reasons— at the very least from the point of view of "aesthetic justice"—recognising alternative forms of aesthetics as equally authentic. When the distinguished Indian painter Gaganendranath Tagore began to experiment with a distinctive but recognisably Cubist style, the British art critic (and former colonial officer) W.G. Archer, accused him of being "un cubiste manqué" and having effectively stolen his ideas from Picasso and Braque rather than seeing his work as not derivative, but as the local reinterpretation of an emerging style, even as the founders of Western Cubism had been heavily influenced by African sculpture (Archer 1959, 112). But there are other dimensions too—the possible existence of multiple modernities, not only in the economic or sociological senses, but also in terms of art and its impact on the evolution of cultural forms (e. g. Clark 1998), the profound fact that alternative aesthetics promote or embody alternative imaginaries, which in turn lead to alternative realities—in architecture for example. What might be thought of as "classical" cultural postcolonialism (as represented by such seminal figures as Edward Said for instance), has been primarily literary in its concerns. It might however be time to produce a companion volume to the early significant study of post-colonial literature—Bill Ashcroft, Gareth Griffith and Helen Tiffin's celebrated *The Empire Writes Back* (2017 [1989]) perhaps with the title *The Empire Paints Back*, or if you prefer, performs back.

The work of many Indian artists of the late colonial and early independence periods shows how this might be accomplished—Tyeb Mehta drawing heavily on themes from Hinduism and Indian classical mythology, Jamini Roy on the iconography of village art, M.F. Husain on both Hinduism and Islam, Amrita Sher-Gil on village life and customs. These are all celebrated "major" artists, whose work is well known internationally. But if one turns to the indigenous art of those villages which form much of the actual civilisation of both historical and contemporary India, one finds immediately spontaneous artist expressions and underlying aesthetics—in the Bengal and Oriyan *Pata* paintings of Eastern India (KCC 2018), the wall paintings of the Santhal people, also of Bengal and the many forms of vibrant indigenous painting that exist throughout the country including Bhil, Warli, Gond, Madhubani, and many others (Dallapiccola 2011), to say nothing of crafts—textiles, pottery, wood carving, vernacular architecture, costume, metalwork and others. If one extends this idea into film, theatre, music (where the aesthetic canons are radically different from that of Western forms) and dance—one of the most celebrated forms of performance in India—, the existence of a polycentric aesthetics immediately becomes apparent. Space does not permit, but a similar investigation can easily be launched into African arts and cinema (Kasfir 1999; Diawara 1992; Niang 2014), the art of the Australian Aborigines, and many other geographical and social situations.

The paradoxes of globalisation: the dialectic of inclusion and exclusion

In their book on Indian tribal arts, Wolf and Wolf (2015) raise many issues pertinent to the current discussion, including that such artists "remain outsiders and are seldom invited to participate in dialogues around culture and regeneration" (Ibid, 144), despite the fact that "Present day indigenous and folk artists are inextricably linked to the modern world, even if they are excluded or located on its peripheries" (Ibid, 128). This is in part because their work tends to be classified by the mainstream art and museum worlds as crafts, and hence not quite qualifying as authentic art. Wolf and Wolf see the solution to this as at least in part in the changing of museum practices which, in their view, have a fundamental responsibility to mediate what they call an "inclusive and authentic pluralism". This might be done through innovative curation and pedagogy and finding more egalitarian ways of fostering dialogue between the mainstream galleries and museums and not only emergent art forms, but in this case, ones that have been around for a long time, but have hardly entered the discourse of art history, criticism or appreciation. In practice these are mostly relegated to the ethnographic museum, rather than to the art gallery. Breakthroughs of this kind have indeed emerged—as with the now widespread appreciation of Australian Aboriginal art (signalled in part not only by its incorporation into art scholarship, but by rapidly rising prices in the commercial art market.) The challenge is not only to "allow" this to happen, but to actively facilitate it, especially in cases such as that of Dalit (formerly termed "untouchable") artists and writers, who have previously been excluded socially and religiously from mainstream Hindu society, and for whom their art and literature has become a vital means of struggle for social justice, self-expression and dignity (Ramakrishnan 2017). At that point of course, "art from the margins" crosses into political discourse as it becomes an important part of a politics of representation and identity.

Globalisation has brought many forms of hitherto separated art forms into contact with one another whether through museums, art publications, biennales, travel, and the migration of artists themselves. Artists have always travelled—Korean temple craftsmen to Japan, late 19th and early 20th Century Japanese and Spanish artists to Paris, contemporary Chinese painters to Singapore and then onwards to New York or London, Singaporean musicians and dancers to Europe, Thai artists to Australia. The internationalisation of art education with Singapore for example having two major art schools with numerous foreign, mainly Asian, students, has intensified this trend (Clammer 2016). German music schools have many Korean students, and the leading art auction houses have not only increasingly represented in particular Asian modern art but have begun to physically move their activities to the region, Christies for example holding its first Indian sales in Mumbai, India, in 2013 and producing a beautiful and collectable catalogue to mark the event. Globalisation has had many effects as we well know, and artistically many of these are still to be traced. They certainly include not only knowledge of "alternative" art forms, but also new patterns of hybridity, charges of appropriation and copying, new forms of artistic entrepreneurship as, for example, Indian tribal artists or Australian Aboriginal ones have begun to discover their marketability. These changes have stimulated new patterns of museum and curatorial practice, and new markets and sales networks, via the Internet for example. In the context of globalisation, the concept of "margin" is likely to be a temporary one, as former margins move to centrestage (for example the aforementioned Australian Aboriginal art), and formerly more central examples fall from notice and become themselves marginal in the eternally cyclical nature of the art market and the discoveries and preoccupations of art historians and critics, as well of artists themselves.

These processes, as with most aspects of globalisation, have both positive and negative implications. Among the negative are the creation of new "margins", excluded groups of one kind or another: refugees and internally or externally displaced persons, and other newly stigmatised groups. Among the positive are the appearance of many new forms of "diasporic" art and performance and the appearance of new nodes of artistic production and display—Singapore, Istanbul, Dubai, Hong Kong, Seoul, Jaipur, Cape Town—which, even if they do not displace the more acknowledged centres (London, New York, Paris), certainly diffuse and spatially democratise the nature of the "art world", a process underlined by the appearance of art magazines and monographs from highly diverse locations (Kaur and Dave-Mukherji 2014). "Flows" rather than discrete spaces then become the focus of interest, as when tribal artists from India show in London and Tokyo, weavers and potters from Latin America show in the USA, traditional Baul and Santhal tribal musicians perform in Amsterdam. And on yet another plane when theatre groups like The Company Theatre from Mumbai present Shakespeare in Hindi with Indian music, dance and costume, demonstrating yet another level of hybridity in which artistic forms from the West are appropriated and transformed into distinctively Asian styles of performance and presentation, or in Australasia, the ways in which motifs from Maori and Australian Aboriginal art have entered into the art practices of many local artists, but of non-indigenous origin (Thomas 1999).

Towards a new cosmopolitanism?

All this suggests the radical expansion of the new forms of artistic cosmopolitanism about which authors such as Nikos Papastergiadis (2012) and Grant Kester (2011) have written, as both note the ways in which old narratives (and notions of what is the "center" and what the "periphery" in a culturally multi-polar world) lose their legitimacy, creating space for new stories and visions to appear. Both document a number of collaborative projects in which artists from very different backgrounds have collaborated to produce work that is in a sense truly "global", and which goes a long way to overcoming any notion of marginal art as opposed to art from some "centre" (see also Schneider 2017). In so far as such projects are truly multinational and transcultural, they represent a new cosmopolitanism rather than any binary of centre and margin.

But there are many other implications: the expansion of the "capabilities" approach to development which includes culture and artistic production as a significant element (UNESCO and UNDP 2013). This notion relates to the ways in which the stimulation of local artistic production, including performance arts, film making and so-called crafts, can substantially promote poverty alleviation and encourage cultural self-respect, while also preserving or even reviving forms of artistic expression that were in danger of erosion or disappearing altogether.

New approaches to performance theory have expanded to include non-Western and non-able-bodied expressions, demonstrating that an expanded aesthetics and the perceptual and ethical revolutions that it implies can take place when symbolic inversion occurs when forms of art and performance that were never encountered before entering the realm of the possible, as frequently happens for example in performance by the differently-abled (Sandahl and Auslander 2005).

An expanded sense of social imagination takes place when creativity is unleashed, and when post-colonial art forms and "minor" and vernacular literatures are re-discovered and given their rightful place in art history. For this to happen of course, a genuine parity of aesthetic forms must be acknowledged, the lingering supposition that the "crafts" are not quite real "art" must be overcome (Buszek 2011), and the dichotomy of "traditional" as opposed to "contemporary" art forms finally dissolved. The "margins", far from being remote geographical or conceptual spaces, are actually the majority, and constitute a space in which socially relevant art is constantly produced and utilised. The recognition of this is not only aesthetically transformative, but also a source of on-going empowerment and recognition, for, as the slogan of the disabled movement in the US so aptly puts it, "Nothing About Us Without Us"; recognition must include inclusion, in this case in the world of art, art history and aesthetics. As Lucienne Peiry (2001) suggests in her detailed study of Art Brut, that form, quite outside the formal "art world" and long ignored by art historians and critics, is immensely rich in the elements that characterise the "margins" in general—as she puts it, intensely communicative works that both decentre cultural and aesthetic values and provide a "poetics of the strange", and which express hidden realms of expression, and point to "an alternative regenerative universe" (Ibid, 253). This statement sums up the fact that it is from the subjugated spaces that new creativity and new visions of the world flow, an insight that while certainly applicable to art, goes far beyond it to describe what is needful for our current troubled civilisation, for as the Mexican poet Octavio Paz once put it: "Imagination—a faculty of our nature to change itself" (Paz 1990, 78). Jonas Tinius phrases this idea a little differently, linking aesthetics not only to art, but also to ethics: "The concept of aesthetics, both in Baumgarten's [1750] original sense of the perceptible, sensible experience, and as a codified set of norms for evaluating and receiving art-forms, implies almost as varied a reality as moral norms or ethical practices" (Tinius 2015, 174). This leads him to the conclusion that in a similar way "a study of aesthetics, similar to that of ethics, especially when studying art institutions, requires attention to the complex set of internal formations of aesthetic traditions, which always also go beyond the 'mere' objects to include practices, rituals and assumptions" (Ibid.).

From the perspective of the present book, this implies two things. The first is the importance of comparative aesthetics, not only applied to other cultures, but also to the "Other" within (the artistically productive, but socially marginalised of any category), in which those aesthetic systems are given equal epistemological and ontological status as the "mainstream" ones which, as Marshall Sahlins argued years ago, are simply themselves forms of local knowledge that have, through various historical processes such as colonialism and the spread of capitalism, become hegemonic (Sahlins 1996). The second is the recognition that, while as is now widely recognised, the art objects or performances must be taken seriously in themselves (de La Fuente 2010), so must their social location and modes of production, consumption and dissemination. The two approaches (the "aesthetic" and the "sociological") are not in opposition. Far from it: when properly balanced they alert us to the proper and informed appreciation of the arts now brought to us through global encounters in their aesthetic richness and local social and cultural locations, making both aesthetics and anthropology genuinely comparative approaches to the variety and beauty of human artistic expressions.

References

Archer, W.G. 1959. *India and Modern Art*. London: Thames and Hudson.

Ashcroft, Bill, Gareth Griffiths and Helen Tiffin. 2017 [1989]. *The Empire Writes Back: Theory and Practice in Post-Colonial Literatures*. London and New York: Routledge.

Balfour, Michael, ed. 2013. *Refugee Performance: Practical Encounters*. Bristol: Intellect.

Becker, Howard. 1982. *Art Worlds*. Berkeley: University of California Press.

Boal, Augusto. 2008. *Theatre of the Oppressed*. Trans. Charles A. and Maria-Odilia Leal McBride and Emily Fryer. London: Pluto Press.

Buszek, Maria Elena. 2011. *Extra/Ordinary: Craft and Contemporary Art*. Durham, NC and London: Duke University Press.

Chakraborty, Aishika and Urmila Sarkar Munsi. 2018. "Moving with a Purpose: Women Dancers in Dialogue with Empowerment, Rehabilitation and Therapy." In *The Moving Space: Women in Dance*, edited by Urmila Sarkar Munshi and Aishika Chakraborty, 238–263. New Delhi: Primus Books.

Chernoff, John. 1979. *African Rhythm and African Sensibility: Aesthetics, Social Action and African Musical Idioms*. Chicago: Chicago University Press.

Chimakonam, Jonathan O. 2017. "African Philosophy and Global Epistemic Justice." *Journal of Global Ethics*, 13 (2): 120–137.

Clammer, John. 2015a. *Art, Culture and International Development: Humanizing Social Transformation*. New York and Abingdon: Routledge.

Clammer, John. 2015b. "Performing *Ethnicity*: Performance, Gender, Body and Belief in the Constitution and Signaling of Identity." *Ethnic and Racial Studies Review* 38 (13): 2159–2166.

Clammer, John. 2016. "Migrating Artists/Migrating Art: Intra-Asian Movement, New Asian Arts and New Sociologies of Artistic Consumption and Education."

In *Global Art and Diasporic Art in Japan and Asia,* edited by Kotaro Shinoda, 246–256. Tokyo: Mori Art Museum, MAM Documents 002 (In Japanese).

Clark, John. 1998. *Modern Asian Art.* Honolulu: University of Hawai'i Press.

Coote, Jeremy and Anthony Shelton, eds. 1994. *Anthropology, Art and Aesthetics.* Oxford: Clarendon Press.

Crehan, Kate. 2011. *Community Art: An Anthropological Perspective.* Oxford and New York: Berg.

Dallapiccola, Anna L. 2011. *Indian Painting: The Lesser Known Traditions.* New Delhi: Niyogi Books.

de la Fuente, Eduardo. 2007. "The 'New Sociology of Art': Putting Art Back into Social Sciences Approaches to the Arts." *Cultural Sociology* 1 (3): 409–425.

de Sousa Santos, Boaventura. 2014. *Epistemologies of the South: Justice Against Epistemicide.* London and New York: Routledge.

Diawara, Manthia. 1992. *African Cinema: Politics and Culture.* Bloomington and Indianapolis: Indiana University Press.

Duggan, Patrick and Lisa Peschel, eds. 2016. *Performing (for) Survival: Theatre, Crisis, Extremity.* New York and Basingstoke: Palgrave Macmillan.

Eze, Emmanuel Chukwudi, ed. 1997. *Postcolonial African Philosophy: A Critical Reader.* Oxford: Blackwell.

Feld, Steven. 1982. *Sound and Sentiment: Birds, Weeping, Poetics and Song in Kaluli Expression.* Philadelphia: University of Pennsylvania Press.

Gell, Alfred. 1998. *Art and Agency: An Anthropological Theory.* Oxford: Oxford University Press.

Harris, Mary Emma. 2002. *The Arts at Black Mountain College.* Cambridge, MA: The MIT Press.

Huggan, Graham and Helen Tiffin. 2010. *Postcolonial Ecocriticism: Literature, Animals, Environment.* Abingdon and New York: Routledge.

Kasfir, Sidney Littlefield. 1999. *Contemporary African Art.* London and New York: Thames and Hudson.

Kaul, Suvir. 2018. *Of Gardens and Graves: Kashmir, Poetry, Politics.* Durham, NC: Duke University Press.

Kaur, Raminder and Parul Dave-Mukherji, eds. 2014. *Arts and Aesthetics in a Globalizing World.* London and New York: Bloomsbury Academic.

Kester, Grant. 2011. *The One and the Many: Contemporary Collaborative Arts in a Global Context.* Durham, NC and London: Duke University Press.

Kuppers, Petra. 2007. *Community Performance: An Introduction.* London and New York: Routledge.

Luis, Sandip K. 2019. "Between Anthropology and History: The Entangled Lives of Jangarh Singh Shyam and Jagdish Swaminnathan." In *Intersections of Art, Anthropology and Art History in South Asia,* edited by Sasanka Perera and Dev Nath Pathak, 139–179. New York and Basingstoke: Palgrave Macmillan.

Mathur, Saloni. 2000. "Living Ethnological Exhibits: The Case of 1886." *Cultural Anthropology* 15 (4): 492–524.

Morphy, Howard and Morgan Perkins, eds. 2006. *The Anthropology of Art: A Reader.* Oxford: Wiley-Blackwell.

Motrescu-Mayes, Annamaria and Marcus Banks, eds. 2018. *Visual Histories of South Asia*. New Delhi: Primus Books.

Niang, Sada. 2014. *African Cinema: Legacy and Transformations*. Lanham, MD: Lexington Books.

Papastergiadis, Nikos. 2012. *Cosmopolitanism and Culture*. Cambridge and Malden, MA: Polity Press.

Paz, Octavio. 1990. *Alternating Current*. Translated by Helen Lane. New York: Arcade Publishing.

Peiry, Lucienne. 2001. *Art Brut: The Origins of Outsider Art*. Translated by James Frank. Paris: Flammarion.

Perdriolle, Herve. 2012. *Indian Contemporary Art*. Milan: 5 Continents Editions.

Purkayastha, Prarthana. 2014. *Indian Modern Dance: Feminism and Transnationalism*. Basingstoke and New York: Palgrave Macmillan.

Ramakrishnan, E.V. 2017. *Indigenous Imaginaries: Literature, Region, Modernity*. Hyderabad: Orient Blackswan.

Read, Herbert. 1997. *A Concise History of Modern Painting*. London: Thames and Hudson.

Sahlins, Marshall. 1996. "The Sadness of Sweetness: The Native Anthropology of Western Cosmology." *Current Anthropology* 37 (3): 395–415.

Sandahl, Carrie and Philip Auslander, eds. 2005. *Bodies in Commotion: Disability and Performance*. Ann Arbor: University of Michigan Press.

Sasaki, Kenichi, ed. 2010. *Asian Aesthetics*. Singapore: NUS Press and Kyoto: Kyoto University Press.

Schieffelin, Edward L. 1976. *The Sorrow of the Lonely and the Burning of the Dancers*. New York: St. Martin's Press.

Schneider, Arnd, ed. 2017. *Alternative Art and Anthropology: Global Encounters*. London and New York: Bloomsbury.

Schneider, Arnd and Christopher Wright, eds. 2010. *Between Art and Anthropology: Contemporary Ethnographic Practice*. Oxford: Berg.

Shohat, Ella and Robert Stam. 2002. "Narrativizing Visual Culture: Towards a Polycentric Visual Culture." In *The Visual Culture Reader*, edited *by* Nicholas Mirzoeff, 37–59. London and New York.

Shore, Bradd. 1982. *Sala ílua: A Samoan Mystery*. New York: Columbia University Press.

Thiong'o, Ngugi wa. 1986. *Decolonizing the Mind: The Politics of Language in African Literature*. London: James Curry.

Thomas, Nicholas. 1999. *Possessions: Indigenous Art/Colonial Culture*. London: Thames and Hudson.

Tinius, Jonas. 2015. "Aesthetic, Ethics, and Engagement: Self-cultivation as the Politics of Refugee Theatre." In *Anthropology, Theatre and Development: The Transformative Potential of Performance*, edited by Alex Flynn and Jonas Tinius, 171–202. Basingstoke and New York: Palgrave Macmillan.

United Nations Educational, Scientific and Cultural Organization (UNESCO) and United Nations Development Program (UNDP). 2013. *Creative Economy Report 2013: Widening Development Pathways*. Paris: UNESCO and New York: UNDP.

Westermann, Mariët, ed. 2005. *Anthropologies of Art*. New Haven, CT: Yale University Press.

Wickstom, Maurya. 2012. *Performance in the Blockades of Neoliberalism: Rethinking the Political Anew.* New York: Palgrave Macmillan.

Wolf, Arun and Wolf, Gita, eds. 2015. *Between Memory and Museum: A Dialogue with Folk and Tribal Arts.* Delhi and London: Tara Books.

Wong, Pearly and Clammer, John. 2017. "Performance and Development: Theatre for Social Change." In *The Aesthetics of Development: Art, Culture and Social Transformation,* edited by John Clammer and A.K. Giri, 291–308. New York and Basingstoke: Palgrave Macmillan.

Contributors

Eriko Aoki is a professor of anthropology at Ryukoku University, Japan. She was granted a D.Phil. at the Australian National University. She has conducted anthropological research in the central part of Flores Island, Indonesia since 1979 and in Japan since the late 1990s. Her theoretical interests are in semiotics, fetishism, modernity and enchantment. Her publications include "The Case of the Purloined Statues" in *To Speak in Pairs: Essays on Ritual Languages of Eastern Indonesia* (Cambridge University Press, 1988) and "Korean Children, Textbooks, and Educational Practices in Japanese Primary School" in *Koreans in Japan: Critical Voices from the Margin* (Routledge, 2000). She also published a single-authored book in Japanese.

John Clammer is a professor at O.P. Jindal Global University, India. After completing his doctorate at Oxford University, he has taught at a number of universities around the world such as the University of Hull, the University of Singapore, Sophia University (Tokyo) and United Nations University. Among his recent books are *Art, Culture and International Development* (Routledge, 2015), *Cultures of Transition and Sustainability* (Palgrave Macmillan, 2016), *Cultural Rights and Justice: Sustainable Development, the Arts and the Body* (Palgrave Macmillan, 2019), and the co-edited volume (with A.K. Giri) *The Aesthetics of Development* (Palgrave Macmillan, 2017). His sociological and anthropological interests include issues of culture and development, art, law, comparative social theory, ethnicity and religion.

Willemijn de Jong is a professor of anthropology at the University of Zurich, Switzerland, where she taught for about thirty years. Her publications concern textiles and rituals in Flores, Indonesia; ageing and social security in Kerala, India; and migration as well as reproductive technologies and families in Switzerland. In recent years she has worked on textiles, art, fashion and globalisation. In 2016 she co-curated the exhibition *Striking Patterns: Global Traces in Local Ikat Fashion* at the Museum der Kulturen Basel and co-edited the book with the same title (Hatje Cantz, 2016). In 2020 she curated the exhibition *Textile Verzauberung: Webkunst aus Flores (Textile Enchantment: Weaving Art from Flores)* in an art gallery in the region of Zurich.

Ilana Seltzer Goldstein is a professor of anthropology and art history at the Federal University of Sao Paulo, Brazil. Some of her international publications are "Visible Art, Invisible Artists?" for the on-line journal *Vibrant v. 10* (ABA, 2013); "From the Forest to the Museum: Notes on the Artistic and Spiritual Collaboration between Ernesto Neto and the Huni Kuin People" for the book

The Expanding World: Ayahuasca Diaspora (Routledge, 2018); and "Économies de l´art contemporain: programmation, financement et gestion dans les institutions culturelles brésiliennes" for the book *Art et société : Recherches récentes et regards croisés* (OpenEdition Press, 2016). Goldstein was an editor of *PROA*, a journal dedicated to the interface between arts and social sciences. She has also curated four large-scale exhibitions.

Andrea Grieder is a social anthropologist and poet. Her teaching (University of Zurich and University of Fribourg, Switzerland, University of Technology and Arts of Byumba, Rwanda) and her research activities focus on genocide prevention, trauma and resilience, arts and anthropology. With Obieora Ike and Ignace Haaz she co-edited *Poetry and Ethics, Inventing Possibilities in Which We Are Moved to Action and How We Live Together* (Globethics, 2018). She is the founder and director of Transpoesis, a poetry organisation specialised in Poetry-Therapy, Performances and Video-Production and the co-director of the International Refugee Poetry Network. Her poems are published in *Carry Your Little Flute* (2019).

Abeer Gupta is currently the director of the Krishnakriti Foundation in Hyderabad and the Achi Association India in New Delhi and Leh. He has directed several documentary films and curated art, education and community media projects. His research is based in the western Himalayas, in Ladakh, Jammu and Kashmir around oral histories, material cultures, and visual archives. His publications include, *The Visual and Material Culture of Islam in Ladakh* (2014), *Discovering the Self and Others in Jammu, Kashmir and Ladakh* (Sage, 2014), *A Sense of Place: Islam in the Western Himalaya* (Marg, 2018) and *Constructing Traditions: The Jamdani within Exhibition Practice of Handicrafts* (Projects/Processes, Serendipity Arts Festival, 2021.

Sachiko Kubota is a professor of anthropology at Ashiya University, Japan. Her main domains of research are gender anthropology, anthropology of art, and contemporary hunter and gatherers in Northeastern Arnhem Land, Australia. Her research also includes a comparative study on Indigenous political claims in Australia and Japan. She is the author of a number of articles and monographs, including *Gender Anthropology on Aboriginal Society: Indigenous People, Women, and Social Change* (Sekaishisosha, 2005), *Who Are 'Indigenous Peoples'?* (Sekaishisosha, 2009), and "Transmission of Knowledge, Clans, and Lands among the Yolngu (Northern Territory, Australia)" in *Entangled Territorialities* (University of Toronto Press, 2017).

Maria Bonome Pederneiras earned a bachelor's degree in social science at the University of Minas Gerais, Brazil, and a master's degree in social anthropology at the Museu Nacional, University of Rio de Janeiro, Brazil. She did research on the intersection of theatre and anthropology, studying masks, art and performance in Bali, where she also conducted her first fieldwork. Her master thesis was an ethnographic account about the Arapaso, an indigenous group inhabiting Northwest Amazonia. Currently, she is studying the nexus between myth, history, kinship and territory in the regional interethnic system of the Arapaso and several other Amerindian groups as a PhD candidate at the Museu Nacional.

Magdalena Sophia Toledo received her PhD in anthropology from the Museu Nacional, University of Rio de Janeiro, Brazil. She is an adjunct professor at the Magísteren Antropologías Latinoamericanas at the Universidad Alberto Hurtado, Chile. Her main research interests are in anthropology of art, especially agency and materialities, arts and politics, performance and diasporic aesthetics.

Matori Yamamoto is an anthropologist and professor emeritus at Hosei University in Tokyo. She holds a BA and a MA from the University of Tokyo and a PhD from the Graduate University for Advanced Studies, Japan. She edited *Art and Identity in the Pacific: Festival of Pacific Arts* (Japan Center for Area Studies, National Museum of Ethnology, 2006). She also edited with Tomiyuki Uesugi *The Perspective of Glocalisation: Addressing the Changing Society and Culture under Globalisation* (CGS Seijo University, 2016). She is the author of *Globalised Reciprocity: Circulation of Valuables and the Chiefly System in the Expanding Samoan World* (in Japanese) (Kobundo, 2018).

Index

A

Aborigin
 Aboriginal arts, iii, ix, xxiv, 43, 44, 45, 46, 47, 48, 49, 51, 52, 53, 54, 192, 202, 203
 Aboriginal people, xiii, 43, 44, 45, 48, 49, 50, 51, 52, 53, 54
acrylic paintings, v, xiii, 48, 49, 51, 54, 94, 115
aesthetics, iv, x, xi, xx, xxi, 3, 7, 9, 10, 17, 18, 23, 41, 44, 61, 62, 78, 103, 127, 128, 130, 153, 154, 164, 177, 192, 197, 198, 199, 200, 201, 204, 211
Africa, xxv, 42, 47, 136, 171, 189, 192, 200
 African diaspora, 129, 130, 133
agency, vii, viii, x, xi, xii, xxviii, xxix, xxxi, 3, 5, 7, 8, 9, 11, 16, 17, 24, 27, 28, 35, 40, 41, 42, 43, 77, 81, 89, 100, 103, 105, 106, 109, 111, 121, 122, 123, 125, 129, 138, 140, 142, 147, 148, 152, 156, 167, 169, 174, 176, 177, 178, 187, 188, 206, 211
Amaryllis Theatre, 196
Amerindians, 106, 107, 110, 130, 131, 138
anthropology, vii, viii, ix, x, xi, xii, xiii, xiv, xv, xvi, xxii, xxiv, xxv, 7, 9, 27, 28, 44, 50, 121, 132, 170, 171, 177, 192, 198, 205, 209, 210, 211
Antilles, 126, 130, 133

antiques, 151, 157
art brut, xiii, xvii, 60
art by appropriation, xvii
art by intention, xvii
art market, xii, xviii, xix, xxi, 5, 40, 62, 65, 70, 71, 76, 103, 202
art theory, 8
art world, iii, vii, xiii, xvi, xvii, xviii, xix, 23, 47, 49, 53, 59, 60, 61, 62, 64, 65, 70, 73, 75, 76, 81, 103, 116, 121, 191, 193, 194, 203, 204
artefacts, 8, 61, 104, 121, 129, 133, 134, 135, 140, 147, 156, 159
artification, xx, 104
artisticity, 121
Auckland, 82, 83, 84, 85, 86, 88, 90, 92, 93, 94, 97, 98, 99, 100, 101
auction, 49, 202
Australia, viii, xxiv, 43, 44, 45, 46, 48, 49, 51, 52, 54, 55, 92, 104, 124, 182, 202, 210
authenticity, xxvii, xxix, 49, 54, 104, 194, 198, 200, 201
authorisation, 104, 175
authorship, 112, 148
avant-gardists, xv, xvi, xviii, 127, 128

B

Bali, 18, 27, 28, 29, 30, 31, 34, 42, 211
Baniwa, Denilson, vi, 103, 106, 117, 118, 119, 120, 121, 122
bark paintings, 45, 46, 47, 48, 49, 50, 53

Bauhaus, 192
Becker, Howard, xvii, xxvii, 60, 76, 191, 205
Benjamin, Walter, xix, xx, xxviii, 62, 63, 75, 76
Bharat Bhavan, xxvi, 192
Bharucha, Rustom, xxvi, xxviii
Boal, Augusto, 196, 205
body painting, 108, 110, 111, 113, 122
Braz, Arissana, 115
Brazil, iii, iv, v, viii, xxii, 27, 42, 103, 104, 105, 106, 107, 108, 114, 115, 117, 118, 119, 120, 121, 139, 209, 210, 211
bricolage, xii, xiii, 137

C

cannibalism, 125, 131
capitalism, vii, xxi, 59, 60, 63, 75, 205
Caribbean, 125, 126, 127, 130, 132, 133, 136, 137, 138, 141, 142, 143
carvings, 8, 45, 48, 50, 90
ceramics, v, 64, 111, 113, 129, 130, 131
 ceramic dolls, 113
ceremonies, 20, 22, 23, 30, 31, 34, 35, 41, 84, 95, 135
Césaire, Aimé, 126, 127, 128, 131, 132, 138, 142
Chow, Rey, xxv, xxvi, xxviii
Clifford, James, xv, xvi, xvii, xxi, xxii, xxviii, xxix, 3, 24, 35, 42, 63, 77, 85, 99, 100, 104, 121, 123, 132, 141, 142
colonialism, xiii, 63, 95, 117, 141, 199, 205
commoditisation, iii, x, xix, 59, 60, 63, 74, 147, 148, 157

contemporary art, iv, viii, ix, xi, xii, xiii, xiv, xvii, 19, 21, 23, 53, 71, 74, 81, 93, 113, 115, 122, 135, 147, 148, 149, 156, 157, 165, 192, 193
counter-orientalism, 3, 21, 22, 23
crafts, ix, xxiv, 6, 30, 36, 45, 155, 157, 158, 160, 165, 192, 193, 205
creole, 129, 132, 134, 138, 142

D

dance-theatre, 29
Dar, Javed, 197
design, xix, xx, xxviii, 11, 22, 73, 85, 89, 92, 93, 95, 155, 192, 193
diaspora, 84, 88, 99, 123, 138, 142, 153, 210
Dogra, 149, 152
Drass, 154
Dubuffet, Jean, 59, 60, 61, 62, 63, 64, 77, 192

E

eco-criticism, 199
efficacy, 10, 11, 22, 25, 27, 30, 31, 36, 37, 39, 40, 41, 169, 170, 177, 178, 186, 187, 189
embroidery, 100, 159, 162
enchantment of technology, xi, 27, 31, 36, 37, 41
Entelechy Arts, 196
ephemerality, 135
epistemicide, 199, 206
Errington, Sherry, xvii, xxix, 47, 54
Esbell, Jaider, 103, 115, 120, 122, 123
ethnicisation, 6, 19, 20, 21, 23
ethnographic turn, ix, xix
ethnopoetics, 169, 172, 188
Extant Theatre Company, 196

F

fashion, xix, 3, 8, 19, 24, 25, 26, 62, 63, 73, 74, 159, 160, 209
fine art, ix, 4, 5, 49, 62, 117, 128
Flores, 3, 5, 6, 7, 8, 10, 11, 12, 18, 19, 22, 24, 25, 26, 59, 60, 66, 75, 209
folklore, 4, 8
Fusco, Coco, 195

G

gamelan, 29, 31, 32
Geertz, Clifford, 35, 42, 121, 123
Gell, Alfred, viii, x, xi, xii, xiii, xiv, xv, xvii, xxi, xxix, xxx, 3, 5, 8, 9, 11, 16, 18, 19, 23, 24, 27, 28, 30, 31, 35, 37, 39, 40, 41, 42, 62, 77, 99, 100, 105, 121, 123, 125, 127, 135, 139, 140, 142, 148, 167, 169, 170, 177, 186, 187, 188, 192, 206
gender, xv, xvii, xxiv, xxviii, xxxii, 6, 9, 19, 20, 21, 24, 25, 70, 78, 95, 173, 196, 197, 205, 210
gendering, 19, 23
gift, xii, xiii, xxxi, xxxii, 10, 24, 25, 78
Gilgit, 149, 167
Glissant, Édouard, 127, 128, 130, 131, 132, 133, 134, 137, 141, 142
global art, vii, xiii, xviii, xxii, 3, 8, 21, 23, 47, 81, 99, 122, 148
globalisation, xiii, xxiii, 3, 21, 148, 193, 201, 202, 203, 209
Gomez-Pena, Guillermo, 195
graphic art, 112
graphic design, 111, 116
graphic repertoire, 112
Guarani, 115, 118, 122

H

heritage, iv, xxxii, 3, 29, 81, 82, 87, 89, 90, 92, 95, 97, 98, 99, 100, 117, 125, 153, 154, 167
Huni Kuin, 108, 116, 123, 209
hybridity, xxvii

I

iconography, 19, 117, 153, 166, 201
identity, iv, xvi, xix, xxviii, 19, 67, 81, 82, 84, 89, 90, 91, 92, 93, 95, 98, 101, 125, 126, 127, 130, 131, 132, 133, 135, 136, 142, 148, 172, 178, 188, 194, 197, 202, 205, 211
India, i, iii, iv, vii, viii, xxiv, xxvi, 6, 17, 113, 147, 148, 150, 151, 152, 153, 154, 161, 162, 163, 165, 166, 167, 191, 192, 193, 195, 196, 197, 201, 202, 203, 205, 209, 210
Indians, 110, 118, 131, 134, 135, 138, 198
indigenous, iv, vi, xi, xiii, xx, xxiii, xxiv, xxv, xxvi, xxviii, xxix, 9, 41, 45, 83, 84, 92, 103, 104, 105, 106, 108, 110, 113, 114, 115, 116, 117, 118, 119, 120, 121, 122, 125, 130, 131, 156, 194, 195, 199, 200, 201, 203, 207, 210, 211
Indira Gandhi Rashtriya Manav Sangrahalaya, 192
Indonesia, iii, viii, xx, 3, 4, 5, 7, 11, 18, 20, 23, 24, 25, 26, 30, 35, 47, 59, 60, 66, 75, 209
intellectual property rights, 72, 74
intellectually disabled, 59, 60, 63, 64, 65, 66, 67, 68, 69, 70, 71, 73, 74, 75, 76

intentionality, 16
Itoga, Kazuo, 59, 60, 64, 68, 69, 77, 78

J

Jammu, 149, 150, 151, 152, 157, 162, 167, 210
Japan, i, iii, iv, vii, viii, xvi, xx, 16, 43, 44, 50, 51, 52, 53, 54, 55, 59, 60, 62, 63, 64, 65, 66, 67, 68, 69, 70, 71, 72, 74, 75, 76, 77, 78, 81, 99, 101, 192, 195, 196, 199, 202, 206, 209, 210, 211

K

Kadiweu, v, 111, 112
Karajá, 113, 124
Kargil, 150, 151, 153, 155, 160
Kashmir, 149, 150, 151, 152, 157, 159, 167, 196, 197, 206, 210
Kaul, Survir, 197, 206
Kayapó, 110, 111
Kester, Grant, 203, 206
Kuikuro, 109

L

Lévi-Strauss, Claude, xii, xxx, 116, 124, 171
Lio, 10, 13
Little Tibet, 148

M

Macuxi, 115, 122
Maguta Museum, 110
Main Bazaar, 148, 149, 150, 152, 157, 158, 166
Malkki, Liisa H., 178, 180, 188

Maori, xi, 82, 83, 87, 89, 90, 93, 97, 203
marginalisation, viii, xiii, xvi, xxiii, 6, 43, 104, 121, 122, 148, 152, 193, 194, 195
marginality, iii, vii, viii, ix, xiv, xxx, xxxii, 4, 5, 7, 170, 180, 195, 196
Marronage, 136, 137, 141
Martinican aesthetic, 127
Martinican identity, 126, 127, 134, 136, 141
Marubo, 112, 113, 123
mask-makers, 29, 30, 36, 37, 38, 39
masks, v, 27, 28, 29, 30, 31, 32, 34, 35, 36, 37, 38, 39, 41, 108, 138
Mauss, Marcel, xii, 28, 42, 50
memories, xxxii, 51, 91, 109, 126, 128, 130, 132, 156, 180, 181, 208
micro-utopias, ix, xiii, xiv
migrant, 82, 83, 85, 86, 95, 96, 97, 151, 161
migrant labour, 151, 161
missionaries, 45, 46, 84, 110, 149
modern art, xvi, xvii, xviii, 44, 46, 47, 53, 90, 202
monastic museums, 152, 153
Morris, William, 61, 79, 192
Museum of Modern Art (MoMA), xvi, xvii, xx, xxxi, 46, 47, 51, 53, 64, 78, 116

N

Namgyal dynasty, 149
Négritude movement, 126, 132
neoliberal, xviii, xix, xx, 75
New Zealand, iv, viii, 46, 81, 82, 83, 84, 85, 86, 87, 88, 89, 90, 92, 93, 94, 95, 96, 97, 98, 99, 100, 101

Index

O

Oceanic art, 81, 82, 85, 86, 87, 88, 89, 90, 92, 93, 94, 95, 97, 98, 99
orientalism, xvi, xxvi, 3, 19, 20, 21, 22, 23

P

Pacific peoples, 81, 82, 83, 84, 90, 92, 93, 97, 98, 99
Papastergiadis, Nikos, 203, 207
Paris, xv, xvii, xix, xxvi, xxx, xxxi, xxxii, 47, 50, 62, 64, 75, 116, 124, 126, 128, 130, 132, 139, 142, 143, 202, 203, 207
pashmina, 149, 150
Pataxó, 115
patterns, 10, 11, 13, 19, 39, 111, 112, 161
Paz, Octavio, 204, 207
Peiry, Lucienne, 193, 204, 207
performance, xxv, 8, 27, 28, 29, 30, 31, 32, 34, 35, 37, 38, 39, 40, 41, 42, 103, 119, 129, 138, 170, 171, 178, 179, 183, 185, 186, 187, 188, 192, 194, 195, 196, 198, 201, 203, 205, 206, 207, 208, 211
personhood, xi, 27, 28, 41
perspectivism, 107, 111, 119, 124
Piano, Renzo, xxvi
plantations, 128, 134
politics, iv, xv, xxvi, xxix, xxx, xxxi, 16, 19, 22, 23, 24, 25, 103, 127, 165, 180, 191, 193, 194, 195, 202, 206, 207, 211
polycentric aesthetics, xxiii, 191, 198, 201
Polynesia, 82, 84
postcolonial, ix, xix, xx, xxv, xxvi, xxxi, 3, 6, 19, 20, 51, 95, 167, 206
pottery, xxiv, 64, 89, 154, 161, 191, 192, 198, 201
primitive art, xvii, 45, 47, 50, 53, 61
primitivism, xv, xvi, xvii, xxxi, 43, 47, 50, 53, 54, 63, 117, 124

R

refugee, iv, 169, 170, 171, 172, 173, 174, 175, 176, 177, 178, 179, 180, 182, 183, 184, 185, 186, 187, 188, 189, 197, 205, 207, 210
religion, xi, xxiv, 19, 22, 24, 30, 31, 62, 141, 152, 165, 198, 209
representations, xix, xxiii, xxvi, xxvii, 30, 31, 43, 44, 45, 48, 49, 101, 107, 110, 119, 140, 147, 148, 152, 165, 178, 194, 200, 202
resilience, 169, 170, 182, 184, 185, 210
resistance, viii, xv, xix, xxiii, xxx, 113, 115, 118, 128, 136, 137, 138, 140, 141
rhizome, 133
Rothenberg, Jerome, 169, 170, 171, 189
Rwanda, iv, viii, 169, 170, 171, 172, 173, 174, 177, 180, 181, 182, 187, 188, 189, 210

S

Samoa, 82, 84, 86, 87, 89, 90, 93, 94, 95
Sansi, Roger, viii, ix, x, xii, xiii, xix, xxxi, xxxii, 74, 78
Sao Paulo, iv, 42, 103, 122, 142, 209
Sao Paulo Art Biennale, 115, 119, 120
Sao Paulo Museum of Art (MASP), 119

Sao Paulo Museum of Modern Art (MAM), 116
Schneider, Arnd, viii, xiii, xiv, xxviii, xxxii, 3, 5, 21, 25, 26, 192, 203, 207
sculptures, 37, 86, 89, 90, 93, 95, 162, 164, 193, 200
shamans, 109, 112, 117, 119, 124, 137, 139, 140
Shangri La, 153, 167
Shankar, Uday, 195
Shore, Bradd, 94, 197, 207
Shyam, Jangarh Singh, 194, 206
sidhakarya, v, 32, 33
Skardu, 149
slavery, 125, 128, 129, 130, 131, 133, 134, 135, 138, 140, 141
spindle, 159, 164, 166
Spivak, Gayatri, 169, 185, 189
Srinagar, 150, 152, 154, 167
Strathern, Marilyn, viii, x, xii, xxxii, 16, 26, 127, 128, 129, 141, 143
subjectivity, 29, 39

T

Tagore, Gaganendranath, 200
taksu, 27, 29, 30, 31, 34, 36, 37, 38, 39, 40, 41
tapa, 84, 85, 86, 89, 91, 94, 100
tattoo, 86, 95, 100
Tautai, 82, 86, 87, 88, 92, 93, 95, 99, 101
technical processes, 30, 31, 37, 40
technology of enchantment, xi, 27, 30, 31, 37, 41
textile artists, 4, 5
textile arts, 3, 4, 5, 7, 10, 22, 23, 192
textile studies, 3, 5, 8, 18
Theatre of the Oppressed, 205
Thiong'o, Ngugi wa, 199, 200, 207
Third Cinema, xxv

Thomas, Nicholas, x, xxix, xxxi, 8, 26, 37, 42, 49, 54, 87, 91, 92, 101, 203, 207
Tibetan Refugee Markets, 151, 161
Tjibaou Cultural Centre, xxvi
Tonga, 82, 84, 85, 87, 89, 90, 93, 94, 96, 100
topeng, iii, v, 27, 28, 29, 30, 31, 32, 33, 34, 35, 36, 37, 38, 39, 40, 41, 42
tradition, viii, xiv, 3, 4, 20, 23, 24, 26, 54, 61, 91, 113, 138, 148, 153, 167, 170, 171, 175, 187, 193
traditional arts, xiii, xiv, 21, 82, 84, 85, 93, 95, 103
traditionalisation, 6, 20, 21, 23
transit, 43, 44, 53, 54, 173
transition, 33, 43, 44, 47, 53, 54, 160, 209
Transpoesis, 169, 170, 175, 176, 179, 181, 182, 184, 186, 187, 189, 210
Treaty of Amritsar, 149

W

Wajãpi, 112
Wauja, 41, 110, 112
Wayana, 110, 124
Weitz, Morris, 61, 62, 79
welfare, xxi, xxvii, 59, 60, 64, 65, 67, 68, 69, 70, 71, 74, 75, 77, 78
Western art, xv, xvi, xvii, xxvii, 47, 60, 61, 62, 81, 85, 98, 99, 105, 110, 119, 122, 199
Wolf, Arun, xxvi, xxxii
Wolf, Gita, xxvi, xxxii
work-life-balance, 70
World War II, 48, 59, 60, 64, 68, 74, 81, 82, 127

X

Xerente, 111, 124
Xikrin, 110, 124
Xingu, 42, 109, 110, 113, 119, 120, 122, 123, 124

Y

Yanomami, 113, 124

www.ingramcontent.com/pod-product-compliance
Lightning Source LLC
Chambersburg PA
CBHW071351290426
44108CB00014B/1506